D1527554

CARIBBEAN CULTURAL IDENTITY

The Case of Jamaica

Published with the cooperation of the
Inter-American Foundation

Studies on Social Processes and Change

CARIBBEAN CULTURAL IDENTITY

by Rex Nettleford

The Case of Jamaica

Foreword by
Claudia Mitchell-Kernan

An Essay in Cultural Dynamics

Center for Afro-American Studies
and
UCLA Latin American Center Publications
University of California, Los Angeles

Center for Afro-American Studies
UCLA Latin American Center Publications
University of California, Los Angeles

Copyright © 1978, 1979 by Rex M. Nettleford

Contents

Foreword   ix

Preface   xvii

Acknowledgements   xix

Prologue   xxi

I.   CULTURAL PLURALISM AND NATIONAL
     IDENTITY   1

II. PRESERVATION AND FURTHER DEVELOPMENT
     OF CULTURAL VALUES   47

III. THE CULTURAL DIMENSION OF DEVELOPMENT   83

     Exploratory Committee on the Arts   87

     The Cultural Mission of the State   91

     Investment in Education and Training in
        Arts and Culture   94

     Institutional Rationalisation: Transformation
        of the Institute of Jamaica   110

     The Jamaica Festival Commission   122

     Voluntary Contribution and Cultural Dynamics   124

     Communications Media, Information and
        Cultural Policy   126

     The Financing of Cultural Policy   140

IV. CULTURAL INTEGRATION AND CO-OPERATION
     IN THE WIDER CARIBBEAN AND LATIN
     AMERICA   149

V.   Epilogue: Cultural Action and Social Change   181

     Index   231

List of Illustrations

I.   The Ancestor—sculpture by Edna Manley   *frontispiece*
     photo by Maria LaYacona

II. Diagrams: State Cultural Institutions
                 Structure of Institute of Jamaica
                 Structure of Jamaica Festival Commission
                 Voluntary Organisations and Cultural Interaction

III. Institute of Jamaica

     West India Reference Library, Natural History Division
        photos by courtesy of Institute of Jamaica

     Folk Museum, Spanish Town and Arawak Museum
        *photos by courtesy of Institute of Jamaica, Jamaica Tourist
        Board*

     National Gallery & Works by Edna Manley, Osmond Watson,
     Karl Parboosingh, Carl Abrahams, Kapo, Christopher
     Gonzales, David Miller, Albert Huie, John Dunkley
        *photos by Dennis Gick and by courtesy of National Gallery
        and Agency for Public Information*

     Cultural Training Centre
        *photos by Evon Williams, Richard Montgomery, Keith
        Morrison, Tony Russell and by courtesy of Institute of
        Jamaica and Design Collaborative*

     Jamaica National Trust Commission, Court House, Morant Bay
        *photos by courtesy of Agency for Public Information and
        Institute of Jamaica*

     Jamaica Festival
        photos by courtesy of Jamaica Festival Commission

     Popular Entertainment
        photos by courtesy of Jamaica Tourist Board

     Traditional Culture
        *photos by Maria LaYacona and by courtesy of Agency for
        Public Information*

Craft
photos by courtesy of Jamaica Tourist Board

Little Theatre and Ward Theatre
photos by courtesy of Agency for Public Information and Little Theatre Movement

The LTM National Pantomime
photos by Maria LaYacona

Jamaica Folk Singers
photos by Errol Harvey, by courtesy of Agency for Public Information

Reggae: Bob Marley, Jimmy Cliff, Big Yout'
photos by courtesy of Agency for Public Information
Toots Hibbert, Peter Tosh, Desmond Dekker, Judy Mowatt
photos by courtesy of Jamaica Daily News

National Dance Theatre Company
photos by Maria LaYacona

University of the West Indies
photos by courtesy of the University of the West Indies

Ancestor and Progeny
photos by Maria LaYacona

Foreword

It is my distinct pleasure to introduce Rex Nettleford's perceptive and critical analysis of social change in Jamaican society to an American audience more aware than ever of the commonality of New World-based struggles for cultural recognition among peoples of African descent. The joint publication of this work by the Center for Afro-American Studies and the Latin American Center at UCLA in cooperation with the Institute of Jamaica and the Inter-American Foundation is a significant progression in the institutional recognition of this commonality of the Caribbean cultural and regional experience. Collaboration on the American edition highlights the relevance of Nettleford's critical perspective beyond the specific case of Jamaica. The final chapter, "Cultural Integration and Cooperation in the Wider Caribbean and Latin America," treats the potential for alliance and cooperation in a region where history has taken a parallel course in terms of struggles against political domination and economic exploitation, and which throughout has experienced the dilemmas of cultural identity and national integration on a base of social conflict and cultural and ideological diversity.

Rex Nettleford has written a book vividly documenting social change and recent trends in the development of Jamaican society. His insightful analysis of the issue of cultural identity in Jamaica succeeds in offering a neglected perspective on the pattern of change unfolding in Jamaica and the Caribbean which is both contrastive and complementary to the more traditional political and economic perspectives. The cultural frame of reference provides a point of departure for the consideration of a multiplicity of problems of social change and creates the impression of a struggle taking place which is multilayered and with profound linkages between the political-economic, social-structural, and cultural theaters.

On one level, culture emerges as a symbolic issue, manipulated by political and economic elites in contention and by social groups long in conflict. Moreover, cultural issues appear to be ascending in the more recently unfolding ideological conflicts which strain Jamaican society today. At yet another level, culture as a shared system of symbols with which to forge a Jamaican national identity and achieve some measure of societal integration is examined as a substantive issue.

Jamaica, like many other areas of the recently decolonized world, has a heritage of cultural diversity. To what extent differences in cultural inventories among groups within Jamaican society are central to social-structural cleavages is apparently an issue on which there is considerable difference of opinion. There is more often than not a good deal of tension within social systems in situations of culture contact. Institutional displacements, social realignments, and cultural exchange are common features of contact situations, as is ideological diversity in response to the dislocations intrinsic to the experience. The cultural problems of Jamaica, where contact is now some three centuries in depth, do not seem to arise from gross disparities in the cultural inventories of different groups, as some would argue. Rather, as I read Nettleford, the problems arise from the legacy of groups meeting on unequal terms, creating from the outset divisions along lines of country and continent of origin, and of free as opposed to bond status. If an opportunistic intercaste group, mediating between the groups in conflict, is added to such an already conflictive mix, the ingredients are available for the state apparatus to manipulate social categories and material resources, keeping large segments of the population economically and politically subordinate. Further, the spice of racism, with its utility as a vehicle for sustaining the ruling caste's political and economic hegemony, combines to assure this caste's cultural dominance. It is through consideration of the interplay of these factors that an adequate description of the situation produced and sustained by European expansion from the sixteenth century onward emerges. The exploitation of antagonisms between groups, the emphasis on cultural distance among them, and the versatile use of racist ideology in the rationalization of the existing order have been highly effective strategies for the preservation of the existing socioeconomic contrasts.

Nettleford deals with these processes by putting in bold relief their effects with specific reference to the subordination of elements in the cultural repertoire of Jamaica that are either indigenous or of African provenience. He draws attention to the beneficiaries of this pattern of subordination and the institutional means by which it has been effected through such devices as language policy and other controls of the criteria of social mobility.

What is perhaps special in Jamaica today is the level of consciousness among Jamaican intellectuals and policy makers about the historical workings of these processes of subordination and their political-economic, socio-cultural, and psychological vehicles. This consciousness, coupled with organized efforts aimed at social change resting on this diagnosis, is graphically described by Nettleford and conveys an impression of Jamaica as a society moving with a firm sense of direction.

Black people in the United States have tended to view the issue of cultural domination as a ramification of economic and political subordination and as tied significantly to their status as a minority enclave. An exception might be the perspective of Harold Cruse in his book, *The Crisis of the Negro Intellectual.* Nettleford's testimony to this same phenomenon on the socio-cultural level in a context in which Afro-Jamaicans are in control of the state apparatus will thus be viewed with a certain irony, but it should also serve as a salutary antidote to simplistic thinking.

Nettleford complains of Eurocentricism in outlook within the upper stratum. He underscores the lack of recognition of indigenous cultural forms, an attitude inherited from the experience of slavery and colonial domination. He rightly inveighs against the conscious and unconscious assumptions held currently by many Jamaicans that things foreign are intrinsically superior and indigenous elements of lesser value in the struggle to transform and integrate Jamaican society within a socialist framework.

But what is Jamaican society? Or, for that matter, what is any decolonizing society that contains peoples derived from every territorial niche over which the British Union Jack formerly cast its colonial shadow? What, indeed, is American society and culture, which today can probably claim an enclave of every linguistic–cum–cultural group in the world? The strategy of the United States in dealing with its cultural diversity has been to institutionalize policies that have required popular assimilation. American cultural orientation was also Eurocentric, and the indigenization process was markedly dominated by the New England states with their self-conscious class of articulate intellectuals whose cultural impact was eventually far to exceed their numbers.

Yet the indigenous and foreign strands did not disappear. These strands have produced substrata in conflict with, and in some areas subversive of, the ideology and culture of the dominant stratum, leading to the creation of a kind of schizoid framework within which bicultural people must live, work, play, marry, and reproduce. Certain cultural paths exist as roads to upward mobility, however strewn with obstacles they might be. Other paths have been a refuge historically from slavery and imposed pariah status. The Afro-American cultural substrata have been and still are the most vulnerable. They present arenas of culture loss, a generating milieu of conflictive designs for living, and a fertile soil for millenarian thought. For the individual, the Afro-American cultural path may be materially impoverished, while the other, mainstream America, may be devoid of spiritual and cultural sustenance. And since neither path can be fully embraced, a kind of cultural limbo has been created out of which the individual Afro-American is forced to fashion (or fail to fashion) a design for life.

To this painful Afro-American crucible, add those competing designs for a socialist transformation that so stir Jamaican and Third World consciousness today, and the excitement of this work can readily be felt. The book has a personal dimension, the fervor of someone who has been literally in the thick of it; it is documentation by an eyewitness and key participant who has survived the rancor of social forces, meeting the frontiers of change while maintaining a spirit of ebullience in the face of complexity and adversity. Although critical, Nettleford's book is full of hope.

How can national integration and cultural identity be defined in a society such as Jamaica? Undogmatically, Nettleford seems to insist only that the experience of three hundred years of culture building cannot be ignored. At the same time, he stresses that the most outcast substratum has the greatest vitality for playing a culturally undergirding role in those transformations necessary to the political and economic spheres. This confidence compels attention.

Nation-states are by definition socially and culturally heterogenous. Jamaica has its measure of ethnic diversity, though this line of cleavage is perhaps not as central as in Guyana and other parts of Latin America; it has its linguistic diversity, if the creole language is given its due; and it has its cultural differentiation generated and sustained by differential access to resources. Nowhere, however, do the lines of social-structural cleavage adequately map the cultural terrain.

The largest substratum is nowhere purely African, but is a mosaic of African, European, and indigenous response to a truly novel reality. A feature of its dominant African provenience may be its continued communal basis, which offers a balance and tension to its cultural character while emphasizing personal autonomy. This autonomy probably emanates from the slavery and postslavery experience of peoples of African descent throughout the New World. Yet so powerful does this ethos of personal autonomy remain that the subordinated cultural strand cannot be easily coopted, vitiated, or diluted through its introduction as a symbol of newly sought national identity.

The stratum has its own cultural devices to confront and deal with superior power and with the economic and social disadvantages it has had to bear. It is highly practiced in "slipping the yoke." Its sense of identity is neither generated nor maintained through institutional means but is rather organic. Therefore, its survival and perpetuation will not be strictly determined by institutional means. Its subjective constructions of reality or culture grow out of its experience. Though it is not without self-pride, this subordinated stratum is not as sentimental about itself as are many of those who would like to hitchhike on its energy or channel it for political ends. It has its own sense of order and a characteristic cynicism about the claims of the existing order. Its vitality lies in its possession of deep roots of personal egalitarianism and devices for achieving equality, at least on the interpersonal level, which should be the envy of many architects of modern socialism. While fertile and a wellspring, it is nonetheless fragile.

It would be naive to neglect in any analysis the inequalities in the political-economic sphere from which the Jamaican cultural repertoire and social structure have evolved. Yet it is equally naive to consider the resulting socio-cultural configurations as phantom in character. Yesterday's fictions can and do become the concrete realities of tomorrow. Nowhere is there a better exemplar of this maxim than in the evolution from ethnic and linguistic diversity of a new ethnic group in the United States, Afro-Americans. Though neither cohesive nor culturally and "racially" homogenous, they exist as a social category with a strong sense of common identity and a force of latent political importance both intra- and internationally.

Anthropologist Robert Blauner aptly captured the special character of their history and current position in noting that it is possible to discern among them a simultaneous Americanization in ideas and action along with a movement toward ethnicity and distinctive cultural consciousness. As paradoxical as this seems, both these tendencies came to the fore with the economic and social change of the 1960s and 1970s. A recreolization occurred in many spheres of activity and social life as Black Americans strained to maintain their distinctive cultural identity and distance from the forces of their exploitation and oppression. This is the reality upon which old alliances have been abandoned and upon which future alliances may be formed which may yet influence change in the modern world.

Nettleford's powerful confidence in the resilience and vitality of the Jamaican masses for social reconstruction and cultural identity is the hallmark of this work. Yet this sense of confidence does not pander to or romanticize the cultural repertoire of the masses. Nettleford aspires to a genuine Jamaican metamorphosis; he does not demand that Jamaica be Africanized, whatever that might mean. He sees a central place for the indigenous arts in the forging of new symbols of loyalty and allegiance to the unfolding socialist transformation. In placing emphasis on the arts, however, Nettleford articulates the fact that culture comprises not simply art forms, but designs for living in all spheres of human activity.

Jamaican culture is geared to the demands of subsistence in a shaky economy and has grown organically to adapt itself to the distribution of power in the society. This cultural repertoire includes means for dealing with the problems of underemployment and of itinerant male labor with its limiting consequences for conjugal relations, family structure, and child socialization. This cultural repertoire succeeds in promoting a measure of dignity through inverting, at least in some spheres, the terms of the dominant value complex. Nettleford does not assume that all within the subordinated stratum is constructive and worthy of nurturance; he recognizes some of its contradictory features and its propensities for self-negation.

Nations in the modern world cannot and probably should not aspire to cultural homogeneity. This is a mode of the past, suited to small-scale, isolated societies where consistency of experience provided the grounds for achieving consistency in value and premise. While Nettleford does not advocate hegemony for any cultural component of the Jamaican repertoire, he does seem intent on elevating the cultural vision emanating from the masses of the Jamaican people. For such a process to unfold in other than a superficial fashion, some necessary and fundamental changes would have to be effected in the material basis of the society and in the distribution of resources. Therefore, more than a cursory glance must be given to the existing social, political, and economic context within which a Caribbean culture identity is attempting to forge itself, and even more careful scrutiny must be paid to the existing situation with regard to its potential for the transformations to which Nettleford aspires.

Claudia Mitchell-Kernan
Los Angeles, July 1979

Preface

Questions of cultural identity are the perennials of history from *civis Romanus sum* to "the African personality". Even where "cultural identity" appears to be settled, changes in society produce new imperatives, thus Beatledom has been given official cultural status by the Queen of England. English youth continue to salute Nelson but recognise the echoes of new social relationships in the popular sounds — popular as Shakespeare. Yet our articulate bureaucracy, still enclosed in Victorian excuses, have refused to embrace Bob Marley and enjoin us to sing homage to Rodney. But matrices change and the Caribbean, which has been changing dynamically for more than four hundred years, produces many puzzles and several rich answers.

In this book Professor Nettleford sets out to analyse and show the dynamics of cultural development in our Caribbean. And he is excellently equipped for the task. Firstly, as an intellectual who has given at least a decade's serious thought to the matter, he focuses on our problems of identity, particularly on "cultural pluralism" and the evils of Eurocentricity. This impressive sweep is underpinned with references to all the relevant texts, including unpublished material. Secondly, as a successful practising artist, he brings both knowledge and sensitivity to the consideration of the role the performing arts have played in the overall development of Jamaica and the Caribbean and the increasing social thrust now required of them.

Refreshingly, Professor Nettleford does not balk at the two key problems of the Caribbean — Race and Marxism. He writes:

> "That Race (and ethnicity) must be worked into the Marxian dialectic to meet the realities of Caribbean existence is a responsibility serious Caribbean socialists must face or find that yet another theory from Europe will have failed to deliver the goods because we would have ignored Marx's own injunction, by not relating our efforts sufficiently to the specificity of Caribbean history and realities."

Preface

This is a useful reminder that will be applauded by the many countries which, *mutatis mutandis,* are trying to use the instruments discovered by Marx as tools in their attempt to dismantle European capitalism and its cultural values.

Caribbean Cultural Identity gives warning to the outside world that Caribbean man has arrived as a functioning totality; and it reminds the developing Caribbean of the need to decide, objectively and with full attention to the details of our existence, what options to choose from the multiplicity offered us by history.

We must not be deceived, by the book's delightful eloquence, into regarding it as a word for an hour. Here is a serious statement, by one of our finest minds, about what, culturally, Jamaica and the Caribbean are, and what they must become.

NEVILLE DAWES M.A. (OXON)
Executive Director
Institute of Jamaica

Acknowledgements

I acknowledge with gratitude the assistance given by UNESCO in the preparation of this volume and to the Inter-American Foundation (Washington D.C.) for making this publication possible.

I am grateful to the Institute of Jamaica for allowing access to documents and other relevant material, and especially to its Executive Director, Mr Neville Dawes, who brought early critical encouragement to the entire effort and has written the Preface.

I acknowledge with gratitude the value of all those Jamaican creative artists and cultural agents who have offered kindness and generosity of spirit over the years and especially the dancers, musicians, singers and creative technicians in the National Dance Theatre Company of Jamaica who have all been a major source of inspiration since 1962.

I am grateful to Mrs Doreen Barrow for the painstaking typing of the manuscript, to Mrs Jean Smith, Mrs Barbara Gloudon and Mr Cliff Lashley for their helpful critical reading, to Mrs Janet Liu-Terry for helpful editing in the first and final stages of writing and to Miss Remalyn Reynolds for the typesetting of the entire volume.

I acknowledge with gratitude the following for the use of photographs: Maria LaYacona, Richard Montgomery, Jamaica Festival Office, Institute of Jamaica, National Trust Commission, Little Theatre Movement, Jamaica Broadcasting Corporation, Agency for Public Information, Jamaica Daily News, Delmar.

THE ANCESTOR by EDNA MANLEY
Photo by Maria LaYacona

Prologue

"... the mass of the population are the real people ... and those who will not unite with them on all fundamental matters are the real aliens in the land ... We believe that the people must consciously believe in themselves and their own destiny and must do so with pride and with confidence and with the determination to win equality with the rest of mankind — an equality in terms of humanity which irrespective of power and wealth, can be measured by the growing values of civilisation and culture ..."

Norman Manley, 1938.

In post-colonial societies like Jamaica and the rest of the Commonwealth Caribbean, the question of *cultural identity* logically gains high priority alongside political independence and economic self-sufficiency in the awesome process of decolonisation or, as some would put it, in the arduous struggle against external domination. It is the triple-threat combination of economics, politics and culture which determines the timbre of the ideological thrust of many who advocate change and which delineates the programmatic stages of growth and development in the region at large. The process is predictably complex, organically textured, and open to a wide variety of interpretation and analyses. Competing claims to intellectual and cultural verities result in colliding approaches to the problem of cultural identity.

The rather seductive Great Tradition versus Little Tradition or high art versus low culture debate has been embraced, no doubt in natural response to the obstinate fact of a society that has been deeply segmented historically in terms of clearly designated superordinates and subordinates. The notion of a *pluralist* society as against a *stratified* social aggregate has had spirited airing in learned journals and academic corridors between those who view Caribbean society as one which functions on the basis of conflict and is held together by force, and others who see in it the hope of peaceful social integration and cultural consensus. Caribbean society is sufficiently dynamic to attract such controversial reflections. The new socialist commitment evident throughout the Caribbean region addresses itself to the 'embourgeoisement' of Jamaican culture and aggressively celebrates the promise of a new orientation reflecting the soul and up-coming proletarian power of the large mass of economically and socially deprived Caribbean peoples. Yet others focus on the more positive achievements of the past three centuries by that very mass of Caribbean people (whether peasant, proletariat or evolved middlestratum) in what is a deceptively innocuous process of shaping an indigenous Caribbean lifestyle and a new, viable, worldview born out of the collective experience of a long dominated but rebellious people – now enslaved, now brutalised, now pressured into cultural submission, now colonised, but never really defeated.

None of the approaches indicated above need be mutually exclusive. Yet many of the protagonists are tempted to stations of arrogance and intolerance in the region's present mood for revolutionary change, which sometimes brooks no skepticism and is in unrelenting quest for the one-and-only-true path to liberation. The dangers are evident, the fears not always unfounded, but the imperative of the journey towards human dignity and fulfillment through economic betterment, political autonomy and cultural integrity dictates the inescapable risks entailed in such a path. Paths are, indeed, *made by walking*. There is no escape and little chance of turning back.

So from whatever perspective or with whatever vision one examines it, certain themes emerge with a constancy which makes the subject of cultural identity, in Jamaica and the Caribbean, perpetually challenging. The following themes suggest themselves and are the basis for discussion in this volume:

(a) cultural pluralism and national unity
(b) the preservation and further development of cultural values.
(c) the cultural dimension of development, and
(d) the possibility of cultural integration and co-operation between the territories of the Anglophone Caribbean on the one hand and the wider Caribbean and Latin America on the other. This has indeed been a factor of great concern to people of the Caribbean with their history of frustrated attempts at political federation, the current experiment in economic co-operation, and a persistent yearning after a common cultural vision dating back many decades.

Such integration and co-operation cannot, however be seriously contemplated without due regard for the deeper issues of Caribbean life — issues which are currently manifesting themselves in terms of the political and economic initiatives being taken to bring about the fundamental transformation of each Caribbean territory from colonial outpost and ex-slave plantation into a viable, independent, and self-respecting national unit.

If the people of the Caribbean own nothing else, they certainly can own their creative imagination which, viewed in a particular way, is a powerful means of production for much that brings meaning and purpose to human life. And it is the wide variety of products emanating from the free and ample exercise of this creative imagination which signifies to man his unique gift of culture.

A bold and certain recognition of this fact is bound to embolden and facilitate all those who set out to build just and civilised communities among us. Such builders come in many guises — as politicians and innovative technocrats, creative artists and innovative scientists, intellectuals of daring and a sensitive, informed and wise citizenry. In 1938, which marks the beginning of a new vision for the Caribbean region, Norman Manley based *his* hope for national unity in his native Jamaica on the view that "the mass of the people are the real people and that those who will not unite with them on all fundamental matters are the real aliens in the land." Our cultural identity, like our food, shelter, clothing and job opportunities, is a fundamental matter. Cultural action is central, then, to effective social change as the Jamaican experience strongly indicates and the final chapter of this book asserts.

In many ways what follows in this volume is addressed to all our Caribbean nation-builders who have dared to be creative as much as to those of our creative artists who, having dared to be themselves, are no longer 'aliens in their land.' It is dedicated, moreover, to all who have gone before but have left behind the

Prologue

legacy of a tradition of struggle and survival which continues to be one of the most reliable sources of energy for creative action in the region's growth and development.

Rex M. Nettleford.

University of the West Indies
Mona
Kingston 7
Jamaica

Part I

CULTURAL PLURALISM AND NATIONAL UNITY

CULTURAL PLURALISM AND NATIONAL UNITY

As a variant of that culture sphere known to social scientists and cultural anthropologists as Plantation America, Jamaica and the Caribbean are often defined in terms of their cultural pluralism. For the Caribbean is the story of "arrivants" from across the Atlantic and beyond, each group bringing a cultural equipage, including for some the legitimacy of power supported by gunpowder, scientific knowledge and a later developed sense of racial superiority. M. G. Smith describes the island of two million souls as a deeply segmented aggregation of descendants of European masters, African slaves and in-between offspring of both. Each group has built up cultural institutions independent of each other but each with its own inner logic and consistency. The advent of latecomers from India and Southern China as well as from Lebanon has only served to intensify the segmentation since they too have created definitive ethnocentric enclaves. This deepening of the diversity, goes the pluralist argument, is a potential breeding-ground for disunity and instability — even violent reactions in the scramble for power. But this is prevented by the pragmatic but tenuous cementing of bonds by political forces. "National unity" is therefore forged not by an organic cultural integration but by the concentration of coercive power in the hands of a political directorate. Needless to say, such a "unity" is sustained by a high sense of self-interest and survival. But let M. G. Smith speak for himself. "It is purely Pickwickian to assert that since no society can exist without a minimum sharing of common values, societies based on conquest, slavery or colonial domination must inevitably possess these common values, since they clearly exist ... From such presumptions, absurdities often follow, as when sociologists emphasise 'the processes making for unity and integration' of plural societies within which social conflict steadily increases in scale and intensity. At that stage their deductive normative theory can only be maintained by asserting that conflict expresses consensus: but this deprives it of any meaning".[1] The depth and nature of the pluralism according to M. G. Smith is therefore a matter that cannot be ignored in any discussion about national unity. Not everyone is agreed on this interpretation since it is felt that such an analysis ignores or at best underestimates the dynamic interplay of forces that has marked the distinctive process of creolisation or indigenisation in Caribbean society over the past three hundred years.[2]

The term "creolisation" is sometimes used in a pejorative sense to denote the tenacious hold that the conceivably super-ordinate metropolitan forces of Europe maintain over the cultural apparatus of the Caribbean. But more properly it refers to the agonising process of renewal and growth that marks the new order of men and women who came originally from different Old World cultures (whether European, African, Levantine or Oriental) and met in conflict or otherwise on foreign soil.

The operative word here is "conflict", at least for the early comers — the Europeans and the Africans. The fact that their presence marked by a violent relationship made marginal or totally redundant the indigenous populations of Amerindians and Carib Indians in places like Guyana and Dominica or totally extinct the peaceful Arawak Indians in places like Jamaica, is part of the irony of the struggle by "usurpers" to gain cultural ascendancy as part of the fight for total power. This has been done as part of a history in which economic exploitation went hand in hand with cultural subjugation by way of deracination, psychological conditioning around to a superordinate-subordinate determinism in the Europe-an-African relationship, systematic cultural denigration and insti-tutional colonization.

For despite the legacy of a textured diversity, that divers-ity has up to now been allowed to exist on the terms set by the

1. Smith, M. G.: *The Plural Society in the British West Indies,* Berkeley 1965 pp. xi, xiii.

2. See R. T. Smith: "Social Stratification, Cultural Pluralism and Integration in West Indian Societies" in *Caribbean Integration* (eds. S. Lewis & T. Matthews) (Rio Piedras, Puerto Rico).
   Brathwaite, L.: "Social Stratification and Cultural Pluralism" in *Annals of the New York Academy of Sciences* Vol. 83, 1960 pp. 816-836.

dominant 'master-culture' in the cultural complex. It is important to recall that for two-thirds of the time since the great waves of migration from Europe and West Africa into the Caribbean, the meeting of peoples from these old civilisations has been on the basis of conflict in circumstances which rendered one set of migrants (the Europeans) as the prescribed superordinate power over another set of migrants (the Africans) brought *involuntarily* and kept in a carefully nurtured captivity. The disintegration of the structural arrangements that, in law, ensured an unprecedented control by masters over the life and limb of servants did not immediately bring a totally new life based on a civilised relationship between men and women deemed to be of equal creative potential. In fact all such potential where manifested among the subordinate group was hounded underground, deprived of legitimacy, and devalued. The paradox of Caribbean life is that the more things change the more they have remained the same. The vault-like ascent by the society from slavery into freedom and then from colonialism into constitutional independence is yet to be matched within the society by a corresponding progress from cultural inferiority of the vast majority to cultural self-confidence. Metro-politan bombardment of the periphery continues, even increases, with the development of modern technology. It must indeed be admitted that Emancipation did set in motion the release of the majority of Jamaicans and West Indians from that trap of cultural dependency and did help to accelerate the process of indigenisation already evident among all segments of the population at the end of the eighteenth century. For the conscious and subconscious crea-tion of a new environment is what the process was and is all about.

It continues apace today. But it continues against the background of persistent forces that would seek to perpetuate the domination of metropolitan Europe and its cultural extension, North America. It also continues within the context of the old-style "plantation system" not only in terms of economic depend-ency but also in terms of an abiding Eurocentrism which puts everything European in a place of eminence and things of indigenous (i.e. native born and native bred) or African origin in a lesser place. This breeds cultural cynicism, suspicion, disrespect and a hankering by Caribbean peoples after values alien to the realities of the Caribbean cultural experience. This persistence of the European/African dissensus born of slavery and mercantilist greed at worst leaves latecomer East Indians, Chinese and Lebanese virtually out of the determination of the cultural ethos and at second best tempts them to side with the symbols of power which are logically those associated with Europe. The war of the Plantation is nowhere ended. Neville Dawes as witness to the war concludes that "a Jamaican is anyone white, black or mixed who grew up in Jamaica and traces Jamaican ancestry back to the period of the institution of slavery in Jamaica."[3]

An effort years ago to find a cryptic phrase to describe the phenomenon, produced "The Melody of Europe and the Rhythm of Africa", for with "Europe" determining the ethos it is melody (following the canons of Western musical aesthetics) which 'makes the music' while rhythm merely provides the atavistic underpinnings. Small wonder that the rider "But Every John Crow T'ink Him Pickney White" had to be added — a point completely missed by some critics who saw the account as an uncompromising apologia for utopian multi-racialism and weak-kneed cultural nationalism.[4] This critical posture is nevertheless understandable since in Jamaica and other parts of the Caribbean cultural nationalism has indeed been an "ideological facade"[5] to cover up the social injustices of induced poverty among the black masses and the continuance of the entrenched privileges of the Eurocentric few. A lop-sided diversity designed to preserve the *status quo* cannot possibly provide the basis of national unity. In fact cultural nationalism is held suspect because it is not practically serviceable:

3. Dawes, Neville: Address to Lions Club Montego Bay, 2nd May, 1974 (mimeographed). Note: Mr Dawes is the Director of the Institute of Jamaica and a writer.

4. Lewis, Rupert: "Black Nationalism in Jamaica in Recent Years" in *Essays on Power and Change in Jamaica* edited by Carl Stone & Aggrey Brown, Jamaica Publishing House 1977, pp. 65-71.

5. Holzberg, Carol: Paper — "Social Stratification, Cultural Nationalism and Political Economy in Jamaica: The Role of the Entrepreneurial Elite" p. 20 (mimeographed — Boston University).

national mottoes such as Jamaica's "Out of Many, One People" are said to be too ambiguous to be useful since it can mean anything to anyone and therefore nothing or little to a nation in search of unity. On another level, the notion of a national identity is dismissed by many persons as an unpardonable indulgence since Jamaicans can claim to have several "identities".[6]

The cultural diversity which is the potential source of enrichment through cross-fertilisation and creative interaction becomes the framework for different groups to hold on to their different ethnocentric or class positions with due invocation of the inheritance of 19th century libertarian principles which persist if only because these in fact have served an entire generation that fought for self-determination and political autonomy. It seems as though M. G. Smith's pluralist theoretical framework is more real than the critics allow, after all. But it is this very reality of a 'perverted' cultural diversity that seemingly drives many Jamaicans to a range of responses and positions — some of them contradictory. Knowing the numerical strength of the people of African ancestry in the Jamaican cultural complex some people of said African ancestry opt for the very pluralism they question. For tactically it would give them a chance to develop a strong Afro-Jamaican tradition unhindered by having to bother with accommodations with the other ethnic groups in the society. The logic behind this is that numerical strength which ultimately means political weight in a one-man-one-vote democratic elective system would guarantee them the levers of power to effect in their favour the *one* out of "the many".[7] But other ethnocultural groups in the society would support the pluralist approach for the same reason — viz: in order to be left free to maintain their own positions especially if they belong to minority groups which hold economic power and wield influence in the corridors of political power. A realisation of the

6. Cumper, Gloria: Review of *Mirror, Mirror, Identity Race and Protest in Jamaica* Caribbean Quarterly, Vol. 17, Nos. 3 & 4, Sept.-Dec. 1971 — pp. 144-5. Gloria Cumper concludes that "no person has a single identity and the search in the terms in which it has been proposed [is] misconceived . . . "

7. The national motto of Jamaica is "Out of Many, One People".

implications of the numerical dominance of the other group has however forced many people back to a nationalist position insisting, as minority groups, that it is the *Jamaicanness* of the Jamaican that really matters rather than his being White (Euro), Black (Afro), Chinese or East Indian. None of this sits well on a growing group of intellectuals who eschew the notion that race enjoys a position of primacy in the socio-cultural equation of Jamaica or the West Indies.[8] The view is that rigid race, ethnic and even class lines are likely to be eroded with the improvement of economic conditions among the disadvantaged black poor, especially with the modernisation of the political system and the increase in political affiliations on the basis of issues rather than on adulatory loyalty to charismatic personages. In this regard the socialist commitment is a ready gift since it replaces race and ethnicity, difficult and inconclusive variables as they are to handle in social analysis, with an economic determinism which neatly transforms denigrated Blacks into the exploited working-class or proletariat.[9] Moreover it extends a wider embrace in places like Guyana and Trinidad to the numerically significant descendants of indentured labourers — the East Indians. Intellectually this is a tactical advance in the fight for distributive justice and economic betterment. But it is likely to prove strategically inadequate in the face of persistent cultural realities rooted in objective history and evident in certain present-day cultural sensibilities.[10] The battle between Europe and Africa continues for an African centrality in the indigenising process, if not for uncontested supremacy: and neither Guyana and Trinidad with their growing East Indian aggregates, nor Cuba with its predomin-

8. See Carl Stone's *Class, Race and Political Behaviour in Urban Jamaica* (Social and Economic Studies, Mona, 1973) also his "Race and Nationalism in Urban Jamaica" in *Caribbean Studies*, Vol. 13, No. 4, 1974.

9. Lewis, Rupert: *op cit* p. 71 especially the following "The struggle for national liberation has real roots in the interest of the exploited classes to challenge the economic system, inasmuch as the struggle against *national liberation* and socialism has roots in the desire of exploiter classes to maintain the status quo. *The solution to the racial question rests on the resolution of this conflict.*" (My emphasis).

10. Cp. the situation in Guyana where the East Indian Opposition Marxist Leader, Cheddi Jagan, whose phenomenal struggle to subsume considerations of *race* under

antly European population or Jamaica with its overwhelming African majority can escape the fact of the African Presence in the national cultural ethos. This is a fact of Caribbean life! The coming of Socialism with its supportive literature from Marx through Lenin to Marcuse could very well be seen as a deepening of that very cultural dependency on Europe, though the influence of Nyerere (and his Ujaama) does carry a legitimacy consonant with the age-long effort to give the African contribution to Caribbean cultural life its proper place. Even so the search outside of Caribbean experience for the solutions may be said to be taking "the struggle" no further out of its Eurocentric cocoon since the colonialist conditioning of dependency will not have been escaped. The argument that the exchange of Edmund Burke or John Locke and J. S. Mill for Marx and Lenin is part of the fertilising process necessary for growth has undoubted merit in the light of the advancement of human knowledge. But what if the fertiliser becomes the soil?

The failure by this author to treat such realities as race and culture largely as "superstructure" in an economic determinist framework receives conventional disapproval from Jamaican neo-Marxist critics. A critique by one such critic[11] of some of the literature of black nationalism betrays the biases usually associated with vulgar Marxism whereby the cultural phenomena are reduced to an ideological reflex of class interests. So one's silence "on how far and in what way [the power of the entrenched oligarchy] will have to be cut" is dismissed as "bourgeois nationalist". (Marx, he might recall, failed to leave behind a programme and not all that Lenin gave as strategy entered the practice of politics in post-Lenin Russia.)

In terms of his own perspectives, this author would

---

the 'universal' creed of scientific socialism though attended by some success, still depends for a good deal of his internal legitimacy on his massive *East Indian* support in the spirit of *apan jaht*. Similarly the Black socialist Prime Minister though he is after national unity under the label of co-operative republicanism finds political security largely in the passionate support of his Black *(African)* compatriots.

See Eddie Green's "Race vs Politics in Guyana — Racial Cleavages and Political Mobilization in the 1968 General Election" (1974).

11. Lewis, Rupert: *op cit* pp. 69-71.

regard the neo-Marxist borrowed technique of polemical labelling not only as an easy way of scoring a debating point but as ironically *Eurocentric*. But this author stands firm by the view that there need to be different and *innovative* ways of approaching social analysis in order to arrive at the truth about Caribbean society as basis for action. And both author and critic are of exactly the same *opinion* on at least one thing — substantively if not methodologically. That opinion, as the critic articulates it, is that "the privileges of the exploiter classes ["entrenched business oligarchy" to this author], including the rights and power accorded on the basis of race and colour, have not been surrendered voluntarily nearly one hundred and forty years after Emancipation."[12]

Of course the concept of *race-and-colour* in Caribbean terms is far more complex and difficult to deal with than many Caribbean Marxists seem ready to admit. The harsh fact is that it is a "reality" that has to be taken into account in any serious analysis of Caribbean society. And without underestimating the primary importance of the economic "class/historical point of view", we might reflect on the state of mind of a renowned Caribbean economist who had reason in 1977 to give out a *cri de coeur* on the subject of "institutionalised racism" which he insists persists in Jamaica.[13] The privileges of the "exploiter classes" have not been surrendered indeed!

A young Black Cuban radical in the sixties had reason to ask whether Marx and Engels were racist and though he may have found no conclusive answer the significant thing is that as a Caribbean man, he felt the urge to put the question. That Race (and ethnicity) must be worked into the Marxian dialectic to meet the realities of Caribbean existence is a responsibility serious Caribbean socialists must face or find that yet another theory from Europe will have failed to deliver the goods simply because we would have ignored Marx's own injunctions, by not relating our efforts suffi-

12. *Ibid.*

13. See Report of Dr George Beckford's statement in the *Jamaica Daily News* of Sunday, May 8, 1977. See also John Maxwell's "No Better Herring" in the *Jamaica Daily News*, Tuesday, May 3, 1977.

ciently to the specificity of Caribbean history and realities. What is more, the cultural hang-up of hanging on to the philosophical drippings of Europe.in the name of intellectual universalism may or may not be itself economically determined, considering that the disease permeates all strata of post-colonial societies like Jamaica.

On another level, the deterioration of social analysis into a consecrated activity for a select fraternity that is intolerant of alternative visions and methodological daring, is not likely to serve the Caribbean well in its desperate search for a new social order, no more than a path bereft of a sense of direction and indecisive in its intellectual foundations can do.

The revolutionary Cubans have not decided by accident to invoke Marxism-Leninism for ideological legitimacy while making José Martí, their native son and national hero, the *soul* of their revolution. National liberation and socialist reconstruction are, after all, joint concerns in the pantheon of concerns among the progressives in the Caribbean region. Referring to the "monstrously efficient" and "invisible" sort of "infiltrating virus" from outside which denies to the Caribbean people their "own creation" and their own "intimate way of being", Nicolás Guillén invokes the memory of Martí who, he says, "allows for grafting from outside, but just as long as the trunk is our own". "On these bases" concludes Guillén, "rests Cuban cultural policy under the guidance of Fidel Castro".[14] The Cuban "strategy" cited above is a typically Caribbean compromise-of-a-solution, since the quest for identity in an inherited diversity confronts the Caribbean territories constantly with the *agony of options.*

For a Caribbean country like Jamaica, the options reside in the very presence in this "open" society of distinctive groups, classes, or segments of "nationals", each with a different cultural focus of commitment born out of abiding historical forces. These are evident firstly among an intensely Eurocentric (predominantly white) upperclass. This class is by no means homogeneous for it comprises Sephardic Jews, Lebanese-Syrians, Whites of Anglo-

---

14. Guillén, Nicolás: Acceptance Speech on the Award of the Musgrave Gold Medal, Institute of Jamaica, 4th December, 1974, in *Jamaica Journal*, Vol. 9, No. 1.

Saxon or Nordic stock, and some 'high-brown Jamaica (functional) Whites'. Their different socio-cultural points of reference disappear in the face of their shared international consumption pattern and, one might add, in the face of the threat to their entrenched oligarchic position in the face of rapid social change.[15] Secondly are the intermediate groups of polyglot souls who are partly Euro-centric [and for this they are sometimes termed as functional whites]. They are also partly creolised in the sense of their racial mixture with the African ingredient quite evident, as well as in the sense of their not always unqualified commitment to homegrown cuisines, native-bred speech patterns where appropriate, endorsement of the now indigenous mating habits and kinship patterns and their support by active participation in the conscious shaping of "Jamaican" classic expressions in such artistic fields as music, dance, drama, the arts and crafts. In addition, they are among the willing recruits into what has been described as the "international consumption pattern",[16] whereby members of the entrepreneurial and professional elites (irrespective of racial/cultural origin) participate in "an international life style" which facilitates their social interaction with expatriates and foreign elements as can be seen in the almost nightly ritual on the cocktail circuit involving the diplomatic corps and in their high visibility on occasions of performances by visiting metropolitan performing-arts groups. Such performances are often misguidedly projected as the blessing of "high culture" as against the ready-to-hand "low culture" of indigenous Jamaican origin or vintage. Thirdly, there are those who would be regarded as the purveyors of "low culture" or as some would say "the little tradition" to be found at the base of the society among the lower classes, who are economically poor and ethnically of African ancestry. Here the situation is nowhere as simplistic as might be implied.[17] The hankering after the classical antiquity of an African past is the *force vitale* of much that is

15. Holzberg, Carol: *op cit* pp. 20-23.

16. *Ibid.*

17. Indeed not; in Marxian forms of social analysis most of these would be classified as

the cultural existence in the ghettos of urban Jamaica, and indeed through the main cities of the Commonwealth Caribbean. But there is also the Caribbean psychic posture firmly rooted in the native-born, native-bred legacy of centuries of transformation of the Afro-Jamaican into a Caribbean man through a process of adjustments, rejection, affirmation and innovation.[18] And this is very evident among the sturdy and independent-minded peasantry of Jamaica. Among them, however, is the strong attraction to things North American as is the case throughout the rest of the society — what with the influence of the cinema and the mass media, (especially radio and latterly television) and the frequent contact that the lower-class household help has with her middle and upper-class mistress. The cultural options are indeed diverse and this is not by any means the case for only a few Jamaicans.[19] Any one individual from whatever group described above is wont to opt simultaneously for more than one opportunity as suits his/her needs in a society that has never been too sure about itself or of its identity — a society which has been described as a labour camp with a transient workforce waiting to flee to better opportunities, as a state of "Babylonian captivity" whose victims are waiting to be delivered into some Promised Land, as a plantation owned by outsiders whose interest and ambition have hardly gone beyond commericial profit, or as a kind of no-man's-land occupied by usurpers whose legitimacy to ownership and control is yet to

petty-bourgeois covering, at least in Rupert Lewis' analysis (*op cit* footnote 2, p. 71) "the small property owning class and the peasantry, small shopkeepers, petty traders, higglers, artisans and craftsmen (who) make up the bulk of the population". Included in my third category would also be the "lumpenproletariat" of the urban ghettos — many unemployed. This note is included to acknowledge the different ways that exist in Jamaica of looking at Jamaican society — itself a significant "cultural phenomenon" in any discussion on cultural identity and national unity in Jamaica and other parts of the Caribbean today.

18. Nettleford, Rex: Editorial Foreword in *Caribbean Quarterly* Vol. 19, No. 3, (University of the West Indies) pp. 4-5.

19. Cp. Jamaica's diversified foreign policy.

be settled and can only be settled by the absolute victory of one set of contenders over the other. Small wonder that the migrating propensities of the Jamaican people have been so great throughout the ages — first among the planters whose absenteeism from their property was almost a condition of West Indian proprietorship in the days of slavery and secondly among the descendants of ex-slaves who hankered after economic prosperity as basis for cultural strength and human worth in lands near and far but away from Jamaica, whether it be Panama (for the building of the Canal), Costa Rica and Central America (for the construction of railways and the planting of bananas), Cuba (for the cultivation of sugar), the United States (for the eking out of fortunes in sundry fields of endeavour), or the United Kingdom (for the running of public transport, the staffing of hospitals, or for working in factories). The exodus in the 1970's of persons from the skilled intermediate groups given to the international consumption pattern in the wake of changes which threatened to deprive them of their culturally dominant position in the society, pales beside the mass migration of those economically marginal Jamaicans who had left the country in the nineteen-fifties and sixties in search of "a better economic life". The call to patriotism and identification with what is believed to be a Jamaican cultural ethos and national unity is not heeded by those who harbour fears about an uncertain political future. But it is in the nature of the diversity in the range and focus of cultural commitment among Jamaicans that the habitual preference of an alternative is said to be manifest even among political leaders who reputedly carry a "green card" giving them permanent residential status in the United States or whatever is the equivalent document that provides landed-immigrant status for Canada. It is not an accident that among these who carry such insurance against future odds are many late-comer Jamaicans, especially of Chinese and Lebanese origin, whose cultural marginality in the Jamaican ethos may very well account for the easily weakened commitment to national unity in time of crisis among these otherwise economically dominant groups of Jamaicans. The result is a confusion that feeds on itself.

The question of whether there can be harmonious integration of cultural diversity with national unity is here strained by the realities of political ideological factors (themselves a cultural variable). The coincidence of cultural marginality in the diverse complex with impending political/ideological redundancy is seen to compound the difficulties of existence among such privileged groups. Flight becomes the solution. This rates some comparison with the phenomenon of the lasting coincidence between the economic marginality of the majority of the populace and the cultural marginality of the same people in an uncompromisingly Eurocentric ethos. Again, the answer was flight for those who could flee back in the fifties and early sixties. They left behind those, who were unable to or who could avoid fleeing, to face the agony inherent in the noxious notion that all things drawn from the experience of Europe, the land of the masters, are good and all or most things drawn from elsewhere (and particularly from the experience of people of African ancestry or from Africa itself) are less than good.

A brief survey of some of the major indices of culture will bear out the point. Take the question of *language* — both the oral tongue and the scribal writ — by which a people's civilisation is known. Linguistic autonomy becomes the pride of a people and some would even die in defence of it. Most Jamaicans speak their native-born, native-bred tongue — "patois" or "Jamaica Talk" — most of the time. But it is Standard English of the metropolitan brand which, though functionally a second language, is culturally mandatory if one is to get on in the society. The institutional guarantee through the O-level/A-level British school-leaving examinations, now being replaced by a Caribbean version, is reinforcing. This has led in the past to a serious neglect (which is now being corrected) of closer examination of the learning needs, language-wise, of the Jamaican child whose first language is, after all, his creole tongue. The question is yet to be answered as to how many are the young humans who have been relegated to stations of lifelong inferiority or a sense of irredeemably low status because their own linguistic potential has not been properly explored? This argument of course could be used as an excuse to deprive the 20th century Jamaican child of an experience as a citizen of the world; and clearly this would be undesirable in the global village that is the world of today. But what excuse can there be for depriving him of his rich native tongue forged out of the specifics of his and his forebears' experience simply to make room for what is consecrated *the* universal and powerful language? Need the two be mutually exclusive? Is the diversity again to be on the terms of the traditionally dominant overlord? Why can't the Jamaican child grow to feel that he is free to use any language-form appropriate to his needs or even to be free to create other forms from his diverse knowledge of different language forms of which Standard English is but one, albeit an important one? Can't he be allowed to think in Jamaica Talk as well as in English, in Yoruba or Swahili as well as in French or Spanish, in Papiamento as well as in Dutch or Portuguese, in Hindi, Urdu, Chinese, or in German, Italian or Greek? Despite the supremacy of the English language in the world at large, what with the eclipse of French, the cultural history of Jamaica and the Commonwealth Caribbean makes the imposed supremacy of Metropolitan English too reminiscent of the cultural bombardment to which generations have been subjected and the subtle psychological conditioning that has deepened the state of the people's mental dependency on Europe in ways that are still evident among so many Caribbean ex-colonials, 'bourgeois' and 'leftist radicals' alike. For the "lingua franca" has virtually become the language of legitimate Caribbean literature and the mastery of it a determinant of progress towards 'civilisation'. Whether it is George Lamming, John Hearne, Vidia Naipaul, Wilson Harris, Derek Walcott,[20] Alejo Carpentier or Aimé Césaire, it is the achievement in the master's language which has earned them their well deserved place in the pantheon of treasured gifts that they undoubtedly are to a still powerless people. But happily they are but one part of the complex story of Caribbean cultural diversity, since ranking high in the adventurous journeys toward the discovery

20. Messrs Lamming, Hearne, Naipaul, Harris, Walcott are from the (Commonwealth) Caribbean, Carpentier is from Cuba and Césaire is from Martinique, a department of France.

of self are such others as Louise Bennett turning out her deceptively simple quatrains in the powerful language of the ordinary folk or Nicolás Guillén[21] matching the spiritual nobility of his deracinated islanders with the earthy passion and musical reverberations of the people of his soil, or Edward Brathwaite,[22] consciously forging aesthetic sense out of the contradictory omens of the chaotic but exciting existence which has been the bane of Caribbean life, or Vic Reid[23] and Samuel Selvon[24] struggling with the language of their people to give a classic scribal expression in a world that, for good or for ill, remains the child of Gutenberg.

They are all at once engaged in the search for solutions to the "problems of language." That problem is not simply the matter of the call for mandatory fulfilment of proficiency in the use of the master's tongue now seen by some to be a universal necessity, but rather the threat that the unrelieved promotion of such a cultural manifesto poses for that self-realisation and hope of independent discovery in the world of human expression through the use of the languages that are themselves the organic linguistic expression of the vast majority of the people in Jamaica and throughout the Caribbean. The negation of a much hankered after cultural diversity is one thing; the continuing effort to effect the final deculturation of masses of Caribbean people another.

In Jamaica reaction against any such effort finds form in the persistence of the Jamaican dialect in myriad forms, from parish to parish, from country to town, from one social group to the next. Conscious change of vocabulary and syntax is itself part of the "politics of protest" in at least one dominant cultural group − the

21. Louise Bennett is a Jamaican poet, folklorist and actress, Nicolás Guillén is Cuba's national poet.

22. Edward Brathwaite is a Barbadian poet-historian residing in Jamaica. His academic work on the creolisation process is reflected in his poetry which explores the cultural dynamics of the uprooted and re-grown Caribbean man.

23. Vic Reid is a Jamaican novelist whose *New Day* is regarded as a watershed event in Caribbean writing.

24. Sam Selvon is a Trinidadian novelist working out of the United Kingdom.

Rastafarians — thus creating greater diversity in the speech patterns and linguistic profile of the Jamaican cultural complex. On another level scholars are continuing work on Jamaica Talk.[25] But there is also now in progress a project designed to document the vocabulary and structure and total framework of Caribbean English directed from the Cave Hill campus of the University of the West Indies.[26] The point of this, *inter alia,* is that Standard English (metropolitan style) has undergone more than a sea-change and now has an independent existence as Caribbean English, creatively forged out of Caribbean experience as has happened with the language in the United States of America and Canada where there are now dictionaries of American English and Canadian English. This at least is a declaration of intent to redress the imbalances and habitual biases in the cultural diversity as far as language is concerned. Whether it will be an effective contribution to the promotion of national unity in the individual territories concerned or whether it will bring the Caribbean closer to regional integration is a matter purely of conjecture at this stage.

It is Edward Brathwaite who gives the timely reminder that Caribbean languages are more than lexicography, that they are

25.   See F. G. Cassidy: *Jamaica Talk* (MacMillan, London for Institute of Jamaica, 1961).

F. G. Cassidy & R. B. LePage: *Dictionary of Jamaican English* (Cambridge University Press, 1967).

Beryl Loftman-Bailey: *Jamaica Creole Syntax: A Transformational Approach* (Cambridge University Press, 1967).

R. B. LePage & David DeCamp: *Jamaican Creole — An Historical Introduction and Four Jamaica Creole Texts* (MacMillan, London, 1960).

Jean D'Costa: "Language and Dialect in Jamaica" in *Jamaica Journal,* March 1968, Vol. 2, No. 1.

26.   S. R. Richard Allsopp in a proposal for a lexicographical centre to be located at the Cave Hill Campus (Barbados) of the University of the West Indies gives the following rationale for the project: "The Lexicography Project which began in November 1971 at UWI, Cave Hill, aims to produce a Dictionary of Caribbean English Usage for which data is (sic) to be drawn from every Anglophone Caribbean territory including Guyana, Belize and the Bahamas. The main thrust of the undertaking is at the regional lexicon in educated use — identifying and cross referencing the particular words and the particular usage throughout the Anglophone sub-cultures of the area . . ."

Proposal for a Lexicographical Centre at the UWI, Cave Hill, December 1974 (mimeographed).

imagery, tone, metaphysical symbolism, and possessing the properties of song/dance/movement even. Basil Matthews, a Trinidadian
scholar at Howard University lists Brathwaite's disclosures of the
African properties in Caribbean literature, such as "the progressive
use of imagery; the use of 'nation-language' or Afro-dialect; the cult
of the word as *sound*; its sound value, as for example, when words
are concocted to make onomatopoeic sense or nonsense; the con-
cretising or the grounding, that is, the fleshing out of ideas; imaginative visualisations; Afro-puns and the calypsonic miming of words
... [and] the philosophic symbolism in which poems and folksongs bring the metaphysical and the mundane into a single unity
of life [as well as] the surreal images of the literature of folk
religion."[27]

Such 'surreal images' are everywhere to be found in the
"folk expressions" of Caribbean countries with their diversity of
language forms. Such diversity need not be incompatible with
national unity though it can present the nation with an endemic
crisis verging on imminent disorder.[28] In the Caribbean it is an
aspect of the characteristic pluralism. Bilingualism, in some cases
multilingualism, is functionally a fact of Caribbean life. In every
case it is a European language, the language of the masters and of
political power, that is the *lingua franca,* though Papiamento is
struggling to be a legitimate second in its native Curacao (Netherlands Antilles). In Jamaica and the rest of the Commonwealth
Caribbean it is English; and here Eurocentric intolerance is likely
to dictate the disqualification of hordes of people from entering
the corridors of advancement if they fail to match plural noun with
plural verb. It is one thing to require of a trainee-teacher proficiency
in the official language of instruction; it is quite another to block
the progress of a talented dancer, sculptor, musician or painter by
denying him/her entry to a tertiary-level training programme

27. Matthews, Basil: "Voice of Africa in the Diaspora" in *New Directions* (Howard
University, Washington D.C.) April 1977, p. 18. Dr Matthews' comment is on the
excellent article written by Edward Brathwaite in *Daedalus* Journal of the American
Academy of Arts and Sciences of Spring 1974, pp. 73-110 and entitled "The African
Presence in Caribbean Literature."

28. Cp. the experience in India and Canada.

because he has failed to attain the O-level passes in English language. Small wonder that social protest manifests itself in language change. For defiance of society includes defiance of its language.[29]

The diversity of *religious forms* is no less a challenge for national unity in Jamaica and the Caribbean. The early efforts to discourage the spread of ancestral African religions led to an active defiance and a startling survival of African forms reinforced by post-slavery infusions from West Africa in such expressions as Kumina in Jamaica, Shango in Trinidad, Cumfeh in Guyana and Obeah all over the region.[30] In Jamaica, as elswhere, a wide range of syncretised religious expressions are to be found under the generic nomenclature of Revivalism but Pukkumina (or Pocomania) regarded as a form more African than the Christianised Revivalism, has had a long track record dating back to the post-Emancipation period – i.e. after 1838.[31] In addition, there are evidences of such "world religions" as Judaism, Mohammedanism, Hinduism, (with large numbers of adherents to these in Trinidad and Guyana), Bahai and even Buddhism. Standing above them all with the authoritative confidence of prior legitimation is the Christian Church from Europe and of late America, covering fundamentalist evangelical, missionary Baptist, Wesleyan Methodist, high Church Roman Catholic, disestablished but deeply entrenched Anglican and

29. Attributed to Theodor Adorno in his famous essay "Prisms" quoted by Martin Jay in his book *The Dialectical Imagination* (Little Brown & Co. Boston, 1973) p. 176.

30. Simpson, George Easton: *Religious Cults of the Caribbean* (Institute of Caribbean Studies, University of Puerto Rico, 1960) especially pp. 11-111 and pp. 157-200.

    Obeah Law of Jamaica in Laws of Jamaica, Vol. 5, 1948.

    Barrett, Leonard: *The Sun and the Drum* – African Roots in Jamaican Folk Tradition, (Sangster's Heinemann, Kingston, Jamaica 1976, Chap. IV).

31. Wadell, Hope Masterton: *Twentynine Years in the West Indies & Central Africa* – A Review of Missionary Work and Adventure 1829-1858 (Frank Cass & Co. 1970, 2nd Ed. Chaps. VI-XIX).

    Wright, Philip: *Knibb, 'the Notorious'* – Slaves' Missionary 1803-1845 (Sidgwick & Jackson, London, 1973).

    Phillipo, James: *Jamaica Its Past and Present State* (Dawsons of Pall Mall, London 2nd Ed. 1970).

    Simpson, George Easton: "Jamaica Revivalist Cults", *Social & Economic Studies* Vol. 5, No. 4 (Dec. 1956) University of the West Indies.

    Seaga, Edward: "Cults in Jamaica", *Jamaica Journal* Vol. 3, No. 2 (June 1969).

more recently the ancient Ethiopian Orthodox Church. The 1970 census revealed the following:[32]

Religion	Male	Female	Total
Anglican	133503	143829	277332
Baptist (Orth)	152319	167421	319740
Brethren	14978	17214	32192
Church of God	141937	163475	305412
Methodist	51293	56842	108135
Moravian	25336	26471	51807
Pentecostal	26139	30916	57055
Presby/Congr.	45041	48096	93137
Roman Catholic	69199	73504	142703
Seventh Day Advts.	54980	62079	117059
Not stated	161309	131620	292929
Total	876034	921467	1797501

The supremacy is underscored by the tremendous prestige Christianity enjoys as the 'religion of advanced civilisation' or Christendom in Western colonial history, and the reinforcement of this prestige by the place of eminence Christian Church leaders enjoy in the hierarchy of Caribbean officialdom. Political leaders have repeatedly declared Jamaica to be a "Christian country". Political creeds are given Christian sources of origin or inspiration when they are to be promulgated and 'sold' to the general mass of people. Europe here again reigns. But Africa rules in the on-going assertion of faith in some Black or African soul-force among the mass of people who, though present in the congregation of the orthodox Christian denominations, continue to be the source of such indigenous forms or religious expression as Rastafarianism,[33] which declares the late Emperor of Ethiopia as God, the land of Ethiopia as the Black man's Promised Land, the West (and especially Jamaica) as Babylon, and themselves as Black Israelites. A cultural response to social and economic deprivation here becomes the makings of a profoundly insightful religion, challenging in serious

---

32. *1970 Population Census of the Commonwealth Caribbean* Vol. 7 — Race and Religion, Editor G. W. Roberts, pp. 93-98.

33. Owens, Joseph: *Dread, The Rastafarians of Jamaica* (Sangster's, Kingston, Jamaica, 1977).

ways the theology of Christian orthodoxy, the religion of status and power.

Is this diversity of religious outlook among the Jamaican populace supportive of national unity?[34] This question was posed in the early sixties on the occasion of social unrest and active cultural assertion by one group of aggrieved Jamaicans.[35] They continue to cry out against discrimination and the victimisation they insist they suffer at the hands of the press and the police because of their religious beliefs. Will freedom of conscience, a long accepted principle in the exercise of civil liberties since 1826 in Jamaican society, be extended to people like the Rastafarians?

The question is not an academic one. In an ex-colonial society doused in colonial attitudes and mores, old practices of colonial vintage die hard. The extension of freedom of conscience even when accepted in principle was not always as speedily applied as might be expected. The law against Obeah is after all still on the Statute Books in Jamaica though repealed in Guyana in 1975. There is no law against the Rastafarian creed though the elevation of marijuana to the status of a Holy Weed by the faithful receives no dispensation from the stringent penalties of the country's Dangerous Drugs Law. In 1977 a Parliamentary Committee appointed to look into the decriminalization of ganja (marijuana) recommended a more liberal official attitude towards the use of the "weed", thus indicating a significant departure from the position taken by the wider society in the sixties and no doubt in deference to the cultural reality of persistent and widespread usage among people, especially young people, of all classes in Jamaica.

34. Ronnie Thwaites, a lawyer, radio commentator, journalist and declared socialist, had this to say: "For the most part the so-called established Churches in Jamaica remain as conservative forces within the community without a clear resolve up to this point of history to challenge their members and the much wider cross-section of persons of goodwill who are mindful of Church teaching and attitude towards the evident righteousness of the aspirations of our people for decency and subsistence". See "The Church and Socialism", *Jamaica Daily News*, Wednesday, May 4, 1977.

35. i.e. the Rastafarians. See *The Ras Tafari Movement in Kingston, Jamaica*, (ISER, UCWI Mona, Jamaica 1960) by M. G. Smith, F. R. Augier and Rex Nettleford.

Taking Rastafarianism into account, the diverse religious forms to be found among the great majority of Jamaicans all draw from the same source — the Holy Bible. Religious diversity then has an underlying commonality in the Word from the Holy Book. The force of the indigenous religious expressions and the growing nationalist awareness since Independence have forced Jamaican Christian orthodoxy nearer to relevance by way of visible adjustments and adaptations in areas of liturgy, style of vestments and the like though not in the substantive aspects of theology and canonical law. Many of the young clergy from a variety of denominations are to be found actively on the side of what would be called progressive politics, supporting social change and consciously seeking ways and means of projecting God with a human face.[36] There is predictable resistance among other representatives of the Christian clergy against the revolutionary rhetoric of socialism and change but the Eurocentric nature of the society assures for Christian orthodoxy, and not indigenous religious forms, a place of top priority in Jamaica's cultural ethos, leaving the indigenous forms to provide a vibrant source of energy for the development of the Arts.

In the area of the *Creative Arts* there has been greater success at relating national unity to the cultural products out of the awesome process of creolisation or indigenisation; though there are still significant groups of Jamaicans from the privileged classes who naturally place the achievements of Europe (or in some cases, the achievements of any external civilisation) over and above the achievement of Jamaica and the Caribbean. Despite this the effort in music, painting, sculpture, dance and drama by a generation or two to forge different expressions reflective of Jamaican experience out of the rich diversity of the country's cultural heritage, has produced results which could very well be the answer to the less felicitous conclusions of M. G. Smith's analysis of Jamaican cultural pluralism. For M. G. Smith insists in

36. Compare the work of CADEC (Christian Action for Development in the Caribbean) in a wide range of adult education, culturally based community welfare, social and economic action research programmes.

his study[37] that "the differing sectional values within a plural society are a profound source of instability". He adds that in such a situation "the subordinate cultural section may either practice escapist religious rituals or create a charismatic leadership as the organ of sectional solidarity and protest". The conscious and sub-conscious 'functionalist' attempts to avoid this by the use of the arts as means to social integration merely reinforce the validity of Smith's point while at the same time seeking to mitigate its viler consequences.

There is in *music*, for example, the tremendously rich output since the late 1950's of original genres in the popular mode which has given to a wide cross-section of the Jamaican people and especially the general masses a sense of positive achievement and identity through indigenous creative action. The international attention the 'Jamaican sound' has attracted, has only served to buttress this new-found confidence. Going by such names as *Ska*,[38] *Rock-Steady*[39] and now *Reggae*,[40] the music has gone beyond fulfilling the universal need for entertainment to attract acute interest in its deeper significance for Jamaican and Caribbean cultural search for form and purpose. As the earlier Trinidad calypso movement threw up internationally acclaimed exponents

37. Smith, M. G.: *op cit* pp. 90-91.

38. Ska is a type of music emerging from among the urban mass population in Jamaica during the mid-1950's, with evidences of influences from American recorded pop music, elements of traditional music (revival and pukkumina) and from Rastafarian drumming. The late Count Ossie, a Rastafarian patriarchical figure, is credited with having been a rallying point for original creators of the music and for the popular exponents who emerged soon after.

39. Rock-Steady is a type of music popular in Jamaica about 1960, intermediate between ska and reggae and based on American rhythm and blues.

40. "Reggae is a type of music that emerged in the mid-sixties, based on ska and usually having a heavy four-beat rhythm using the bass, electric guitar and drum, with the scraper coming in at the end of the measure, and acting as accompaniment to emotional songs expressing rejection of established (white-man: or Babylonian) culture". This definition is suggested by Frederick Cassidy (1976). Chief exponents of the reggae in the seventies have been the internationally acclaimed Bob Marley, 'Toots' Hibbert, and Jimmy Cliff.

such as Lord Kitchener and Mighty Sparrow, so now the Jamaican revolution in music produces for the international charts such stars as Don Drummond, Desmond Dekker, Toots Hibbert, Jimmy Cliff and Bob Marley whose names have travelled from the ghettos of Kingston via the electronic media and the giant recording industry to distant lands including those of Africa and the Orient. The lyrics of many a reggae tune is the raw stuff of protest coming from the "subordinate culture section" of Jamaican society and expectedly the sound of the music is ancestral echo itself.[41]

Ancestral echoes find reality mostly in the traditional music that is to be found among a robust peasantry and the urban ritualists of Jamaica. The work among them by artists like folklorist Louise Bennett, anthropologist Edward Seaga, the Cudjoe Minstrels of the 1940's, the Frats Quintet of the 1950's and since Independence the Jamaican Folk Singers led by Olive Lewin, a Jamaican folkmusic collector and arranger, has created what is likely to be of lasting interest among future generations of Jamaicans in the diverse musical heritage of Jamaica. Edward Seaga had this to say in speaking of the Folk Music Research Unit which he established in the Jamaica School of Music in 1966 to collect the wide variety of folk music material which existed in Jamaica: "Folk music coming as it does from folk society, is usually plagued by the social and cultural gaps which separate folk society from the rest of society in developing countries . . . It is necessary to bridge [those gaps], otherwise the material collected from within the confines of folk society which creates it, or which carries it on as a tradition, is exposed across a bridge into those other areas of society which have not had the firsthand experience of witnessing or participating in the folk rituals or the folklore."[42] Although a

---

41. In preparation is an independent study of the development of the Jamaican popular music since the late fifties by Garth White, a Rastafarian and graduate of the UWI. Also in preparation is a compilation by Tony Laing *et al* of lyrics, recordings, sheet-music, and biographies of artists over the period from 1959-1979. This is under the aegis of the Institute of Jamaica.

42. Seaga, Edward (Hon): Welcome Address to the Twenty-first Conference of the International Folk Music Council, Kingston, Jamaica, August 1971. Mr Seaga was Minister of Finance (and Culture).

collector and researcher, he saw other important uses for the traditional music of the country. He went on: "It is necessary, therefore, to create a central pool of material where firstly the researcher can go for further information, but also where the creative artist can go, so as to be able to get his material which he uses as a point of departure in the creative process, to enable him to create in the performing arts, material which properly reflects the folk basis of his performance".[43]

This strategy of exposure has best served the group organised by the Folk Music Officer, the Jamaican Folk Singers, who have complemented the Festival Commission's own plethora of annual competitions in choral music and have succeeded through radio recordings and live performances to maintain an active interest in the traditional music of the country, not only in Jamaica but overseas. It is a paradox that before the Jamaica School of Music was reorganised in 1973, students passing through that institution missed the fruits of the new collection by the Folk Music Research Unit. The reason lay not merely in the proverbial clash of personalities that plague cultural movements anywhere, but as much· in the dilemma over what are the cultural values in music to be preserved and developed in Jamaica. One Minister of Government seemed clear in his own mind but the ethos of the then music school did not reflect agreement on this point. From the society could come a letter as late as March 1974 deploring the decline of classical music among the students at the School of Music. The writer saw such music as being something which is "good for people, and even (if) not wanted, . . . should be persuaded upon people". He noted the absence of a "National Symphony Orchestra", a fact which dissuaded Jamaicans from taking to classical music as a profession but lauded the introduction of a course for music teachers in the public schools. He was sure that there was greater demand for classical music among Jamaicans than appeared on the surface judging from the capacity audiences at recitals by the School itself. In any case "those who love classical music are not likely to write to the stations about it, whereas

43. *Ibid.*

the maid, cook or yard-boy will get a postal card, take a stub of pencil and protest hearing classical music and expressing the urge to hear the latest pop 'ting'." The inherent snobbery in the Jamaican cultural complex emerges in the writer's reference to a "better type person" (sic) who lives for experiencing an appreciable amount of classical music, "whether by performing himself or by hearing others in live performances." As to who the "better type person" is in the Jamaican scheme of things there is no doubt in the mind of the letter writer who further in his treatise volunteered the following discovery: "Some years ago an anthropologist published his studies of cultures in which drumming played a major role (in Africa and India) and those cultures were stagnant."[44] All the above illustrate the stereotype of a classical plantation position and hopefully the position of a dying breed. But this letter was written in 1974 at a time when a popularly elected government was shouting socialism and participatory democracy and twelve years after Independence! European classical music is still regarded as necessary to life and is reserved for the 'better-type person.' A national *symphony* orchestra in a country where people make their own indigenous music which need not require 'symphonic instruments', is invoked. Yet the Jamaica Philharmonic which was founded and directed by the Jamaican Sibthorpe Beckett has been struggling long before Independence with less than adequate support from the devotees of so-called "good music", a fact which prompts speculation as to whether the leader's musical background, social antecedents and objective class position, such as they were, could have given him the recognised authority among the "good-music" Establishment in the hey-day of colonialism. The drum, once described as an "unsubtle instrument", and the dominant musical instrument of Africa and India from which vast hordes of Jamaicans come, denotes cultural stagnation! In 1976, the argument was still being pushed though less crassly. An expatriate European music teacher publicly offered the following views to Jamaicans on his impending departure after many years of influence in Jamaican music circles: "most of the great music that has

44. Letter from a Resident in Jamaica.

proved lasting comes from a handful of European countries.
Jamaica has not, as yet, produced an outstanding composer of
such international repute ... Until Jamaica and other countries
develop worthwhile art music of their own, performers and
audiences have no alternative but to enjoy only Bach, Beethoven,
Brahms and Britten, etc." This represented a typical Eurocentric
conceit that has informed the colonial relations and still plagues
the post-colonial cultural consciousness.[45] This was to prompt a
reply which stressed the importance of the display of excellence in
the world of music over the claims to exclusive achievement by
"classical composers". "Long live Beethoven, Bach, Bob Marley
and the Mighty Sparrow" concluded the rejoinder.[46] It is clear
that what is essentially a non-issue to those who are committed to
good music from anywhere, including the Caribbean, gets blown
into proportions of great socio-cultural significance because of the
continued denigration of the genuine potential and actual output
of the Jamaican creative imagination and the sustained inferiority
complex to be found among many native Caribbean people who
may or may not be exposed to the product of Europe's own
creative genius.

The Jamaican musical heritage is itself the result of
centuries of cross-fertilisation of the sounds and rhythms of Africa,
Europe, the creolised Caribbean itself, the Orient and modern
America. There is no escape by our young instrumentalists and
composers working in the Jamaica School of Music from the influence of a wider world of music and the far more challenging realities of the process of indigenisation, based on Jamaican and Caribbean material. Any other approach is likely to perpetuate the
reproduction of imitators equipped with Licentiates and graduate
diplomas certifying a quite ordinary level of competent craftsmanship but offering no guarantee of the enrichment of Caribbean life

45. *Daily Gleaner,* Kingston, Jamaica, Letter to the Editor July 24, 1976 from Barry
Davies. See also letter to Editor August 25, 1976, from Geoff Fairweather. See
Editorial, July 3, 1976 and letter replying from Rex Nettleford (July 16, 1976).

46. *News Analysis,* Radio and Television (Jamaica Broadcasting Corporation) July 26,
1976 by Rex Nettleford.

by the exercise of a lively creative imagination. The dependency on other people's talents will also perpetuate the importation to the colonial periphery of palm-court musicians parading as Stravinskys; and the transmitted mediocrity and pedestrianism will in turn perpetuate itself in smug audiences who will relegate reggae to the baser instincts of the Jamaican ghetto-bred or who will regard traditional music as the romantic outpourings of noble savages to be replicated in 'cultural concerts' by folksingers, and who will mistake as high art the light operas and popular classics which jam the airwaves at select hours of transmission and are introduced from the liner notes of the record jackets to those who like "good" or "serious" music.

Dance and dance-theatre have fared somewhat better, but only somewhat! There can be little doubt that there is a Caribbean dance-theatre that is distinctive in content, style and technical potential. It draws heavily on the African memory in its rhythmic contours and, depending on the colonial power, reflects the influence of the manners of the European court simulated by the Great House balls of the plantation gentry or the masquerade revelries of a more robust fieldhand populace.

It is from this source of rituals, masques, set-dances and revelries that has come a varied repertoire of traditions explored by Beryl McBurnie of Trinidad in the 1940's and 1950's and internationalised by the skill of Boscoe and Geoffrey Holder[47] in Metropolitan England and America, though Berto Pasuko,[48] the Jamaican, preceded the Holders in England. They formed the basis for experimentation and creative-dance departure by Ivy Baxter during the 1950's in Jamaica. This was to be a historic departure from the distinguished and imaginative work in classical ballet by

47. Boscoe and Geoffrey Holder are well-known names on both sides of the North Atlantic, Geoffrey more so since in 1975 he won awards for his direction of the Broadway Musical "The Wiz" (a Black version of "The Wizard of Oz") to which he brought all the colour and flair of the Carnival of his native Trinidad. Both brothers are also accomplished painters and a son of Boscoe is a principal dancer in the major American ballet company — the Joffrey Ballet — in New York.

48. See Ivy Baxter's *The Arts of An Island* (The Scarecrow Press) Chap. 20 which deals with the development of dance in Jamaica from 1938-1962.

Hazel Johnston who had studied music and dance in London in the thirties.[49]

Over in Haiti the work of action analysis, classification and technical refinement developed during the fifties under the direction of Lavinia Williams,[50] a former dancer with the American Black anthropologist and dance creator Katherine Dunham who used Jamaica, Haiti and Brazil as the main sources of her widely acclaimed repertoire of African-American dances. Jean Leon Destine[51] meanwhile popularised the Haitian art in the United States. In other places the transmission of field work to stage proceeded with varying degrees of success from Grenada and the Grenadines to Martinique and Guadeloupe.

In post-revolutionary Cuba the newly acquired dignity of the Cuban Black found similar exercises in Conjuntos Folk-loricos[52] with strong emphasis on the African heritage while a Modern Dance Company dating back to the 1950's revealed a mix between the indigenised Cuban popular and traditional dance-forms on the one hand, and American Modern dance and ballet techniques on the other. The National Ballet of Cuba under the direction of the international Cuban ballerina Alicia Alonso began to stretch, in tribute to the revolution, the classical ballet beyond its natural thematic boundaries to Cuban sensibilities and body preferences.

49. *Ibid.*

50. Yarborough-Williams, Lavinia: *Haiti-Dance* (Bonners Druckerwi Frankfurt-am-Main).

51. Haitian dancer and choreographer, founder of the National Folkloric Group of Haiti. He has lived and performed in the United States since the late forties.

52. The Cuban professional dance-theatre community displays typical aspects of the "Caribbean dilemma" in the European, creolised mulatto, and African levels of cultural perception. The Alonso Ballet attracts to it largely Cubans of obvious European ancestry; the modern dance company betrays a predominant Euro-African type, and the conjuntos folkloricos are largely black-skinned. The "solution" of three "national companies" is a different approach to the Jamaican, Trinidadian, Barbadian or Guyanese approach where experimental work is done on the indigenised dance-forms of the Caribbean itself and the inherent 'techniques' isolated. The Cuban situation is clearly a function of the persistence of "the plantation" in Cuban life. This author has had very spirited discussions with officials of the Cuban cultural directorate on his visits to Cuba.

In Jamaica the advent of Independence was the occasion of the flowering of all that had gone before in the strong "creative-dance movement", the classical ballet which had English and Russian influences, and the existing traditional dances embedded in religious rituals, ring-games and action songs. In 1962 the National Dance Theatre Company of Jamaica[53] (NDTC) was launched with 'the blessings' of the Jamaican government. Since then it has built up an extensive repertoire of dance-dramas, dances based on Jamaican Caribbean folk and ritual dance, as well as pure-dance compositions to indigenous and other kinds of music. It has toured extensively, earning an international reputation and a large following at home. In 1970 it founded the Jamaica School of Dance, now the national school. It has been the chief source of inspiration for the development of an indigenous dance-theatre in Jamaica and other parts of the Anglophone Caribbean.[54] As a result the dance since 1963 is a major area of competition in the annual festivals, which have in turn helped to spread the interest of dance among the young. The dance flourishes in varying degrees of "indigenous" expression as an art form all over the Caribbean and more importantly continues with vigour and regenerative force in the rituals, masquerades and carnivals of the indigenous culture.

The prejudices of Eurocentrism are not by any means dead, however, despite this vigour and force.[55] Little Caribbean girls are still encouraged by their mothers to hanker after the image of a European ballerina; and class connotations that still attach

53. Nettleford, Rex: *Roots and Rhythms* (the story of the Jamaica National Dance Theatre) Andre Deutsch, London, 1969.

54. e.g. The Barbados Dance Theatre, the Guyana Dance Movement since Carifesta I, 1972.

55. See the Leandro cartoon which places 'Jamaica' in Tutu on 'pointes' waiting for the hand of the rival suitors, the leader of the Opposition and the Prime Minister both placed in the posture of the Danseur noble! The idea of dressing them in Caribbean dance garb was probably too much for the cartoonist who on the other hand may have been dutifully communicating to the cultured readership of the country. Dance-art to many 'cultured' Jamaicans is still considered to be European classical ballet. *Daily Gleaner,* Tuesday, November 23, 1976.

themselves to this 'high art' of Europe might well have killed the art in the wake of rising nationalism and Black Power politics of the sixties had it not been for the good sense of a few teachers as can be found in revolutionary Cuba or even in Jamaica where concessions have long been made to at least treating *Jamaican* themes through the idiom of the classical ballet. Uninformed critics however are wont to use the canons, idiosyncracies and clear culture-determined aesthetics of this style of European dance-theatre to measure *all* indigenous efforts to find a 'classic' Caribbean dance expression. The unending debate that rages on the matter is merely an aspect of the wider argument over the debasement of all creative effort of the people of the Caribbean in favour of a continuing dominance by all that emanate from the former colonising power. The implications for the internal social dynamics of the society are too obvious for further comment. As far as the dance itself is concerned, it is a paradox that the circumstances of colonial history dictate that a dancing-people, as the majority of the Caribbean peoples undoubtedly are, must get approbation and critical affirmation from a non-dancing metropolitan country like Great Britain to convince themselves that they can achieve excellence in an art native to them. The answer increasingly lies in the development within the Caribbean itself of a tradition of criticism[56] alongside the development of the region's dance-art as well as a tradition of scholarship on dance itself and gleaned from among the relevant disciplines such as history, anthropology, ethnomusicology, non-verbal communication, anatomy, physiology and sociology. In a culture-complex which is in the process of sorting itself out, the danger of relegating the dance to being the 'divertissement' of the arts, the frill and frippery of culture is very real. But this is a second-order problem soluble in terms of the Jamaicans' willingness to liberate the dance from the 'minstrelsy syndrome' to which it deteriorated on the Plantation and restore it to its place of primordial necessity as ancestral Africa, like ancestral Man, knows it.

---

56. Dance criticism in Jamaica is on the whole inexpert, misinformed and often cluttered with a miscellany of marginal matters (e.g. comparison with ballets from dance-theatre experience in Europe of the 1920's and 30's).

As with dance, so with *drama* and what is misnomered the 'legitimate theatre'. The misnomer took on special significance in a British colonial outpost where Shakespeare was made to rank virtually with the Good Book among those who were literate and the tritest of English soap opera or situation comedy from the cultural memory of English expatriates armed with a settler-mentality and a yearning for provincial England, was mistaken for 'good art', 'desirable art' and even excellence. Therein lay the perennial colonial problem which was hardly answered by the period of quite distinguished touring companies from North America and England giving to Kingston, the capital city of Jamaica, cosmopolitan pretensions from the turn of the 20th century right up to the mid 1930's. Henry Fowler in an informative article in *Jamaica Journal*[57] gives a thumbnail sketch of these developments going back to the early English settlement and drawing on Richardson Wright's excellent source book on Jamaican theatrical history, *Revels in Jamaica* for the period 1682-1838.[58] But it is Wycliffe Bennett's critical "preliminary overview" of the Jamaican theatre[59] which points up the cultural dilemmas of a Eurocentric tradition reflecting the great dependency on the unquestioned supremacy of the metropolitan centre and the corresponding apologetics or alternatively over-solemn pursuit of indigenous theatrical experimentation. This dilemma is nowhere totally absent from the contemporary Jamaican theatrical experience.

Shakespeare, whose greatness cannot be denied, is still often mistaken as the national playwright by some people and the latest successes on the commercial Broadway theatre are given facsimile productions in Kingston with commerical success. The English undergraduate-type revue which offers a vehicle for political and social satire has flourished in Kingston's intimate 'theatres'

57. Fowler, Henry: "A History of Theatre in Jamaica" *Jamaica Journal* Vol. 2, No. 1, March 1968.

58. Wright, Richardson: *Revels in Jamaica 1682-1838* (Dodd, Mead & Co. New York, 1937).

59. Bennett, Wycliffe: "The Jamaica Theatre — A Preliminary Overview" *Jamaica Journal*, Vol. 8, Nos. 2 & 3, Summer 1974.

with a growing audience appeal from among the prosperous middle strata. Imitation of metropolitan fashion is accepted. "Nureyev and Friends" a Broadway invention designed to introduce a great classical ballet star into American modern dance and to give such modern dance 'friends' wider attention, becomes in Jamaica "Louise Bennett and Friends."[60] The daily contact the nation has with New York reflects itself in the instant imitativeness of the Broadway theatre and the public relations gimmicks used in advertising which admittedly receives positive audience response from the urban middle-strata which have long hankered after metropolitan life-styles and aesthetic norms.

Such a situation might have been deemed hopeless had it not been for the evidence of a competing alternative in the work of many Jamaicans who strive to "found a theatre dedicated to native aspirations". Among the first to address themselves to this responsibility was the great visionary and Jamaican National Hero Marcus Mosiah Garvey.[61] Garvey would undoubtedly agree with Wycliffe Bennett's reminder that "to change the character of any theatre, you must first of all change the basic assumptions of the people who produce it."[62] The basic assumptions were palpably changed back in 1937 at the beginning of the nationalist upheaval when "a great theatrical experience" was created by none other than the leaders of the Roman Catholic Vicariate in Jamaica. The event was the pageant "Jamaica Triumphant" and the expatriate (American) director found it necessary to make heavy weather of the ethnic diversity of performers as follows: "They were ranged through the whole gamut of nationalities, of ancestries, of colours, of religions and social groups . . . there were men of coal black and then through the scale of purest white; there were Chinese and one or two East Indians . . . And during the pageant they put aside

60. A 'nostalgic' variety show entitled "Come Back to Jamaica" was designed to urge Jamaicans residing in the USA to come back to Jamaica. Organised by Air Jamaica Ltd.

61. Others were: E. M. Cupidon, Una Marson, Frank Hill, Roger Mais and Archie Lindo.

62. Bennett, Wycliffe: *op cit.*

everything except the desire to make it a success . . . I have never felt community spirit rising to finer heights and more devoted self-sacrifice."[63] The following forty years was to see the growth of drama in search of an indigenous line out of the soul of Jamaican and Caribbean traditional and contemporary life. With the establishment of the University of the West Indies in the late forties came a Department of Extra Mural Studies which appointed Staff Tutors whose tour of duty in Jamaica resulted in the production of West Indian drama which included plays written about Jamaica by Jamaicans and English residents in Jamaica. The Federal Theatre Company under Errol Hill "led a [controversial] crusade against the preponderance of imported scripts on the Jamaican stage" for Europe continued to govern with an assured supremacy. The very first Secondary Schools' Drama Festival in 1950, for example, was a festival of excerpts from Shakespearean plays coached and adjudicated by an English actor-director lent by the British Council whose objective was to transmit British culture.[64] But the later fifties saw the emergence of Sam Hillary, who caught the tragi-comedy of Jamaican life in his early work.[65] The period also saw the early work of St. Lucian Derek Walcott on the Mona campus of the University. What this influential Caribbean poet-playwright-director attempted in his undergraduate years he was to express on his first return to Jamaica with his Trinidad-based company of players: "The Poor Theatre, Grotowski's phrase for his own bare style, has never been more applicable to our own situation here in the islands, both as economics and as a chord of compassion for theatre artists, playwrights, actors, musicians and craftsmen continue to labour under embittering conditions. Our culture needs

63. *Daily Gleaner,* April 10, 1973, quoted by Wycliffe Bennett, *op cit.*

64. The adjudicator was Nugent Monck, English actor/director, founder of the Maddermarket Theatre in Norwich, England. The Secondary Schools' Drama Festival which has changed its character considerably since then still exists. This author was in the first festival, playing Bassanio in an excerpt from "The Merchant of Venice" for Cornwall College, a Jamaican high school situated in Montego Bay.

65. Sam Hillary won the Ministry of Education playwriting competition over Derek Walcott with his "Geva Charlotte" (1957). He was to follow up with "Chippy" (1960) and "Departure in the Dark" (1965).

preservation and resurgence, our crises need an epiphany, a spiritual definition, and an art that can emerge from our poverty, creating its own elation. Our resilience is in our tragic joy, in the catharsis of folk humour, our art for the time being, because it emerges from and speaks to the poor, will find its Antaean renewal in folktale and parable. We present to others a deceptive simplicity that they may dismiss as provincial, primitive, childish, but which is in truth a radical innocence. That is what our fable is about . . ."[66]

This introduction to the Walcott masterpiece *Ti Jean*, "a folkmusical", came over thirty years after the Little Theatre Movement, Jamaica's community theatre movement, had spearheaded and developed in Jamaica an indigenous folkmusical called a "national pantomime" which at first followed faithfully the narrative, conventions and staging of imported English Christmas pantomimes. But under the intuitive eye of the LTM's founder, Greta Fowler, and the organisation of her husband Henry Fowler, the pantomime was to find its feet in the Jamaican folk arts. By the 1950's the Anancy cycle[67] based on the stories of the Jamaican spider folk hero, and skilfully interpreted by the great Jamaican folklorist and actress Louise Bennett and the master-comedian Ranny Williams, transformed what started out as something for the amusement of the carriage-trade into a genuine *people's theatre.* To date it is the only piece of Jamaican theatre that has managed to compete with the powerful cinema and win. Anything between 60 and 70 thousand people see the folkmusical every year which opens on Boxing Day (December 26th) and has never missed a deadline since 1941.

The early shaping of this important Jamaican theatre form was done by directors like Noel Vaz whose creative work in Jamaican theatre, and with the University in the entire Eastern

66. Walcott, Derek: *Introduction to Ti Jean* in Programme Brochure, Jamaican Season of Plays, April 1973.

67. "Anancy and Busha Bluebeard" (1949) co-authored by Louise Bennett and Noel Vaz and directed by Noel Vaz, is considered as the watershed between Eurocentric English pantomimes and Jamaican folkmusicals. An earlier attempt in 1943 with the staging of "Soliday and the Wicked Bird" directed by an Englishwoman named Elinor Lithgow did not inspire sequels in the years that followed.

Caribbean throughout the fifties and sixties, has contributed significantly to the development of Caribbean theatre arts. The Little Theatre pantomime was to be the testing ground of many actors, singers, dancers, directors, playwrights. All major performing artists today have at some time or other worked on the pantomime. It certainly convinced many of the acceptability of indigenous Jamaican theatre, despite the criticism levelled against it for what is felt to be a too settled formula.

Playwrights like Dennis Scott and Trevor Rhone could enjoy an ambience of understanding awaiting them by the time they were ready in the late sixties to deal with serious Jamaican themes.[68]

Popular theatre with comics like Ed Bim Lewis, Clover, his wife and Bam his long-time partner, attracted large crowds of people as did and do the variety concerts staged on public holiday mornings at the larger cinemas in the main towns.

The popularity of the cinema among the Jamaican people would prompt one to assume that an indigenous film industry would be a natural development. Lack of funds and lack of easy accessibility to the knowledge of the technology are very effective constraints. Two full length features, "The Harder They Come" [by Perry Henzell] and "Smile Orange" [by Trevor Rhone], both Jamaican films, have had international exposure. The Jamaican audiences warmed particularly to the former which dealt with the sounds and pressures of urban ghetto life in the sixties. Its Jamaican and international success can probably be explained by the following critical review coming out of the United States: " 'The Harder They Come' is far more effective in conveying the texture of alienation in a world of socio-economic injustice than are the 'didactic message' films of Costa-Gavras or Godard's recent unfeeling, over-

68. Trevor Rhone has won international acclaim for his film "Smile Orange" and Jamaican and Caribbean-wide recognition for such plays as "The Gadget", "Music Boy" (musical pantomime), "School's Out" and "Smile Orange". Dennis Scott, a poet and dancer, also has a long list of credits from national and international recognition. A play for the deaf and dumb at Washington's Kennedy Centre was preceded by his showing of "Echo in the Bone" at the Nigerian Festival of Arts and Culture (FESTAC 1977).

intellectualised explorations of capitalist marauding ... I would claim that no ethnographic report, novel, or play with which I am familiar captures the style of West Indian urban life as vividly as 'The Harder They Come.' "[69]

Yet the field of drama has not itself produced any distinctive line for Jamaica as say what the Ugandan Players which visited Jamaica in the early seventies seemingly do for Uganda,[70] though the folkmusical in the form of the LTM pantomime and the popular Ed Bim Lewis farces do carry a definite Jamaican character. The Jamaica Festival which is strong on dance, choral music and speech is weakest on drama; and a national drama company, similar to the national dance theatre, has failed to materialise despite repeated efforts dating back to the mid-sixties. Work on the Mona campus of the University of the West Indies continued with a certain fresh and youthful vitality throughout that period and the introduction of a Christmas term "festival of plays" called "Tallawah" has offered a special dynamic to the campus activities. But the occupation in 1970 of the University's Creative Arts Centre by students calling for relevance did have an adverse effect on the development of a strong West Indian or Jamaican theatre for a while.

The founding of the Jamaica School of Drama may in time correct this. Yet the Jamaican theatre is not short on output which includes Broadway or West End of London "hits", locally written plays, satirical revues, musicals (local and foreign), Jamaican farce, operettas (imported) and experimental work, all of which offer vitality in the capital city of Kingston and hold out hope for more exciting developments in the next decade. Perhaps like Derek Walcott, the Jamaicans will have to try "for a staging that would be easy under some backyard tree as with the devices of the rich theatre. The wealth of this bareness is in the nakedness

69. Lieber, Michael: Review of 'The Harder They Come' in *American Anthropologist* March 1974, pp. 199-200.

70. Robert Serumaga brought his Uganda Players to Jamaica with *Renga Moi* and *Amarykitti* in 1973 and 1974 respectively. Mr Serumaga taught at the Jamaica School of Drama in the 1974 Season.

of spirit, in the pliant and magical metamorphoses of the body."[71] That wealth of bareness was duly sought after by a movement towards "the Yard theatre" in the early seventies as part of a revolutionary assertion for an independent aesthetic. It attracted interest and excitement while it lasted but may well have failed because it sought to gild the anthurium. For Jamaica's yard-theatre exists naturally and organically in the Pukkumina (pocomania) meetings, the revival gatherings, the Kumina and Bruckin party settings, the Rastafarian groundings. As Ras Jose of the Mystic Revelation of Rastafari once said in reference to his group "we are not entertainers but communicators."[72] Minstrelsy is here denied and the might of the Message invoked. Marcus Garvey, a major prophet to the Rastafarians, would have approved. Between 1930 and 1932 Garvey had himself written and mounted theatrical events with such titles as "The Coronation of an African King" (a 3-Act Play with a cast of 100), "Roaming Jamaicans" (with a cast of 80), "Slavery from Hut to Mansion" (with a cast of 120) and "Wine, Women and War."[73] The Garveyite theatre of struggle, Rastafarian lessons in being whole, and Walcottian metaphors all betray the need that lies deep among many Jamaicans to see the drama grow through the nurturing of playwrights, actors and directors for the celebration of the Jamaican and Caribbean people's language, life and spirit.

Painting, currently a lively and passionate artistic expression in Jamaica, has thrown up many artists themselves passionately committed to their art but also to the notion of its central place in building the consciousness and pride of a nation and people. In this someone like the late Karl Parboosingh had no

71. Walcott, Derek: *op cit.*

72. See Liner Notes to Recordings "Tales of Mozambique" by Count Ossie and the Mystic Revelation of Rastafari. Published by Sheila Music, 1975 Dynamic Sounds, Kingston, Jamaica.

73. Hill, Errol: "Plays of the English-Speaking Caribbean, Part I: Jamaica (A Bibliography and Check List)" *Bulletin of Black Theatre* Vol. I, No. 2, Winter 1972. Garvey who spoke for the total liberation of the Black man would naturally have seen artistic expression as a key instrument in the struggle. He composed poems and songs as well.

rival.[74] The energy of output and commitment have in turn prompted tangible responses from among a growing audience who flock to the many art exhibitions held annually in the capital city of Kingston. The presence of a National School of Art, a National Gallery of Art and the existence of a long-standing art-teaching programme (covering painting, craft, pottery) in the primary and secondary schools has provided some preparation for wide audience appeal and appreciation.[75] Today the Jamaican art-movement can celebrate such masters as John Dunkley, Albert Huie, George Rodney, Carl Abrahams, and Osmond Watson[76] whose artistic confidence in the certainties of a personal and Caribbean aesthetic makes them the universal artists their work declares them to be.

74. Karl Parboosingh – born in Jamaica and educated in New York, Paris and Mexico City. He was an artist in the United States army for four years. Returned to Jamaica and taught at the Jamaica School of Art. He had exhibited in Europe, the USA, Mexico and Puerto Rico and extensively in Jamaica. He was co-founder of the Contemporary Jamaican Artists Association and a great advocate of Caribbean co-operation in the field of arts and culture. He died in 1975.

75. The Denham Art Shield Competition for Schools was organised in 1937 by Theodore Sealy of the Gleaner Co. with the assistance of Edna Manley and H. B. Molesworth of the Institute of Jamaica who formed a group known as the Jamaica Arts Society. In 1945 the Institute of Jamaica took full responsibility for the Exhibitions held annually. The Competition was retired in 1970 and replaced with the Annual National Exhibition of Art in Schools. The Denham Shield was replaced by the Institute (of Jamaica) Trophy.

76. *John Dunkley,* a barber by profession, born in 1891, died in 1947; travelled in his early years to Central America, returned to Jamaica in 1926 and developed a unique painting style as a self-taught artist. Was helped in his development by Molesworth of the Institute of Jamaica and Edna Manley, the sculptress.

   Albert Huie (born Falmouth, Jamaica); has been painting since age 16. Studied in England and Canada. Recipient of several awards – both Silver and Gold Musgrave Medals, Int'l Award for Painting in Havana, Cuba (1959) and both the Badge of Honour and Order of Distinction (Commander) from the Government of Jamaica.

   George Rodney, a graduate of Jamaica School of Art and Arts Student League, New York. He is a painter and graphic designer. He is a Silver Musgrave Medallist.

   Carl Abrahams started out as a cartoonist but was encouraged to take up painting seriously by Augustus John, the great British painter. He did this on his return from World War II (he was in the Royal Air Force). He is recipient of several awards including the Silver Musgrave Medal and the Order of Distinction.

   Osmond Watson has been painting since age 9. A graduate of the Jamaica School of Art, and St. Martin's School of Art (London). Has exhibited extensively at home and abroad. He is a Silver Musgrave Medallist.

David Boxer, the curator of the Jamaica National Gallery, exercises caution in writing of a "Jamaican art movement." He reminds his readers that "a history would hardly begin with the first Jamaicans, the Arawaks, for they contributed little to the Jamaica we know today. To be sure they were exceptionally fine sculptors in wood; unfortunately, however, very little of their work survived, and those that did such as three superb pieces found in 'Charpentier's Mountain' in 1972 were spirited away to the basement of the British Museum."[77] If Jamaica lost out on the Arawaks they were to gain, albeit four centuries later, from the work of Edna Manley[78] who has been a source and inspiration to two generations with whom her remarkable gifts of vision, commitment, craftsmanship, sense of place, self-discipline and aesthetic balance were generously shared. Later there emerged Mallica Reynolds – Kapo[79] – from the roots exuding ancestral echoes and taking the nation's sensibilities back to the woodcarvings of ancestral Africa and probably the Arawaks. He fitted perfectly into the dynamic modern movement linked to the search for identity. There was indeed, "the effort to establish an independent artistic expression of Jamaican realities which Edna Manley spear-headed in the closing thirties and which bore fruit in an enormously vital and self-sustaining movement of people, ideas and work, perhaps without parallel or equal in the emerging tropical nation States."[80] Apart

77. Boxer, David: Introduction to *Ten Jamaican Sculptors,* 1975, in Brochure (National Gallery).

78. Edna Manley, widow of Norman Manley and mother of Michael Manley, Prime Minister of Jamaica, is the single most influential person in the plastic and fine arts in Jamaica over a period of 40 years. Born in England of Jamaican mother and English father and studied in London and primarily with Maurice Harding, the animal sculptor. First recipient of the Gold Musgrave Medal for outstanding contribution and leadership to the arts in Jamaica. See Wayne Brown's biography of her, entitled *Edna Manley: The Early Years,* Deutsch, London, 1976.

79. Kapo, (Mallica Reynolds) is a Shepherd of a revivalist cult. A self-taught sculptor, he began painting in 1967. Has exhibited in the USA, England and Jamaica. He is a Silver Musgrave Medallist for painting and sculpture.

80. Smith, M. G.: "Introduction" Brochure on *Edna Manley: Selected Sculpture and Drawings 1922-76,* March-April, 1977.

from Alvin Marriott who remained a fine traditionalist and academic
sculptor in the strongly European realist mould, the movement in
sculpture followed in the wake of the burgeoning of spirit, energy
and skill from the late thirties; and it is the combination of Edna
Manley's craft, sanity and inspiration and the ancestral intuitiveness
of someone like Kapo that will seemingly inform the future
successes that can be expected from younger sculptors and carvers.[81]

The related art of *Ceramics* is not without its special
appeal to a people to the majority of whose ancestors pottery was
second-nature. The master that Cecil Baugh has become to
Jamaican art-lovers provided a model for the scores of young
potters and ceramicists who have since followed in his wake with
the benefit of his inspiration to which many were exposed at the
Jamaica School of Art where he taught for many years. The work
of Edwin and Maribel Todd, American residents in Jamaica, com-
plements the work of Baugh and others. Not least among "the
others" are the scores of native potters who for decades provided
the ordinary Jamaican with the domestic yabba pots and home
gardeners with flower pots and other containers made from clay.[82]

The craftwork of the basket weavers, workers in straw,
sea shells, beads made out of seeds of tropical trees, of embroi-
derers, seamstresses and woodcarvers reflects the diverse influences
on the Jamaican "transplanted population." That these varied
cultural expressions they wrought and/or developed over time
could be mobilised into activities in the service of welding a people
together as one, was fully realised from early by people like Marcus
Garvey and most certainly by one of the founders of modern
Jamaica, Norman Washington Manley. Even before he entered
politics, the promotion of cultural activities through the creative

81. For example, Christopher Gonzales, Winston Patrick, David Miller, Hylton Nemb-
hard, Fitzroy Harrack and the master-painter Osmond Watson. See Brochure on
Ten Jamaican Sculptors, Commonwealth Institute, London 1975 (National Gallery).

82. See R. C. Ebanks' account of the Yabbah collection in the Old King's House
assemblage of artifacts. "The size of the yabbah collection and the local clay earthenware assemblage indicates that there was a well developed potting industry" says
Mr. Ebanks. *Jamaica Journal* Vol. 8, No. 2 & 3; Summer 1974, p. 2.

arts and craft development was part and parcel of his Jamaica Welfare Limited in 1937. Hence emphasis was placed on the exploration by the people themselves of their own creative potential and the force of creative application on the products of the natural environment around them.

In the great thrust towards self-government and national self-determination, Manley with the crucial support of his artist wife was to put the creative urge and cultural activities as one of the main planks of his platform for national unity.

The august Institute of Jamaica established by the colonial government in 1879 for the encouragement of arts, science and literature was in full bloom. But its concentration in effect was more on the management of the art, science and literature of the colonial rulers or at least what expressed itself from the point of view of metropolitan perspectives. Norman Manley saw the need for change of focus in national terms. In 1959, a Ministry with responsibility for cultural affairs, like the National Trust Commission was created by him.

By the 1960's an entirely new generation had grown up as true beneficiaries of the Manley cultural vision. Not only were they constitutionally independent; they were also anxious to experience cultural independence consonant with the provisions in the constitutional instrument of authority transferring power from Britain to the Jamaicans. A young voice carrying the name of Edward Seaga from a new Administration articulated the urge and the inclusion of an aggressive cultural policy as part of the Five Year Plan. The thrust was a conscious and vigorous promotion of the popular and traditional arts. The recording industry was mobilised in the service of the former while the co-ordination of existing parish and village festivals into a national festival (Jamaica Festival Commission) was designed to serve the latter. The creation of other institutions like a Folk Music Research Unit, Things Jamaican (for craft development) and the new interest in cultural tourism, added positive dimensions to the cultural dynamics of the nation. The mobilisation of cultural resources drawn deliberately from the mass of Jamaicans in the service of national identity drew disapproval from some Eurocentric compatriots during the Seaga leadership as it had raised eyebrows under N. W. Manley before him.

But this very fact signalled the strength which this continuity of effort between Administrations of different political party persuasions brought to national development. For further continuity was assured with the advent to power of Michael Manley, son of N. W. Manley. One of his first acts was to set up an Exploratory Committee on Arts and Culture, the report of which was to form the basis of the initial policy on cultural development dating from 1973.[83] It continued under the auspices of a special portfolio for Culture, still within the Prime Minister's Office but under the direct responsibility of a Minister of State for Culture (and Information) until 1977. A full Ministry was established in January, 1979.

Soon Michael Manley was saying publicly that in a country like Jamaica "with the imbalances which history has wrought on the majority of our people, it is essential that every Jamaican, black, white, Chinese, Syrian, Jew — should find a point at which he relates in a positive and soul-satisfying way to the social structure of the Jamaica of today.   It is in this hard-to-define area known as 'culture' ", he declared, "that I feel so many of the answers to our problems can be found."[84]

There is a certain rightness about much of this development because of the inherent logic that resides in that long struggle for the people of Jamaica and the Caribbean to have what they have to have, as one great Caribbean poet puts it.[85] It was that great Jamaican visionary Marcus Garvey who in the 1920's and 1930's spoke to his fellow-Jamaicans — and indeed to all people of African ancestry in Plantation America — in a language other than Europe's. As Sir Philip Sherlock once stated it, "he challenged us to smash the old stereotype, to put self-esteem in the place of self-contempt, to put self-confidence and self-reliance in the place of dependence and self-distrust . . . Most of those who had position

83. *Report of Exploratory Committee on the Arts,* 1972.

84. Manley, Michael: "Address" at Opening of National Gallery, Jamaica, Nov. 14, 1974.

85. Guillén, Nicolás: Poem *TENGO* (I have), translated by Keith Ellis and published in *Jamaica Journal*, March 1973.

and power rejected him. [But] *the common people never did . . .
The work of self-liberation had begun.*"[86]

That Garvey understood the centrality of the cultural process to the liberation struggle is borne out by the Garvey scholar, Rupert Lewis. He states that "Garvey approached the question of art [for example] not as a cheap propagandist or a political demagogue but from a very deep sense of the individual worth of artistic and creative work. In his 1934 address, he made the important point: 'You can still find in Egypt lasting monuments of Negro Art which still remain a puzzle to the world . . . As much as we are trying to develop ourselves in business, religion, politics and so on, we have to build up ourselves in Art.' "[87]

The work continues and after forty or so years of dynamic interaction between the cultural process and the politics of nation-building, there are clear indicators in Jamaica of (a) a continuation of a dynamic interplay between these processes into the foreseeable future and (b) the inescapable commitment that all who represent or speak in the name of the people must have for the preservation and further development of cultural values.

86. Sherlock, Philip: Address on the occasion of the launching of *Ten Jamaican Sculptors* – Commonwealth Institute, London, 1975. Published in *Jamaica Journal*, Vol. 10, Nos. 2, 3, 4, 1977.

87. Lewis, Rupert: "A Political Study of Garveyism in Jamaica and London, 1914-1940", (unpub. M.Sc. thesis, UWI, 1971).

Part II

PRESERVATION AND FURTHER
DEVELOPMENT OF
CULTURAL VALUES

PRESERVATION AND FURTHER DEVELOPMENT OF CULTURAL VALUES

Despite the efforts over time to give a national stamp to cultural expression, not everyone is satisfied with all that has developed nor is universal acceptance automatic in the case of every cultural event that may claim significance in the name of the society. Many Jamaicans do make a virtue of diversity, even at the risk of creating instability. The "natural pluralism" of Caribbean society may indeed be an overriding factor in the way that Jamaicans go about their business or in the way that multiple institutions are created and played one against the other. Moreover, the best of all possible worlds are habitually pursued with zeal and an ardent sense of purpose. Jamaicans clearly have a preference for options. They would quickly opt for *everything* that can be had *both* inside *and* outside of the 'revolution'.

In addition, the Caribbean artistic sensibility is liberally peppered with 19th century European notions about the very special individuality of the artist and about his uniqueness in the society in the sense of his special grasp of and insights into the deeper meanings of existence. He must therefore be left free, goes the argument, to function according to the dictates of his own conscience — a position which few, if any, Caribbean artists would abandon lightly. But the further indulgence of the notion that the artist need have no commitment or relevance to Caribbean society, begs questions of gigantic proportions and is sometimes used to justify the perpetration of a debilitating Eurocentrism — a stance which traditionally denies the value not only of things African but of things created out of the stuff of Caribbean life and experience. The universality of art is here argued, as well, in defiance of the incontrovertible fact that the specificity of human (individual or collective) experience has a priority over the realisation of "universality"; and this is here stated without wishing to deny the validity of the experience gleaned from contacts with the achievements of other civilisations, from personal reflection or even day-dreaming.

But when a Caribbean person, in the exercise of his creative imagination, shuts out his own indigenous experience rooted in the soil of the Caribbean, what he produces is not likely to earn him the status of prophet, visionary, guide or "artist" to the Caribbean of today or to any other people at anytime.

Much of the grand posturing of 'the unique artist' who is to be left free of mundane obligations, is reinforced by the tradition of class prejudice in colonial Jamaican society with its manifestations of contempt for the creative output from the labouring classes though social pressure and the "irreverence" of the young weaned from among the middle strata do force the appropriation of the popular forms by the more privileged groups in the society. As the street dances went to Court and the folk tunes found their way into the classics in Europe so have reggae, mento, Rastafarian drumming and style of painting wended their way from the ghettos and the hillsides into the Jamaican Establishment. This inevitable process is fast becoming the accepted and anticipated way of harmonising popular participatory democracy with cultural reality.

Of course the process is nowhere as simple as this, especially since the older challenges of giving form and substance to what is created out of the experience and activity of all the people without a feeling of inferiority in the face of the master's expression, are still to be met.

The positive thrust since the early seventies towards a Jamaica that will serve the common man and have the country's institutions of growth reflect this thrust, has alienated many erstwhile "leaders" not only in the fields of commerce, business, and of party politics but also in the area of cultural action. The legitimacy of "natural leadership" in setting cultural standards, determining cultural content, defining cultural goals and manipulating cultural symbols is seen by many in the established middle strata as being usurped by "wicked" politicians, "lesser artists" drawn from the Rastafarians, the lumpenproletariat or the new Black intelligentsia. It is now virtually lost to a new aesthetic that challenges past Eurocentric indulgences and the indigence of the accompanying cultural dependency. That the party in power which had a tradition of support *of* and *for* the middle strata should betray its "own class" with the proletarianisation of culture, is seen by certain of the middle strata as one of the unforgiveable sins, pardonable if committed by the old Jamaica Labour Party which anyhow did pander to the "headless mass" but intolerable coming from the People's National Party. For was it not this party which gave Jamaica not only its vision of self-determination and the legendary intelligence of N. W. Manley, but also the touch of "class" which that founding father is supposed to have brought to public life for some thirty years? Only now it was being betrayed by his populist-politician son.[88] That such a position is out of line with the stark realities of contemporary Jamaican life in terms of the dialectics of change that the country has been undergoing for two generations, is difficult to grasp by those who have a vested interest in the cultural norms that were set in the old Jamaica.

In the light of this and the facts of history, the argument that a commitment to an indigenous cultural ethos is a vital necessity for building a nation or achieving national unity in Jamaica has got to be put, before the matter of the preservation and further development of cultural values in Jamaica and the Caribbean can be seriously considered.

For the questions that must be asked are: *whose and what cultural values must be preserved and for whom and what must they be developed?* Such questions are the substance, if not the sum, of Rastafarian protest dating back to the 1930's and coming to a head in the late fifties and early sixties.[89] By the late sixties, some intellectuals and young students saw the light and the Mona campus became a cauldron of steaming protest starting with the so-called Rodney Affair of October, 1968,[90] and culminating

88. i.e. Michael Manley, Leader of the PNP and Prime Minister of Jamaica since 1972. The view is common among many of the entrenched middle-class Jamaicans – educated and creolised but with a strong Eurocentric bias. They believe that populist politics has sent the country "to the dogs" and since 1974 they have been migrating to Miami and Toronto if they can afford it. Many can!

89. Nettleford, Rex: *Mirror Mirror – Identity, Race and Protest in Jamaica* Sangsters-Collins, 1970: Chap. II.

90. Girvan, Norman: "After Rodney – The Politics of Student Protest in Jamaica", *New World Quarterly* Vol. 4, No. 3 (1968) pp. 59-68.

in the student 'capture' of the Creative Arts Centre in February 1970.[91] The heavy involvement of non-Jamaicans drew xenophobic scorn from the Jamaican establishment (official and otherwise), but more importantly it signified the potential importance of the events to the wider Caribbean. Paradoxically, the occupation of the Creative Arts Centre on the grounds that it had failed to be responsive to the true cultural sensibilities of Jamaica and the Caribbean came in the wake of two now historic plays about rebellion and revolt—"Marat Sade" and Genet's "The Blacks"—in which many of the more vociferous protagonists had participated. The event, as events of this kind always do, gave rise to unexpected alliances within the world of literature, arts and culture and attracted to 'the cause' ideologues and academics with a nose for the 'right' causes, as well as genuine social protesters from the off-campus community. The upshot of the whole affair was the ultimate greater participation by the students in the Centre and the airing, through lively debate which was both acrimonious and scholarly, of the questions as to whose and what cultural values ought to be preserved and for whom and what they should be developed.[92]

The answers then as now were never easy to find. The reality of diversity is a gift for speculators, adventurers, cultural

91. The Creative Arts Centre was established in 1968 on the Mona Campus of the University of the West Indies under the Vice-Chancellorship of the Caribbean poet-historian Philip Sherlock. It was intended to help develop work of excellence in the arts and serve as a bridge between the campus and the community through practice of the arts. Student objections first started over the use of the facilities especially the theatre. They soon spread to cover questions about the relevance of the pro-gramme of activities which some students and staff-members regarded as too Euro-centric for a West Indian university. See "Facts about the Creative Arts Centre" *Sunday Gleaner*, March 15, 1970, p. 10. The 'occupation' in February 1970 by students should be seen as part of the wider student protest dating back to October 1968. See Sylvia Wynter ("Issues Behind Creative Arts Centre" *Sunday Gleaner*, March 8, 1970) who asked "Is the primary role and function of the University to be the maintaining of the high standards that they have borrowed from Europe? Or, is it their primary role and function to respond to the needs and priorities of Carib-bean society, and through their response, serve as a catalyst for new and relevant standards?"

92. Among the main critics to surface in support of the group of students were Sylvia Wynter, a novelist and lecturer in the UWI's Department of Spanish; Trevor Munroe,

opportunists as it is for the talented, honest and most sincere of creative persons. Caribbeanwide, the heterogeneity of the European heritage embraces the old imperial connexions of Spain, Britain, France, the Netherlands and of late the new imperialism of Euro-centric North America. The heterogeneity of the African ancestral complex is itself self-evident in the cultural continuities of Akan, Yoruba, Fon and Ibo civilisations of West Africa. However each betrayed a cultural unity in their diversity. Moreover, the raw facts of plantation life in terms of its economic priorities and power arrangements forced on each common points of reference and the sharp polarization that manifested itself over time. Each territory became a variation on a THEME.

The Jamaican variation is played out strongest in the racial and ethnic composition of the society. By the end of the 18th century people of African ancestry (black or brown) were estimated to form 84% of the population.[93] Certainly in some parts of the country black slaves outnumbered whites ten to one.[94] By 1844, Blacks formed 77% of the population, browns 18.1% and white Europeans 4.2%.[95] The 1944 and 1960 censuses revealed very little change except for the addition of figures for the post-Emancipation Indians, Chinese and other migrants and for issues that were the result of miscegenation between East Indians

lecturer in the Department of Government and later trade union leader and Marxist activist; Marina Maxwell, a poet, teacher and postgraduate student who spearheaded the "yard theatre" idea in the early 70's. Alex Gradussov, an expatriate editor of *Jamaica Journal* obliged with a piece on what he called the "Crematorium" and Henry and Greta Fowler, producers of the annual LTM pantomime, lent moral support to the students' cause. It is out of this empathy that came the ambitious but only partially successful Wynter-Gradussov pantomime "Rockstone Anancy" in late 1970. The irony is that among the "victims" of the "occupation" was the University's Staff Tutor in Drama, Noel Vaz, who was largely responsible from the forties to the sixties for the "West Indianisation" of theatre in Jamaica and the Eastern Caribbean where he worked with Errol Hill.

93. Broom, Leonard: "The Social Differentiation of Jamaica", *American Sociological Review*, Vol. 19, 1954, p. 116.

94. Brathwaite, Edward: *The Development of Creole Society in Jamaica 1770-1820*, Oxford: Clarendon Press 1971, p. 152.

95. Roberts, George: *The Population of Jamaica*, Cambridge University Press 1957, p. 65.

and Blacks or Blacks and Chinese. The 1970 census revealed an increasing claim by people to being 'black' with the worldwide black consciousness movement of the late sixties.[96] The fact is that while nearly 80% of the population are unmistakably black some 95% of Jamaicans are people with some degree of African blood. This in Caribbean cultural terms cannot be taken lightly. The phenomenon takes on an odd though lasting significance, however, because of the continuing correlation of blackness with poverty and of poverty with low status — hence the correlation between blackness and things created by blacks as low-status. There are of course, sizeable numbers of evolved Blacks in the middle and high-status professional classes and political elites but they are virtually recruits to the hegemonic Eurocentrism in terms of the received cultural values measured against the cultural expressions of the impoverished mass. Not all are total victims of the fractured vision for many of these evolved Jamaicans are to be found in the vanguard of the movements to indigenise cultural values, paying due concern not only to the ancestral African heritage but to the creative manifestations that have emerged and continue to emerge from the Jamaican peasantry and black urban poor.

Their efforts meet success in the wake of constitutional Independence. But the centuries of psychological conditioning and the inescapable on-going cultural bombardment from the North Atlantic sometimes transforms what is at one moment an object of national pride into a product of doubt, ridicule and low worth. That hierarchy of excellence, with Europe at the top and the indigenous at the base, asserts itself with imperial majesty in the colonial mentality that is too timid to be itself. So Brahms, Beethoven, Bach are declared superior to Marley, the Mighty Sparrow

96. Figures taken from **1970 Population Census**

Population by Ethnic Origin for Major Divisions:

Negro Black – 1634686; East Indian – 20736; Chinese – 11781; Amerindian – 304; Portuguese – 85; Syrian – 907; white – 11841; mixed – 103725; other races – 1381; not stated – 1865; Total – 1797401.

and Jimmy Cliff. "Serious music" becomes a term used exclusively on local radio stations to describe the music of Europe. The 'models' continue to be outside of the Caribbean. The awe of what is undoubtedly the great achievement of Europe in art, music, dance, literature and science succeeds in bludgeoning people into cultural subservience rather than helping to stimulate those, who come in contact with it, to similar excellence. The awe-struck Jamaicans are more concerned with the product rather than the process. The fault is clearly not Europe's — at least no longer. The job of self-liberation from self-doubt and lack of self-confidence is the Jamaican's responsibility. His transformation from third person is *his* challenge and not that of his former masters. It is not a question of whether Mahler is superior to Marley. More to the point is the fact that they have each attained excellence in their respective genres of musical expression.

The powerless mass of creative souls from ghettos and mountain ridges do not have the economic means or political power to command the attention of the world towards their creative efforts and when one of their numbers manages to gain recognition within or outside their shores it is not without the assistance of the economically and politically powerful. Persistent poverty among the Black mass serves further to entrench the European cultural hegemony. Up to 1973, 71.5% of wage-earners received less than $20 per week. Unemployment is high (23-25%)[97] as the following table shows.

Unemployment by Age Group and Sex
October 1976

Age grp.	No.	Both Sexes Rate of Unemploy- ment (%)	No.	Male Rate of Unemploy- ment (%)	No.	Female Rate of Unemploy- ment (%)
Total	261,400	24.2	71,800	14.7	144,600	35.6
14-24	113,100	45.2	41,500	30.7	71,600	62.2
25-34	45,400	22.8	12,900	12.5	32,600	33.6
35-44	25,600	17.1	6,700	9.2	18,800	24.8
45-54	17,700	13.2	5,100	7.1	12,600	20.2
55-64	7,700	7.7	2,000	3.2	5,700	15.6
65 & over	6,900	11.1	3,600	8.4	3,300	17.1

97. See "General Employment Strategy, Foreign Economic Relations" (Production Plan) — *Daily Gleaner*, May 16, 1977, p. 17.

There is a now legendary economic inequality where the highest 5% of Jamaican income-earners in 1974 received 25% of the total income.[98] The heavy reliance on exports and imports, Jamaica's vulnerability as a primary-producing nation (agricultural products and bauxite) in the Western economic system, the worsening of the economic situation following on the government's policy since 1974 to make the country more self-reliant, and the reports of political violence in the internal struggle for power over the post-colonial territory — all these have brought further difficulties to what was always a desperate economic situation, for the Black poor, that is. It is understandable, against this background that scholars like Carl Stone, the political sociologist, should feel that the problems of cultural identity in Jamaica can only be viewed "in the context of solutions to the poverty, unemployment, low education and income and general material and social dispossession that pervades larger sectors of the manual classes."[99]

This point of view has a relevant cogency for the preservation and development of cultural values. Already many Jamaican youths in the thrust towards meaningful change in an economically and socially unjust society are questioning the validity of the very achievements rooted in the consciousness of self that gripped their progressive counterparts two generations ago. In this mood of solemn search, nothing within the searchers' path will escape scrutiny. And rightly so. The valuable trees and shrubs along the way will be in danger of being destroyed either by the awkward aim of the inexperienced machete-wielder, the accidental trampling of the clumsy clodhopper, or the deliberate strike of the zealous pathfinder who sincerely feels this or that must go. Whatever happens, it is going to mean for Jamaica and the rest of the Caribbean the exercise of good sense, consummate skill and deep understanding of the process of cultural growth in "preserving and

98. See "National Income & Product" Department of Statistics, Kingston, Jamaica 1974, p. 14.

99. Stone, Carl: *Electoral Behaviour and Public Opinion in Jamaica* Published by Institute of Social and Economic Studies 1974, (quoted in article "European Melody, African Rhythm or West Indian Harmony? Cultural Orientations of Leaders in a New State" by Wendell Bell & Robert V. Robinson, Yale University. Typewritten, p. 8).

developing" the cultural values which inhere in the collective experience of Jamaica and Caribbean peoples for some four centuries.

Governments are naturally part of this but it is the job of the entire nation of private individuals and public leaders working together in the process to attain the product.

The economic determinism that assumes that the improvement of the economic lot of the mass of the people is a pre-requisite for the cultural identity of the nation is a powerful reminder that no one wishes to identify with the poor and the dispossessed. For poverty and dispossession are not human virtues on which anything positive can be built. Yet this, hopefully, is not an argument to deny to cultural values the possibility of an existence separate from their economic base, nor the independent dynamic force that such values can have in development even to the end of helping to bring about economic betterment for many from the masses.

The promotion of literacy among the poor by the JAMAL Foundation (the Jamaican Movement for the Advancement of Literacy) is clearly designed to provide the disadvantaged with basic skills deemed crucial to economic (and social) self-advancement. The development of education for the poor through the JAMAL programme and the normal school system may be seen as a way of preserving and opening the idea of education as a cultural value in response to the facts of Jamaican social and economic life.[100] The creation by the Jamaican Government of training-schools in the Arts which provide opportunities for talented persons from the disadvantaged masses so as to gain them accreditation and recognition despite their lack of conventional academic qualifications but with provisions for the development

100. JAMAL Foundation was established in 1973 as sequel to the National Literacy Board which was launched in 1972. It is to eradicate illiteracy from among the estimated half million said to be unable to read and write. Some 25% in 1976 were said to have been made literate. The work is done through a network of staff that runs throughout the 18 zones and 53 areas coinciding with the electoral districts. The organisation has a paid arm and a section of volunteers. It is planned for the Foundation's work to develop into a national continuing (adult) education programme.

of their proven native talents in terms of their own experience, is another guarantee for economic betterment. This comes by way of employment in a variety of fields ranging from school-teaching (dramatists, dancers, musicians, artists), through own-account enterprises for painters and carvers, performers (on television, radio and tourist industry) and designing (manufacturing of jewellery, furniture, textile, etc.). The Jamaican Government's positive support since 1963 of a Jamaican music recording industry, by way of a protectionist policy, has resulted in a guaranteed local market for what was to become a burgeoning supply of indigenously created and manufactured musical material providing monetary returns for a large number of talented persons drawn predominantly from the mass of the poor. One such beneficiary of this significant development in the 1960's and 1970's found no solace in the fact of economic betterment and international fame. He could from the outward security of fame and fortune still write with controlled passion of the inward anguish which is the Jamaican/Caribbean reality:

> "You stole my history
> Destroyed my culture
> Cut out my tongue
> So I can't communicate
> Then you mediate
> And separate
> Hide my whole way of life
> So myself I should hate . . ."[101]

Such lyrics are the result and occasion of "real historical relations of a particular epoch,"[102] in this case the Plantation epoch of Caribbean/Jamaican history. But who is to say that coupled with the music that makes these words the special delight they are to contemporary Jamaica, this artistic product will not in future times convey a "transhistorical aesthetic value" despite its

101. Cliff, Jimmy: Song "The Price of Peace". Jimmy Cliff reflects the anguish of the "colonized" Caribbean man in the Fanonian sense of the term.

102. Staden von, Heinrich: "Nietzsche and Marx on Greek Art and Literature" *Daedalus* Vol. 105, No. 1, Winter 1976 p. 83. The Plantation epoch of Caribbean history has not ended with the advent of political (constitutional) Independence.

"specifically based historicity"?[103] Economic determinists are nevertheless wont to deny to art any claim to unqualified autonomy and to the artist any omnipotence that could be divorced from relation to the material world. But not even Karl Marx, the patron saint of many Caribbean economic determinists, could escape having to admit the possibility and fact of "the unequal development of material production [on the one hand] . . . and art" on the other.[104] Marx, we are told, was to be led right back to the conventional view of the "aesthetic normativeness of Greek antiquity" thus perpetuating that "traditional Romantic idealization of Greek art"[105] which figures prominently in the Eurocentrism with which Jamaican and Caribbean perception of art and culture is tightly saddled.

A founding father of modern Jamaica at the very beginning of the movement for nationhood in the late thirties declared thus: "The immediate past has attempted to destroy the influence of the glory that is Africa, it has attempted to make us condemn and mistrust the vitality, the vigour, the rhythmic emotionalism that we get from our African ancestors. It has flung us into conflict with the English traditions of the public schools *and even worse it has imposed on us the Greek ideal of balanced beauty*"[106] (my emphasis). Thirty seven years later and long after the steps taken by voluntary and official effort to redress the imbalance, the anxieties have remained, albeit in a diminished degree. For just as the resisted traditions of Graecophilism defeated a revolting sociodeterministic Marx, so have the resisted traditions of Eurocentrism "continue[d] to score sporadic victories over their subjugators through unperceived metaphorical, metonymic and conceptual tyranny."[107]

103. Staden von, Heinrich: *op cit* p. 82.

104. *Ibid* p. 82.

105. Staden von, Heinrich: *op cit* p. 83.

106. Manley, N. W.: "National Culture and the Artist" *Manley and the New Jamaica* . . . (ed. Rex Nettleford) Longman Caribbean, London 1971, p. 108.

107. Staden von, Heinrich: *op cit* p. 85.

One has only to look at the conventional way in which we approach the study of the history of Jamaica and the region, to experience the force of that conceptual tyranny.[108] Historiography has tended to claim for itself conventional purity by insisting on "pure historical data" to the exclusion of those used by social and cultural anthropologists or of data from the oral tradition deemed unreliable for good history, but which are the source of action and perception of the vast majority of the people who emerged from the plantations. So it is the written records of the literate scribal masters which determine the substance of much of the recorded history of the Caribbean people. Historians like Elsa Goveia and Eric Williams have used conventional material with creative genius to produce controversial and brilliant interpretations;[109] C. L. R. James has brought the power of polemics and Marxian incisive analysis to the history of the great Haitian revolution;[110] and

108.   See *Sunday Gleaner,* May 29, 1977 (pp. 6-7) article "The Biased Slant in West Indian History" by Samuel Washington who does a content analysis of the 1976 W.I. History Ordinary Level General Certificate of Education question paper to "illustrate the Eurocentric emphasis in our history, an emphasis which is part and parcel of the metropolitan orientation inherent in our nation."

109.   Goveia, Elsa: *A Study in the Historiography of the British West Indies to the end of the Nineteenth Century,* Mexico, D.F., Pan-American Institute of Geography and History, 1956. This is solid scholarship, and brilliant exposition from an outstanding Caribbean mind which influenced an entire generation of Caribbean history graduates in the matter of self-perception and Caribbean identity.

Williams, Eric: *Capitalism and Slavery,* Chapel Hill University of North Carolina Press, 1944. A controversial book that sought to explode the myth of humanitarian determinism in the abolition of slavery and to demonstrate that economic considerations rooted in British commercial self-interest played a primary role. It prompted much debate among West Indian scholars and readers and forced many to take another look at slavery beyond the concerns of William Wilberforce et al. Williams' later book entitled *From Columbus to Castro: The History of the Caribbean,* (Andre Deutsch, 1970) drew comments from Samuel Washington *(op cit)* on the 'Eurocentric' orientation of the book, since the title suggests that Caribbean History begins with the coming of the Europeans.

110.   James, C. L. R.: *The Black Jacobins: Toussaint L'Ouverture and the San Domingo Revolution,* New York, Vintage Books 1963 (the first edition was published in 1938). James added a piece to the second edition entitled "From Toussaint L'Ouverture to Fidel Castro" (pp. 391-418) the two being links in a chain of resistance against imperialist domination, which is the story of a good deal of the life of the Caribbean. This would of course include the indigenous Indians who were

Edward Brathwaite has struggled beyond the conventional records to his poetic imagination to find clues to what the non-scribal African slaves might have felt judging from the cultural manifestations in their songs, stories, rituals and folk customs.[111]

This attempt has prompted an interesting and revealing critical comment from a Caribbean colleague – himself a writer and artist. In reviewing Brathwaite's *Creole Society in Jamaica 1770-1820,* the critic warned against any exaggerated claims scholars and readers would wish to make on behalf of Caribbean plantation society which consolidated itself in the late 18th century. The nature and texture of a society, the energies of which were concentrated on commercial profit and the exploitation of one set of migrants for the enhancement of another, had no time to create any historic institutions or the calibre of ideas that would give to a society historic dimensions. History, then, is not the discipline through which any claims of the society's collective creative acts can be justly validated. He, however, suggests that the very failure of history to do the work provides opportunities for sociology, psychology and poetry.[112] But this very concession begs the question as to the nature of history, as to who makes that history and whether the inherited canons of European historiography are any longer reliable or totally useful for 'discovering the truth' about the Jamaican or Caribbean past. Brathwaite's emphasis on the process of creolisation assumes that the phenomena that this process spans, demand more than the conventional tools of historical analysis to make sense of the unruly and sometimes concealed or transmuted mass of material which he believes to be a significant experience.

Yet Jamaicans and their Caribbean counterparts are still perceived by themselves and others as extensions of Europe, historically speaking. Their actions are seen as 'responses' or

part of the liberation struggle against settlers and conquerors. James as a Marxist would not have missed the point.

111.   Brathwaite, Edward: *op cit* esp. pp. 212-239.

112.   Hearne, John: "The Jigsaw Men" . . . *Caribbean Quarterly* Vol. 19, No. 2, pp. 143-149. See also Editorial *Ibid* pp. 3-4.

reactions to the initiatives of Europe. Columbus is still supposed to have 'discovered' America; indigenous Amerindian civilisations are said to have a pre-Columbian history; the story of the fight against slavery devised in 1976 for popular consumption on the powerful television medium, deals largely with the campaign against the slave trade and later of actual slavery by the English humanitarians led by Wilberforce in England and with less than adequate focus on the internal struggles by the enslaved within the slave plantations.[113] Could this be a simple matter of lack of available written records? Here the past is truncated 'and the future (our present) is depleted as a result.

Part of the responsibility in preserving the cultural values and developing them, is to change the perspectives of conventional historiography as bequeathed the Jamaicans and by taking cues from the work of a Goveia, a Williams or a James, look at the society boldly from inside. Some younger historians like the Guyanese, Walter Rodney,[114] see a need for a total reconstruction of the history of the uprooted African starting at the Beginning which was *in* Africa, outside of the baracoons, and not just when he came bound in chains, or when he started in physical and mental consciousness to regain his freedom, or when he more recently entered, aroused and with hope, into his kingdom of self-government and Independence. Walter Rodney would probably agree with the Jewish historian Walter Benjamin who proclaimed that "only that historian will have the gift of fanning the spark of hope in the past who is firmly convinced that even the dead will not be safe from the enemy if he wins."[115] The enemy here in the Caribbean is a combined entrapment of agelong dependency

113.   Jones, Evan: "The Fight Against Slavery", Television Documentary BBC/Time-Life series 1975 (there is a book version of this co-authored by Evan Jones and Terrence Brady).

114.   Rodney, Walter: "African History in the Service of Black Revolution" *Bongo Man*, No. 1, Dec. 1968 (cyclostyled Journal of African Youth). Dr Rodney went on to write *How Europe Underdeveloped Africa*, Bogle-L'Ouverture, Pub. London 1972.

115.   Quoted in a Review article "The Revolt of Gershom Scholem" by Leon Wieseltier in *New York Review of Books*, March 5, 1977, p. 23.

(economic and psychological) born of colonialism, and the persistent denigration of the African (and some would add all non-European) presence rooted in slavery and indentureship. Historical consciousness has been known to hold the oppressed together at other times and in other places. Why not now in the Caribbean? African Studies at all levels of learning and in all their multidisciplinary and cross-cultural modes, are vital for the preservation and development of key cultural values like self-confidence and a sense of heritage among the masses of people in Jamaica and the Caribbean. Moreover, such studies in African history and culture must be pursued with sustained vigour and with the rigour of scientific inquiry as well as with the compassion of a sensitive artist, scholarly precision and integrity, though not with that smug and timid objectivity which historian Benjamin says can destroy history. One only has to recall the strength of the historical consciousness of the European in Caribbean outposts where no one speaks of pre-Columbian Britain, France or Spain. Indeed, generations of Jamaicans have, for example, had to master the English language, memorise Shakespeare and passages from the King James version of the Bible, know the British constitution and be familiar with the names of royal heads, or perish. In such a situation of cultural one-upmanship it was (and is) natural for the latecomers to reveal a vested interest in keeping their own cultural records straight or at least to protect them by religious preservation or endogamous mating patterns, etc., unless forced by circumstances to do otherwise. Circumstances have forced many to do otherwise and such circumstances are part of the stuff of Caribbean history. But the future generations of the region will need to know this history.

The role of history syllabuses then, carefully designed for schools, colleges and universities, in the area of continuing education as well as of on-going historical research is self-explanatory in the preservation and development of cultural values in Jamaican and Caribbean life.

For the development of a sense of history in nation-building "is a deliberate act of intelligence"[116] and a cultural value

116. Manley, N. W.: "Conservation and Culture: A Sense of History for Nation Build-

worth developing and preserving as it has indeed been over a span of thirty years through:

(a)   research and dissemination of findings by Caribbean scholars into the history, sociology and cultural dynamics of Jamaica and the region

(b)   acquisition and increasing use of voluminous Caribbean primary and secondary material by the West India Reference Library in the Institute of Jamaica

(c)   focus on historical personalities through the creation of the Order of National Heroes and the award of this to prominent historical figures;[117] also focus on events and dates of historical significance which have fired the imagination of the general populace – e.g. Labour Day, commemorating eventful labour riots of 1938, Independence Day (the first Monday in August which bears emotional connections with the old August first Emancipation Day) and National Heroes Day in October, the month of the historic Morant Bay Rebellion of 1865

(d)   the encouragement of writing on the nation's cultural heritage by the Institute of Jamaica through its Publications Division which publishes the Cultural Heritage Series and through the African-Caribbean Institute which is responsible for monographs and occasional papers as is the University of the West Indies

(e)   the preservation of historical sites and monuments as well as the encouragement of archaeological excavations by the Jamaica National Trust Commission.

In Jamaica alone the output and range of activities over

ing" in *Manley and the New Jamaica* . . . (ed. Rex Nettleford) Longman Caribbean, London 1971 p. 117.

117.   e.g. George William Gordon and Paul Bogle of the Morant Bay Rebellion (1865) Marcus Garvey of the Black nationalist movement (1917-1940), Alexander Busta-mante and Norman Manley (1938-1967) founding fathers of modern Jamaica, Nanny of the Maroons (1930's) and Sam Sharpe, leader of the 1831 revolt against slavery (Baptist War).

the decade between 1967 and 1977 have been large and impressive. With them have developed institutions which provide the means of preserving and developing Jamaican cultural values. These are discussed below as part of the overall cultural policy which is a dimension of national development strategy. Central to this positive approach must be the genuine belief that all of the people by definition possess cultural values and that the notion of making "culture accessible" to "the people" is a misguided sense of obligation in the context of the so-called Great Tradition/Little Tradition debate. This is borne out by the experience of the Jamaica Festival Commission, the chief agency of community cultural activity in the country. Since 1963 the Festival movement has offered tens of thousands of creative Jamaicans of talent from all walks of life the opportunity for widespread audience exposure and development, stimulation and challenge through competitions as well as recognition through a system of graded awards (medals – bronze, silver, gold and Certificate of Merit). The activities extend to music (traditional, classical and popular), dance (traditional, Jamaican, creative, folk varieties of other lands, dramatic, classical ballet), drama (Jamaican and West Indian as well as works from established international repertoire), arts and crafts, photography, costume design, fashion (with emphasis on local designs and execution), culinary arts (with emphasis on the innovative aspects of indigenous cuisines and recipes) and beauty contests (which were abandoned since, *inter alia,* they served to exacerbate the angry debate over standards of beauty in a country which though predominantly of African descent has succumbed repeatedly to the European ideal of classic beauty as part of the cultural contradictions of colonial life).[118] The Festival Commission was in effect the official co-ordination and rationalisation of a well established tradition of village, parish, urban municipal and county festivals dating back to the turn of the twentieth century.[119] The great lesson learnt from that

118. Jamaica has produced two "Miss Worlds", neither of obvious African ancestry. One was a "Miss Jamaica" (Carol Crawford, 1965) chosen through the Jamaica Festival competitions, the other (Cindy Breakspeare, 1977) was an independent entrant. The event each time caused controversy of national proportions.

119. The co-ordination was spearheaded by Mr Edward Seaga, Minister of Social

experience produces in turn a cultural value worthy of preservation and development. This pivots on the realisation that the cultural dynamics of such artistic expressions in music, dance, drama, arts and crafts depend on the constant return to the roots, the source of energy. This is not lost on the many sophisticated urban groups who have addressed themselves to the challenge thrown out in 1939 by founding-father Norman Manley who called for the reflection of Jamaican culture in "the painting of pictures of our own mountains and our womenfolk, in building those houses that are most suitable to live in, in writing plays of our own adventures and poetry of our wisdom, finding ourselves in wrestle with our own problems."[120]

Many have heeded the call since those heady days of the late thirties when the "new national spirit" gripped those who were young, adventurous and progressive. To them, the building of a nation has indeed been an "act of intelligence." But acts of intelligence depend in turn on the development of the mind; and in this the creative arts and other cultural activities will continue to play a major role in Jamaica as anywhere else in the world. It is a paradox that it was the Francophone Caribbean Marxist, Frantz Fanon, who finally opted for culture rather than material conditions in effecting the revolution he felt must come. Such an option is almost natural to the Caribbean character though there is a strong enough body of Caribbean radical opinion that would dismiss anything resembling 'cultural nationalism' as too sterile to deal with the harsh realities of the economic deprivation of the masses. It should therefore be pointed out that Fanon's revolutionary culture was intended to be liberated from the preciosity of romanticised folklore and the vulgarities of chauvinism, racism or the self-indulgence of the Black intelligentsia operating from the metropolitan salons or from pseudo-Bohemian outposts in the "colonies." But like N. W. Manley[121] who also saw a national culture in a national conscious-

Development and Culture and later Minister of Finance 1962-72 in the JLP Administration.

120.   Manley, N. W.: "National Culture and the Artist" *op cit* p. 109.

121.   *Ibid.*

ness transcending narrow nationalism as he felt his favourite Jamaican novelist Roger Mais had undoubtedly done,[122] Frantz Fanon expected from his revolution, which he saw as an essentially *cultural* phenomenon, a new humanism and universality.[123] And these are yet further cultural values worthy of preservation and development in Jamaican and Caribbean society. They are indeed evident among conscious artists and among many progressive politicians who inform their search for an appropriate ideology with a strong moral suasion in their commitment to *people vis-a-vis* property. But from the popular streams of the society the above values that Fanon dreamt of emerge strongest in the religious creed of the Rastafarians and the maxims of prudence they enunciate as guide for their daily life.[124] The divinity of all men and the objectives of peace and love are sound enough moral bases for the political aspirations to such ideals as equality and social justice. The force of this contemporary spirit of authenticity is second only to the ancestral cultural goods to be found among the sturdy peasantry on the hillsides and in the valleys of rural Jamaica.

The question still arises, however, as to whether the individualism of artistic cultural expression should not be rescued from the now prevalent revolutionary view that cultural truth can only be seriously pursued and realised within a commitment. At least two Jamaican artists (a novelist and a poet) have pointedly referred to Fidel Castro's reputed injunction to his artistic community — "Inside the revolution, everything; outside the revolution nothing." To some Jamaicans, this is not the stuff of creative autonomy and individual freedom as a distinguished Jamaican poet who sometimes pinchhits as a political journalist implied in a newspaper piece on the great Cuban classical ballet dancer Alicia Alonso.[125] Many Jamaicans would share similar misgivings about

122. Manley, N. W.: "The Creative Artist and the National Movement" being Foreword to a collection of novels entitled '*The Three Novels of Roger Mais*', *op cit* p. 112.

123. Burke, Edmund: "Frantz Fanon's *The Wretched of the Earth*" *Daedalus* Vol. 105, No. 1, Winter 1976, p. 135.

124. Owens, Joseph: *Dread — The Rastafarians of Jamaica*, Sangster-Jamaica, 1977.

125. Morris, Mervyn: "Some Cuban Answers" *Jamaica Daily News*, March 31, 1977.

the determinism of the direction of the creative imagination of their compatriots. Yet a great number would sympathise with and support what could be regarded as engaged art – the sort that Caribbean countries can be said to encourage and be developing in the drive towards *decolonisation* (the negative side of the struggle) and creolisation or indigenisation (which is positive).

The fear of consequences leading to a narrow nationalism, parochialism and pedestrian postures in our cultural life is common enough among the intelligentsia to reveal an unabated debate – omnipresent, always simmering and ever ready for willing protagonists and antagonists. Letters to the press, public statements, individual and group manifestos bring much heat, if not enduring clarity, to light. The battle continues between Europe's superordinate culture and the subordinate specimens that are the African expressions and their dominant continuities in Caribbean creolised cultural forms. The highly sophisticated Jamaican novelist, John Hearne, once "despair[ed] of the "mission-school ignorance" that was "allow[ed] to pass" three times in an article by that engaging Jamaican woman of letters, Sylvia Wynter, who placed Schiller's "Ode to Joy" into Beethoven's Third Symphony (The Eroica) instead of into the Ninth (The Chorale) where it belongs. Not to be outdone, Ms Wynter delivered a priceless retort, admitting the error of her ways and even implying a "freudian" slip. But she made the following point tartly – "John Hearne's very valid and important correction is betrayed by the anguish at what he obviously considers sacrilege; and rather brings out my point about the fetishism of the super-culture worshippers."[126] Hearne may not have been interested in anything more than a respect for accuracy and facts which most civilised Western men regard as important to human progress. But Wynter's point about the fetishism of the

Fidel Castro is credited with the following: "For us, a revolutionary people in a revolutionary process, the value of cultural and artistic creations is determined by their usefulness for the people, by what they contribute to man, by what they contribute to the liberation and happiness of man . . ." (Quoted in *Memories of Underdevelopment: the Revolutionary Films of Cuba*, ed. Michael Myerson, New York, 1973 – dedicatory page).

126.   Letter to the Editor *Jamaica Journal*, June 1969, p. 2.

super-culture worshippers does accurately reflect the problem of Caribbean culture being courageous enough to define itself in its own terms without having to worry seriously whether (as John Hearne in his note of "despair" said) "Priam was Hector's son or that it is Lear who asks 'To be or not to be?' "[127] Put this way the question of European cultural domination may very well be begged. But it is a fact of life that must be faced when the matter of the preservation and development of cultural values is being discussed. *Whose* culture and *whose* values, *what* culture and *what* values become pertinent queries in search of pertinent answers.

One kind of answer found passionate articulation in a newspaper article by the said Sylvia Wynter in March 1970. She expressed the view shared by many of the enlightened products of her generation and educational background that while the rejection by Jamaicans and Caribbean people of the excellent artistic achievements of any civilisation would be self-maiming and self-negating, "to insist as we have hitherto done on any one part — i.e. the European — to the total exclusion of *any* or *all* of the others, is to humiliate and exile a part of ourselves . . . [and] to betray, by distortion, even that part which we accept — i.e. European — since we presume to pass off a part of mankind's experience, however rich and vivid, as the whole of it, as the total sum of possibilities and potentiality."[128] With the now legendary sophistication of the Caribbean world-citizen, she could declare without fear of contradiction that "to understand West Indian history, we must turn to the history of Africa, Asia, of the indigenous peoples of the American continent, [and of] Europe."[129]

Back in 1939, N. W. Manley had put it succinctly and to the point: "We can take everything that English education has to

---

127. *Ibid.*

128. Wynter, Sylvia: "New Standards or High Standards — a Matter of Emphasis" *Sunday Gleaner,* March 15, 1970. On the same page of this day's issue was an article giving the facts of the varied and 'relevant' events which took place at the Creative Arts Centre in the previous 18 months. Another article entitled "Our Root Elements of Culture", by Millard Johnson, an Africanist, on the opposite page all together betray the importance of cultural matters to Jamaican concerns.

129. *Ibid.*

offer us but ultimately we must reject the *domination of her influence,* because we are not English and nor should we ever want to be." "Instead", he went on, "we must dig deep into our own consciousness and accept and reject only those things of which we from our superior knowledge of our own cultural needs must be the best judges."[130] The commitment continues to be a challenge for succeeding generations of Jamaicans and Caribbean peoples in this twin process of decolonisation and indigenisation.

What is the nature of this process? It is a "complex process of transformation through adjustments, rejection, affirmation and innovation."[131] The complexity itself defies the rigidities of imported dogma or the caprice of individual self-indulgence and struggles to celebrate the inherent cogency of the interplay between diverse elements in seeking to give directions to new forms and styles of life in the Caribbean. In forging "for itself its own frame of reference out of the mass of experience over time and in quite unique circumstances . . . the process takes on its own intrinsic dimensions and enriches the texture and meaning of Caribbean life in quite unprecedented ways."[132] Nothing seems to escape the imperatives of the dynamic — whether it is the imperial game of cricket testing the subordinate's skill and psychological prowess against his master's will and legitimacy, or literature which "has long served as an effective instrument for plumbing deeply into Caribbean dimensions at once revealing the anxieties of the exiled African and the anguish of the West Indian born White in the Mother country",[133] or religion and secular belief systems which have been among the most spectacular manifestations of the process, both in terms of results and the methods whereby such results

---

130.   Manley, N. W.: "National Culture and the Artist" *op cit* p. 109.

131.   Nettleford, Rex: Editorial Foreword *Caribbean Quarterly,* Vol. 19, No. 3, p. 5. It is *not* the creolism of Latin Caribbean writers of the thirties who saw themselves as Europeans overseas. See "Problems in the Creation of Culture in the Caribbean" by José Luis Méndez in *Caribbean Quarterly,* Vol. 21, Nos. 2 & 3, (1975) p. 11.

132.   *Ibid.*

133.   *Ibid.*

are achieved; whether it is historical and sociological studies despite the moral turpitude of an early society whose *raison d'etre* hardly went beyond the objective of commercial profit, or even the acultural world of Caribbean business which ignores, at its peril, the cultural context within which it operates.

The range of the phenomena that falls within the ambit of the process is the source of its very strength and is itself a hope for the richness and variety of cultural products that can emerge from it all. What is more, the possibility presents Jamaican and Caribbean peoples with the over-arching challenge to preserve and develop among themselves a *sense of process* that will result not only in greater understanding of the deep issues of their history and contemporary life but also will bring to the challenging task that discipline, hardwork, industry, and sustained application which must inform any struggle "to be."

For the process in the final analysis must concern itself not merely with the black-white dissensus of a vintage Plantation Caribbean. It must of necessity embrace, as well, the experience and more recent history of the "late-comers" like Orientals (East Indian and Chinese) and the Arabs. The ingrained denigration of the African Presence in Caribbean life will have to be obliterated if only to save the present indigenisation process from continuing to promote that cultural intolerance and suspicion betrayed towards late-comer ingredients, particularly the rich East Indian complex which has gained increasing self-consciousness since the Independence of Mother India in 1947[134] and whose increasing importance in Trinidad and Guyana is underscored by the fact of population increase over and above the segments of Trinidadian and Guyanese population which are of African ancestry. It is Maureen Warner-Lewis who wisely reminds her compatriots of the "primal awareness of the changes wrought by time; the apprehension of the other world, the problems posed by war, death, new environment; the need to adapt, the nostalgia for the past — all are basic to human

---

134.   Jha, J. C.: "Indian Heritage in Trinidad and Tobago, West Indies" *Caribbean Quarterly*, Vol. 19, No. 2: pp. 28-49.

experience, regardless of race."[135] The declaration is clearly not intended to deny the exiled African in the Caribbean his black essence; rather it may well be to celebrate his *human* essence which, once denied him in the degradation of slavery continues to be denied him in the persistence of material dispossession, cultural denigration and sheer powerlessness.

Of importance in all this is the matter of the *cultural process* itself — its nature, shape and the range of activities and actions which it encompasses. To conceive it as a manifestation of fragmented segments known as "high art" and "folk art" is to perpetuate some of the worst elements of Plantation society where elitist Eurocentrism lords it over the collective consciousness of the African-folk and where the Great House stands in contempt of the village plot. Better if the cultural process were seen as a growth process with the source of life beginning in the roots sending up shoots which eventually bear fruits which ripen, fall back to the roots to grow again in a never-ending regenerative process. There is such a plant that grows in Jamaica and the Caribbean: it is the banyan tree. This on-going recycling of effort is the dynamic of the cultural process and has no place for elitism as it is understood in a class-ridden and status-conscious society. It is therefore understandable when Arnold Bertram, the young Minister of State responsible for Information and Culture in the Prime Minister's Office, declared in May 1977 at an international colloquium on cultural development in the Caribbean that "You will understand why we as a post-colonial society can neither afford the luxury of misunderstanding the role of culture in the process of national liberation, nor use the term as others do, to suggest the 'refined' aesthetic sensibilities of the elite. We have no time for these petty conceits by which an elite bolsters its courage since our political objective is to eliminate this elitism. We therefore use the term culture in a far wider sense, in which it implies all the means by which a society expresses itself. It is these means to express ourselves that colonial societies deny the majority which accounts for our cultural

---

135.   Warner-Lewis, Maureen: "Odomankoma Kyrema Se", *Caribbean Quarterly*, Vol. 19, No. 2: pp. 51-96.

backwardness."[136]

It is for cultural development policies then, to bring to the people not only an understanding of the power and necessity of the roots but also a full grasp of their responsibility to nurture those roots so that they can bear fruits to enrich the quality of life through replanting and reproduction. The promotion of cultural exclusivity among any one group of nationals to the exclusion of another as colonial policies and practices did in the pursuit of European dominance, would be to repeat the errors of history to the further impoverishment of the heritage.

As indicated above, this is not an argument to avoid the inescapable responsibility of redressing the imbalances of ages by focusing, where vital and necessary, on the conscious *revaluing* of things African and things created out of the collective experience of Jamaicans of African ancestry. For such is the requirement of that self-confidence that some 90% of the people of Jamaica must have in order to become the resourceful productive citizens they are required to be for effective national development. In Jamaica, the focus finds form not only in the community's own aggressive celebration of the African patrimony through Rastafarianism, Black Power protest and the popular resurgence of interest in Garvey and Garveyism, but also in official policy as seen in the elevation of Garvey and Nanny of the Maroons to the Order of National Hero, the establishment of the African-Caribbean Institute of Jamaica and a museum of African arts and crafts, the encouragement of African Studies in the educational system at all levels of learning, the establishment of diplomatic relations with countries of Black Africa, the firm stand taken by Jamaica on the international scene against apartheid and the active support given to movements for the liberation of Black Africa from white colonial rule,[137] and the encouragement since Independence of exchange

136. Bertram, Arnold B.: "The Process of Self-Discovery – A Jamaican Perspective on the Role of Culture in National Liberation", Address to Festival Mondial du Théatre, Nancy, France, May 1977.

137. Jamaica, through Prime Minister Manley, has assumed leadership among the Caribbean nations in the fight for the liberation of Zimbabwe and Namibia. The keynote

visits between African leaders (including the late Haile Selassie, Samora Machel and Tanzania's Julius Nyerere) and their Jamaican counterparts (including the present Jamaican Prime Minister and former Leader of the Opposition and Prime Minister, Hugh Shearer).[138]

Yet for this not to deteriorate into racial exclusivity, cultural chauvinism, or inverted snobbery, cultural policies must place this new-spawned 'revolution' in the perspective of that deeper process of indigenisation or creolisation. In other words, the African Presence must be given its proper place of centrality in that dynamic process of adjustment, adaptation, rejection, renewal and innovation. For the products of this cultural process are what constitute the mandates for a national cultural expression. The Carnival which is one such product out of the experience of the twin-island state of Trinidad and Tobago is cited as the mandate for a national theatre by one of its leading dramatists.[139] In Jamaica the process finds form in the quite robust and resilient traditional and definitive culture of the peasantry and to a positive extent in the modern pop culture of the urban ghettos and back-streets. Such constitute the mandate for the creative work by theatre groups like the National Pantomime, the National Dance Theatre Company, the Jamaican Folk Singers and for that enter-tainment genre of Jamaican popular music, the exponents of which have emerged as "stars" of international significance. And such are the ways in which the country's cultural values are preserved and developed through artistic creation. In no way can the "happenings" on or off Broadway, in West End London, in Paris, Rome or Moscow be the soil for the growth and preservation of Caribbean

address to the historic United Nation International Conference in support of the People of Zimbabwe and Namibia, held in Maputo, Mozambique on May 17, 1977 was delivered by the Prime Minister of Jamaica (q.v.).

138. Since becoming Prime Minister in 1972, the Hon. Michael Manley has visited Africa several times.

139. Hill, Errol: *Trinidad Carnival: Mandate for a National Theatre*, University of Texas Press, 1972. Dr Hill was the first Staff Tutor in Drama to be appointed to the UWI and did much to indigenise West Inidan theatre in the fifties and sixties.

artistic cultural values. There is even a cut-off point to the pleasures of exile enjoyed in the fifties (for good and proper reasons) by many Caribbean literary figures. The paucity of publishing houses in the Caribbean region notwithstanding, the mountain must now come to Mohammed or Mohammed must find his own mountains around him.

Yet the manifestations of lifestyles among the middle strata (and professionals) are largely imitative of metropolitan culture or are versions of that international consumer pattern already referred to. This is not to deny the existence of a developed creative imagination among such middle strata people. In fact, there is overriding evidence of a great deal but those who have made an impact are undoubtedly those with a full grasp of and feel for the strength and significance of the collective consciousness of the folk people of Jamaica as well as of the actual life lived by all people in the country. In any case they are most of them a generation or less removed from this very "folk life". Not to be written off since it encompasses some of the knowledge and skills of modernisation integral to national development, the "imported culture" of the bulk of the middle strata nevertheless cannot be the prime source of energy for an indigenous cultural expression. They are still the most influential transmitters (and interpreters) of cultural values through their control over schoolrooms, parsons' pulpits, professorial lecterns, legal chambers, affluent households with household helps, and the print and electronic media. Their organisational skill and technical know-how give them promotional leadership in crucial areas of cultural expression, e.g. in theatre management, film distribution, impressario work and the management of the recording industry. That these skills are necessary to facilitate the wider spread of cultural products is obvious. The owners of such skills will therefore have to be accommodated and fully acknowledged as part of the cultural process.

But where a sense of place, aesthetic sensibility and sensitivity are clearly lacking, care must be taken to avoid unfair exploitation by the possessers of such skill of the primary creative talents, whether these be of a peasant community rich in folksongs, dances and stories but vulnerable in the face of "unscrupulous researchers" pursuing the folk heritage for purely commercial gain or film directors bypassing trained professional talent in order to obtain cheap labour in the name of 'people-talent', people's theatre or democratic exposure. The creative talents may also belong to a group of ritualists whose place is best in their natural yard-temples rather than in a resort hotel ballroom where they are "given exposure" in the name of "cultural tourism". There is even doubt whether such "ritualists" (if their rituals retain seriousness of purpose) should be processed on to village festival stages to "compete" for medals. Then there is the talented musical composer and lyricist whose songs can achieve international acclaim but may fail to do so without a kickback (payola) to some disc jockey on a local radio station. The wanton pirating of works of art inside and outside the country, instead of preserving and developing certain cultural values may contribute decisively to their vulgarisation and subsequent decline. The introduction of a Copyright law that can command support in the international and regional communities understandably assumes an urgency that is evident in Caribbean nations like Trinidad and Jamaica today.[140]

To avoid many of the temptations cited in the above the need for a high degree of discipline and moral suasion is necessary. The philosophical predilections of a 19th century liberal tradition would send many Jamaicans into passionate advocacy of self-discipline over external coercion. This is not an academic indulgence for a society that is trying to achieve through collective endeavour what the *laissez-faire* commitment has failed to do since the emancipation of slavery. The seduction, then, by that point of view which sees the "future as a set drama, leading through catastrophe to a final enlightenment" is very easy among pockets of both young and wrinkled revolutionaries. But there remains the popular belief among an individualistic generation of descendants of slaves the equally strong view that "each man must choose his own ends of action."[141] This could be a solemn challenge for any

140. A new Copyright Law in Jamaica was passed in 1977.

141. Hampshire, Stuart: "The Future of Knowledge" *New York Review of Books,* Vol. XXIV, No. 5, March 31, 1977, p. 18.

STATE INSTRUMENTS OF
CULTURAL ACTION — JAMAICA

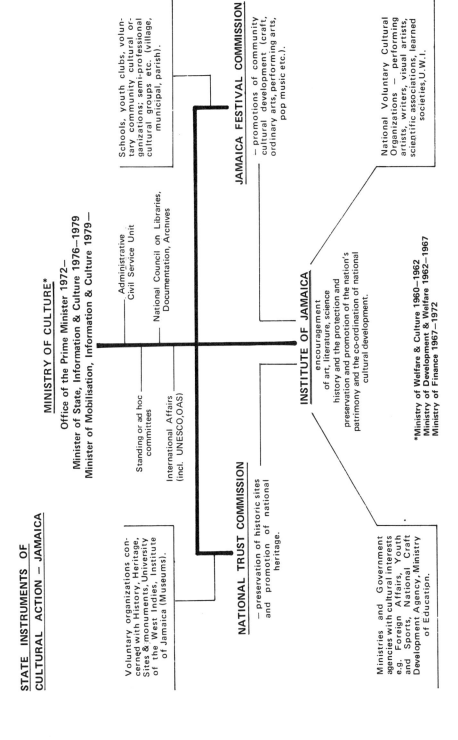

MINISTRY OF CULTURE*

Office of the Prime Minister 1972—
Minister of State, Information & Culture 1976—1979
Minister of Mobilisation, Information & Culture 1979—

Administrative
Civil Service Unit

National Council on Libraries,
Documentation, Archives

Standing or ad hoc
committees

International Affairs
(incl. UNESCO, OAS)

Schools, youth clubs, voluntary community cultural organizations; semi-professional
cultural groups etc. (village,
municipal, parish).

JAMAICA FESTIVAL COMMISSION

— promotions of community
cultural development (craft,
ordinary arts, performing arts,
pop music etc.).

National Voluntary Cultural
Organizations — performing
artists, writers, visual artists,
scientific associations, learned
societies, U.W.I.

INSTITUTE OF JAMAICA

encouragement
of art, literature, science
history and the protection and
preservation and promotion of the nation's
patrimony and the co-ordination of national
cultural development.

*Ministry of Welfare & Culture 1960—1962
Ministry of Development & Welfare 1962—1967
Ministry of Finance 1967—1972

NATIONAL TRUST COMMISSION

— preservation of historic sites
and promotion of national
heritage.

Voluntary organizations concerned with History, Heritage,
Sites & monuments, University
of the West Indies, Institute
of Jamaica (Museums).

Ministries and Government
agencies with cultural interests
e.g. Foreign Affairs, Youth
and Sports, National Craft
Development Agency, Ministry
of Education.

THE INSTITUTE OF JAMAICA 1975 —

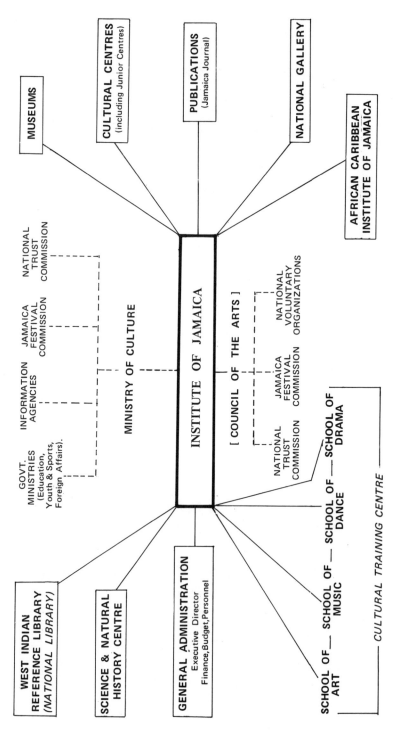

MUSEUMS

CULTURAL CENTRES
(including Junior Centres)

PUBLICATIONS
(Jamaica Journal)

NATIONAL GALLERY

AFRICAN CARIBBEAN
INSTITUTE OF JAMAICA

GOVT.
MINISTRIES
(Education,
Youth & Sports,
Foreign Affairs).

INFORMATION
AGENCIES

JAMAICA
FESTIVAL
COMMISSION

NATIONAL
TRUST
COMMISSION

MINISTRY OF CULTURE

INSTITUTE OF JAMAICA

[COUNCIL OF THE ARTS]

NATIONAL
TRUST
COMMISSION

JAMAICA
FESTIVAL
COMMISSION

NATIONAL
VOLUNTARY
ORGANIZATIONS

WEST INDIAN
REFERENCE LIBRARY
(NATIONAL LIBRARY)

SCIENCE & NATURAL
HISTORY CENTRE

GENERAL ADMINISTRATION
Executive Director
Finance, Budget, Personnel

SCHOOL OF — SCHOOL OF — SCHOOL OF — SCHOOL OF
ART   MUSIC   DANCE   DRAMA

—————— CULTURAL TRAINING CENTRE ——————

NOTE: Each division is managed by a Board of Management whose chairman sits
on the Institute's Council of the Arts (formerly the Board of Governors).

THE JAMAICA FESTIVAL COMMISSION

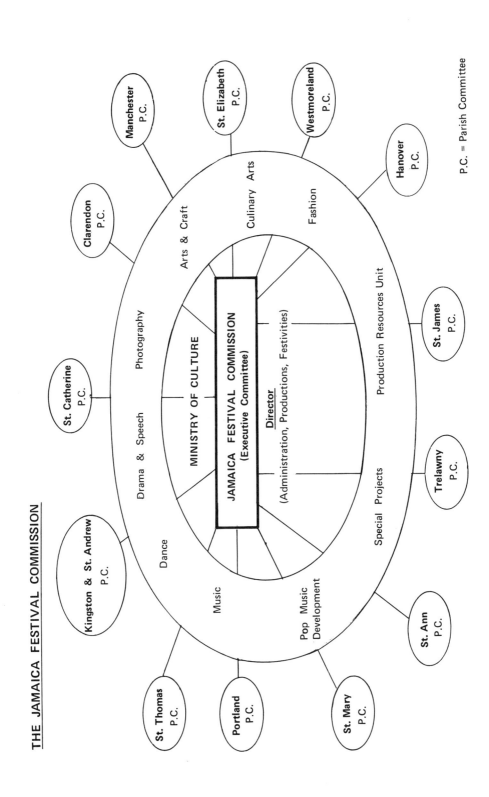

MINISTRY OF CULTURE

JAMAICA FESTIVAL COMMISSION
(Executive Committee)

Director
(Administration, Productions, Festivities)

Arts & Craft
Culinary Arts
Fashion
Photography
Production Resources Unit
Drama & Speech
Dance
Music
Special Projects
Pop Music Development

Manchester P.C.
St. Elizabeth P.C.
Westmoreland P.C.
Clarendon P.C.
Hanover P.C.
St. Catherine P.C.
St. James P.C.
Kingston & St. Andrew P.C.
Trelawny P.C.
St. Thomas P.C.
Portland P.C.
St. Mary P.C.
St. Ann P.C.

P.C. = Parish Committee

NETWORK OF VOLUNTARY CONTRIBUTION
TO CULTURAL ACTION IN JAMAICA

government which is serious about integrating cultural development into its over-all strategies of national development. One could find a way out by emphasising those cultural activities that naturally depend on collective action for expression. Indeed, this probably accounts for the widespread popularity of the performing arts. But does this necessarily mean the impoverishment of literature by censure, of lyrics by banning (the accompanying sound is always inviolate), of painting and sculpture by demolition, and of even the performing arts by dictated commissioning? Not necessarily so, if there is widespread consensus in the leadership and throughout the populace of the need for the indigenisation of our cultural expression and processes. But how wide is widespread?

One of "the problems of the creation of culture" in the Caribbean as the Puerto Rican scholar José Luis Méndez puts it, turns precisely on this. He resolves the conflict that Caribbean artists may feel themselves to have with the phenomenon of fundamental social change thus: "In the same way that specialists in particular fields of endeavour must demonstrate high quality and efficiency, the writer who decides to work for a revolutionary cause must realise that literature is a *form of action* with its own laws, though not autonomous, employing specific techniques and particular tools which must be known, explored and improved. He must realise, too, that the best way to make literature serve a revolutionary cause *is to regard it seriously as an art* . . . (my emphasis) . . . Truly important art is not flight but pursuit, is not apathy but commitment, is not refuge for inaction, but action which responds imaginatively to the most important and significant historical tensions. This is why in artistic works of the highest quality we see manifested not only the individual creative capacity with its peculiar biographical problems, but also, and particularly so, the social groups, with their particular conceptions regarding morality, art and science."[142] Such a reflection on cultural expression by a Caribbean scholar betrays the on-going concern of many practising artists in Jamaica today; and views on which cultural values are to

142. Méndez, José Luis: "Problems in the Creation of Caribbean Culture" *Caribbean Quarterly*, Vol. 21, Nos. 1 & 2, pp. 7-8, reprinted from *Casa*, Havana.

be preserved and developed will naturally turn on the resolution of the problem. One thing is certain: the old "cultural value" which divorced the creative imagination from thé realities of practical existence cannot serve the needs of the region in its desperate search for itself.

Another cultural value to be developed and preserved is that of an understanding of science and technology, for the kind of world in which the Caribbean people now find themselves makes this not only important but necessary. In the popular imagination in Jamaica, 'science' and 'higher science' carry cultural connotations of divine magic, ritual witchcraft and religious wonder.[143] The persistent posture may simply be underlining the faċt that Jamaicans are part of that human struggle against the reputed destruction by science, of the "most precious of [man's] un-renewable resources — a sense of the world's wonder" as a science writer so aptly described one of the dilemmas currently confronting the science sensibilities of Western man.[144] The ordinary Jamaicans themselves have long entered Western modernity with its motorised transport, electric power, its revolution in antibiotics, its jet propulsion and nuclear energy. The cultural impact of science and technology is after all part of the drama of modernity everywhere. What Jamaica must do with science and technology is to use it and not be dominated by it. The 'wisdom' of the Jamaican peasant's knowledge rooted in experience fighting the agricultural extension officer's

143.   The performance of Jamaican children in the science subjects of the London and Cambridge high school examinations (General Certificate of Education) is traditionally unsatisfactory. The following tabulated results speak for themselves:

	London		Cambridge	
	Sat	Passed	Sat	Passed
Mathematics	1752	300	4617	1831
Biology	1355	131	4246	1796
Physics	204	20	1297	629
Chemistry	210	28	1859	911

See *Statistical Year Book 1976;* also article "Deal With It" by Audley Kidd in *The Star*, May 30, 1977 for further discussion.

144.   Hapgood, Fred: "The Reformation in Science" *Atlantic Monthly* Vol. 239, No. 3, March 1977, pp. 107-110.

peddling of a new fertiliser is often an expression of the distrust of absolute power. For the entire tradition of science and technology has been sifted to us through the imperial might of Europe and reinforced by the latter-day global power of North America. It is said that Western domination has been built on science whose strength lies in its power to predict the behaviour of natural phenomena with precision, to reduce trial and error to a minimum and thereby achieve an unprecedented economy of effort.[145] But it was out of this that emanated that spirit which sent Europeans into colonies which were seen as objects to be explored, penetrated, assaulted with impunity and *mastered*. The notion that Nature (the analogy of colonies) could be approached on its own terms, embraced and respected rather than brutalised and dominated, was foreign to that spirit of conquest. That spirit became entrapped in a determinism which all but negated that other side of the scientific tradition which sees the exploration of observable data as a liberating influence through the further doubts such exploration creates and the ignorance it reveals. It is this knowledge that we do not know that goads human curiosity on to further exploration and discovery and keeps Man in a dynamic state of tolerance and humility without hopeless surrender to hypostatized natural forces or abandonment of the capacity to believe in self.

Science as a cultural dimension of development is, in any case, as ambiguous for the developing Jamaicans as it is for the developed North Atlantic. Perhaps the Jamaicans who need to be rescued from the arrogance and hubris of scientific determinism are those to be found in that very segment of the population who have had the "advantage" of a thorough European education and are marinated in the learned debates of European political ideas. To many of these people the very utterance of the word "scientific" as in "scientific socialism" gives them instant claims to authenticity over all other thinkers in what is still a politically fluid and culturally insecure situation. The wholesale importation of Marx and Lenin from Europe is one thing; it is quite another to harbour

145. See Mendelssohn, Kurt: *The Secret of Western Domination*, Praeger, New York, 1976.

the danger of dogmatism parading as "scientific" legitimacy but which robs the fertile minds in a groping Caribbean of the capacity or will to recognise and *take into account* the rich texture of human existence in all its contradictions, dynamic constant flow, its historical specificity (an element not lost on Marx as far as the Europe he studied was concerned) and in the capacity of people (Jamaicans included) to cope with diverse environmental situations with resourcefulness and inventiveness. The appropriate scientific spirit for Jamaica is clearly the one that will facilitate the exercise of such resourcefulness and inventiveness among the Jamaican people, drawing on their own rich resources rooted in their collective experience. Those resources, it is important to add, reside not only in the negative aspects of plantation and colonial oppression but also in the positive innovations by the resourceful oppressed in the form and purpose they have given to their existence in the Caribbean environment for over three centuries. Herein lies the dialectical thrust of Caribbean existence; and the systematic study and analysis of this is the stuff of the social sciences and of historical research which are important tools to development (economic and socio-cultural), bearing in mind the diverse and dynamic nature of the *phenomena involved.*

Finally and by way of recapitulation, it needs to be restated that to preserve and develop the cultural values deemed crucial to the people of the Caribbean, that process positively expressed as creolisation (or indigenisation) is one that cannot logically be omitted from the calculus of change, whatever may be the political or socio-economic strategies devised around, or designed to achieve the fulfilment of, that process. For it is not only the cultural values enshrined in the region's many language-forms, religious expressions, kinship patterns, artistic manifestations, scientific research capabilities, and collective historical experience that must be indigenised. Political and economic systems must also be made to grow out of the native soil, however inescapable or desirable the fertilising boon of imported creeds and practices are seen to be.

The claims of socialism (to name just one creed) are undoubtedly going to gain increasing currency in Jamaica and the

wider Caribbean, (a) with the timely emphasis on economic reconstruction (whether through Marxian class struggle or parliamentary
tactics or both), social justice and equality over and above the now
programmatically weak "nationalism" which served an earlier era
and (b) in combative defiance of the prevailing capitalist experience
known for its well chronicled economic exploitation, social injustice, and the continuing hegemony of the North Atlantic powers
over ex-colonies like Jamaica and the sister territories of the region.
The sense of struggle that inheres in this situation is the same that
resides in the cultural process in that fateful journey from domination to liberation through a dialectical interplay of forces rooted
in Jamaican history as Michael Manley acknowledges not only in
utterances but in the policies which the Jamaican government, he
now heads, formulates in the field of cultural development.[146]

Such acknowledgement is instructive since political
rhetoric and vision do not always serve the realities of the cultural
issues which are now as deep-set as the economic and political ones
in the Caribbean. In fact, they all *together* form an organic matrix
of concern and any arbitrary separation of the one from the other,
is likely to rob country and region of the sort of clues that can
lead to the appropriate strategies needed for meaningful development.

---

146. Manley, Michael: Address to Mystic Revelation of Rastafari Opening of wing to
    MRR Cultural Centre, East Kingston, June 1, 1977.

Part III

THE CULTURAL DIMENSION OF DEVELOPMENT

" . . . the functions of the Institute [of Jamaica] shall
be

(a)   the research into study, encouragement
      and development of culture, science and
      history

(b)   the preservation of monuments as national
      monuments for public benefit

(c)   establishment of museums, and

(d)   the discharge of such other functions as
      may be conferred upon it by this Act or
      any other enactment."

Institute of Jamaica Act, 1978

" . . . I would like to emphasize that this Bill represents
continuity of effort in one area of Government where
both Sides of the House have had an intelligent
understanding of the importance of cultural development as a tool in national growth . . .

As in all revolutions born out of an awakening
of patriotism and from a deep-seated desire for
change in the existing social order, the Jamaican
artists were in the vanguard of the movement of
1938, in which both Norman Manley and Alexander
Bustamante played such prominent roles."

Minister of State, Information & Culture
Hansard, House of Representatives, 1978.

" . . . We conceive the cultural development of the
country as one not to be divorced from the political
life of the country but one in which the political
experience is not dictated into the cultural experience.
By that I mean that an artist creates as he feels; he
creates out of the reservoir of his talents. Artists do
not create because of some ideological experience. He
may create because of some political experience, and
indeed many interesting and profound works of art
have come out of the motivation of the political
experience, but it is an entirely different thing from
laying down political guidelines which say culture
must carry a single political message."

Leader of the Opposition
Hansard, House of Representatives, 1978.

THE CULTURAL DIMENSION OF DEVELOPMENT

The foregoing account and analysis of the Caribbean cultural dilemma need no genius to conclude that the sense of crisis which is engendered by the situation challenges the shapers of the new Caribbean society to a strategy of change that will restore to the vast majority of its people human dignity through their own cultural growth and development. But this test for the society's capacity for change is also the test for the society's capacity to develop. In fact, cultural development is but one aspect of the overall developmental imperative too frequently seen in terms purely of economic growth and political modernisation. That many Caribbean countries have sought to integrate the cultural dimension of nation-building into the total strategy of national development is an indication of the cogency of cultural realities in the history and contemporary life of the region. In this the Jamaican experience is of particular relevance to the rest of the territories in the Commonwealth Caribbean. For ever since the nationalist ferment of the late thirties, leaders have seen the need for a conscious role of creative artists and cultural agents in nation-building. Some would regard the very act of nation-building as a product of Jamaican creativity itself. Today cultural development represents one of the few effective areas of continuity of effort between succeeding political Administrations, giving to the activity not only a strong foundation based on bipartisan good sense but a moral authority that is likely to withstand the more abrasive confrontations that in a situation of rapid change are bound to occur between different generations, ideological adversaries, or persons of different racial origins and class backgrounds.

The place of the arts and culture in national development has itself not escaped controversy on a national scale despite the continuity of effort. The early nationalist movement under Norman Manley which articulated very strongly the centrality of arts and culture to self-government and nation-building came in for serious questioning by at least one among the first set of Independence politicians who defeated Manley's party at the polls in 1962. The criticism came out strongly in the 1963 Five Year Plan, the brain-child of Edward Seaga who was to become Minister in charge of Development, Welfare and Culture — all areas in which the older Manley had himself excelled during his years in power. The JLP Five Year Plan admitted the dynamic created by the ferment of the late thirties but concluded that the efforts resulted in an "urban middleclass" affair which had "fostered a western-oriented con-temporary school which flourished at least in productivity if not in originality of ideas and expression, while the traditional school, grown out of a predominantly rural folk . . . for lack of encour-agement and social status of its exponents, remained largely sterile".[147] The Five Year Plan continued: "The artistic traditions of Africa especially were treated with ambivalence. It was an elusive heritage to the sophisticated performer or creator and there was no dynamic to propel it and inspire creativity. As a result it dwindled in performance so that a whole new generation born of the folk people themselves became largely unfamiliar with the songs, stories, ring games, digging sports and religious rituals of their fathers".[148]

The older Manley made a scathing counter-attack against the attack[149] of what was his earlier thrust to foster a national culture. But much of the assessment bore the truth: Europe had continued to reign while Africa ruled in denigration. The older Manley's optimism and faith in the ordinary Jamaican people blinded him to some of the persistent perversities of Plantation Caribbean life, yet he was not altogether unjustified in rising to a defence. For it is true that many of the painters and sculptors of the early period nurtured by the encouragement of his efforts and those of his sculptress wife, Edna, were indeed drawn from the grass roots.[150] This debate is instructive for it reveals, and indeed

147. *Five Year Independence Plan,* Kingston Jamaica, 1963, proposed by Hon. Edward Seaga, then Minister in charge of culture. p. 48 ff.

148. *Ibid.*

149. See *Manley and the New Jamaica* (ed. Rex Nettleford) Longmans, London 1971, pp. 239-332.

150. *Ibid.*

reflects, the issues that stand in the heartland of the on-going debate about development. Some years later Michael Manley unwittingly contributed to the debate when he declared that although the country's "dynamic artistic movement is part of the process by which we first attained and later experienced independence. But this has tended to be a small, though intense, part of the total social experience. Artists have sprung from all sections of Jamaican society but the audience has tended to be predominantly amongst the intellectual middleclass".[151]

The fruits of the First Development Decade went on a global plane to the rich while the poor countries became relatively poorer. Similarly, within the developing countries the privileged classes became more privileged and the disadvantaged more disadvantaged. Cultural goods and cultural products served the better-offs while the masses of poor people benefited little even when they were the primary producers of a wealth of customs, religious rituals, songs, stories, dances, spirit and the very life they lead. "To the creators and performers in this movement, folklife was veiled in a mystique that was never penetrated and they saw through the veil in terms of their own value systems".[152] Such value systems drew their source of energy from the Eurocentrism of colonial cultural conditioning and perpetuated themselves in a style of life that relegated the vast majority of the poor (and black) masses to stations of inferiority or at best exoticist folksiness.

The implication for national development strategy is self-evident. For such a sense of inferiority would only continue to deprive a vast populace needed for production and patriotic commitment, of a sense of place and purpose in their own society. The sense of territory which was achieved in theory by the entire nation through the self-government movement but in reality enjoyed by only a few, had now to become the universal experience of all Jamaicans. Despite the 1963 Five Year Plan and the real progress made in the development of cultural institutions structured to serve

151. Manley, Michael: *The Politics of Change: A Jamaican Testament* Andre Deutsch, London, 1974, pp. 155-156.

152. Seaga, Edward: *op cit.*

the entire nation,[153] the efforts of the Administration which lasted from 1962-1972 fell prey to the very economic (and by extension social) "sins" of which it had accused the Party it had displaced in 1962.[154] The strong materialist gains in terms of steel and mortar structures were impressive in the first decade of Independence but the cultural realities of persistent class/colour differentiation challenged by the protest of a growing Rastafarian movement[155] and the disturbances of 1968[156] and coinciding with the deepening and widening mass poverty and the highly selective though somewhat increased prosperity, swept the Opposition Party to power and with it a leader (Michael Manley) whose own personal cultural sensibilities were unquestionable.[157] "If the whole society is to develop in an egalitarian way, *art must reflect the total social experience and be appreciated by the society as a whole,*" he said. "Often the failure of the artist to communicate with large areas of the society is a consequence of lack of training

153.   See below for discussion of the institutions introduced during the first ten years of Independence under a policy of active 'Jamaicanisation .

154.   In Independence Year 1962, the nationalist Peoples National Party (PNP) which had been in power since 1955 was voted out of power and replaced by the labourist-led Jamaica Labour Party (JLP). This party lost power badly in 1972 back to the PNP which resurrected its old socialist commitment (1940) and declared for democratic socialism in 1974. It again won power in 1976 by an even greater victory. The campaign was marred by much political (partisan) violence.

155.   Nettleford, Rex: *Mirror, Mirror: Identity, Race and Protest*, Collins Sangster, 1971.

156.   *Ibid* especially the chapter on Black Power, or Notes from a Horn.

157.   Behind a distinguished career as a trade union leader and later populist politician, the Hon. Michael Manley was known as a keen and critically astute devotee of such artforms as sculpture (his mother is Jamaica's leading sculptor and patron of the arts), dance, the theatre and music. The inheritance of aesthetic sensibilities from an artist mother and a sensitive father who linked cultural development with nation building was rooted in his early exposure and his later reinforcement and education of the common people's collective creativity through his work in the trade union movement. On his own account, he skipped classes at the London School of Economics where he read Economics and Government to visit the National and Tate Galleries as well as Royal Albert and Wigmore Halls looking at art and listening to music and with strong temptations to study art criticism.

See Michael Manley: *A Voice at the Workplace* (Reflections on Colonialism and the Jamaican Worker) Andre Deutsch, London 1975, p. 16.

coupled with a failure to make art available to all kinds of audiences in all geographical locations," he suggested. "In other words," he continued, *"the educational process must first recognise art,* in the widest sense of painting, sculpture, poetry, drama, literature, the theatre, music, dancing and the rest, as an indispensable element in the *process of transformation"* (my emphasis). "Thereafter exposure to art must be planned," he concluded.[158]

1972 Exploratory Committee on the Arts

The pledge to rehumanise the society in the thrust towards meaningful development, in terms of people rather than property, found expression in the appointment by Prime Minister Michael Manley on 7th April, 1972, of an Exploratory Committee of the Arts charged to assess the cultural situation and recommend action. The Prime Minister's charge covered the following main areas:

(1) The role of Government in the development of arts and culture in ways that would be consistent with freedom and without prejudice to the proven importance of the private input into the creative process

(2) The rationalisation and maximisation of existing resources provided by Government and the private sector

(3) The decentralisation and spread of resources into areas outside Kingston

(4) The provision of increased opportunities for the greater participation of the large majority of the people in such a way as to make every citizen aware of a point at which he can relate to his own culture and creative endeavours

(5) The development of means to bring the country's cultural heritage into perspective bearing in mind the imbalances of history and the contemporary response to this phenomenon especially among the assertive and self-aware youths

(6) The introduction into our strategies for educational development, the natural concept of creative arts in education

(7) The economic implications of artistic and cultural activity in terms of employment potential, and the protection of the livelihood of creative artists

158. Manley, Michael: *The Politics of Change,* Deutsch, London, p. 156.

(8)   The consideration of sports as an important component of the country's cultural development programme [159]

Through a series of sub-committees, the Exploratory Group dealt severally with education, architecture, music, fine art, theatre, dance, cinema, literature, craft, the environment, the business community and the arts, libraries, youth groups, the church, broadcasting, sports and recreation. The emphasis was on *human resource development,* one of the classic areas of concern in the field of development today. Certain questions were regarded as essential to the discussion on all the areas listed above and are worth quoting from the Exploratory Committee's final report. They are:

(a)   How are Jamaicans of various ages spending their leisure?

(b)   What are the forces which create trends in the use of leisure?

(c)   Does the youth population of Jamaica, because of its size and increasing sophistication due to urbanisation. etc. have new leisure patterns which need special new organisation and attention?

(d)   Are there specific anti-social attitudes in our culture which should be faced; what are the principal agents affecting them and the cultural agencies that can help us overcome them?

(e)   How can the various arts, crafts and cultural agencies be strengthened so as to have maximum appeal to the community?

(f)   Are there some activities which should be nourishing our culture which have not yet received adequate recognition (African Studies – Jamaican publications – more opportunity for broader education and upgrading of skills thus deepening the individual's outlook on life)?

(g)   Are our museums or galleries, etc. playing a sufficiently significant role?

159. *Report of the Exploratory Committee on the Arts,* Kingston, Jamaica 1972, pp. 1-2. The Committee was chaired by Rex Nettleford, Cultural Adviser to the Prime Minister, with Mrs Jean Smith of the Prime Minister's Office as Secretary. Membership included persons from the fields of education, literature and creative journalism, the Church, business, cinema, media, library science, tourism and the different fields of the arts (literature, theatre, plastic arts, dance, film directing, folklore and popular music).

(h)   Should the non-competitive aspect of sport and recreation be given greater attention?

(i)   Relative to all these points, what positive creative part should be played by:
      (i)   Government
      (ii) the Mass-media
      (iii) existing public organisations
      (iv) existing cultural groups?[160]

Before referring to the final recommendations in the Report, it is necessary to draw attention to the fact that the Jamaican committee members in addressing themselves to the questions listed above were particularly concerned about the observed attitudes of many Jamaicans to work and their particular life-styles. The high mobility from rural areas to urban ghettos and from towns to foreign lands is now known to be not simply an economic phenomenon. Not infrequently, the move reflects a dissatisfaction with a daily life that provides little in the way of spiritual satisfaction and a sense of personal fulfilment. If one's daily work does not provide outlets for creative urges then compensation must come with leisure activities. In fact the urban areas of Jamaica and particularly Kingston have built up a textured cultural and artistic life on the basis largely of leisure-time activities on the part of large numbers of voluntary workers.

Indeed the Committee took pains to point out that "the responsibility is placed *on the community* rather than on Government exclusively since the Committee saw the arts not as an instrument of propaganda but as an instrument of cultural growth and personality development".[161] To some this may have been begging the question since it was part of the Eurocentric fallacy (the realities in contemporary Europe notwithstanding) that Government should not be allowed in on artistic and cultural life. It may have been prompted in part by that habit of thought which transforms

---

160.   *Ibid.* The questions emanated from Henry Fowler, educator and founder of Priory School, Chairman of the Little Theatre Movement, consultant to the Minister of Education 1972-76 and, at the time of writing, Jamaica's representative to UNESCO in Paris.

161.   *Report of Exploratory Committee* p. 5.

governments into "necessary evils" or mere "honest brokers," or it may have been the result of genuine belief that from experience man's cultural expression especially in the area of the arts were best left as free as possible to flourish. For "the need for imaginative expression of emotions in careful and elaborate focus is as deeply planted in human nature as is the sexual instinct, with which it is linked."[162] Such elemental sensibilities may by their very nature defy the command of government edict or legislative mandate. Despite this widespread belief, none of the Jamaicans "exploring" the state of the arts in 1972 were unrealistic enough to believe that State support for the arts cannot do what court patronage and private patronage used to do in Europe and in the case of Jamaica what private patronage, to a large extent, still does![163] In any case the intervention of government into several areas of cultural activity during the first ten years of Independence without strangling artistic endeavour challenges views that would see danger from a democratic socialist government charting the course for a cultural policy.

The Committee members conceded that "Government through practical help and constructive guidance, can act as catalyst to help an activity which flourishes best if left to ferment on its own." This, the Committee concluded, "were best done by linking cultural development organically with social and economic development through the country's educational policy, adult education and youth community programmes as well as through direct assistance to national cultural bodies and groups"[164] from the country's rural regions.

"In any case," it was further conceded, "central to cultural development is a cultural policy that can entertain some integrated general planning that would continue to strengthen national awareness and 'facilitate the growth of a way of life' which

162.   Hampshire, Stuart: "The Future of Knowledge" *New York Review (NYR) of Books* pp. 14-18.

163.   *Ibid.*

164.   *Report of Exploratory Committee*, pp. 5-6.

will meet both the deepest aspirations of the people and the requirements of the modern world, without depriving the country of the
benefit of free artistic expression."[165] The deepest aspirations of
the people and the requirements of the modern world at once
declared both a commitment to meeting the need of the majority
of Jamaicans, traditionally the victims of cultural marginality, and
an acceptance of the reality of contemporary life as well as the
fact that Jamaica has to be seen as part of a wider world. This is
itself a significant enough factor especially in relation to cultural
development as *part of national development.*

The Cultural Mission of the State

In the 1977 Budget Speech before the Jamaican Parlia-
ment the Minister of Finance in justifying the large expenditure on
"education, training and cultural development" said that "human
resource development was 'the lynchpin of our strategy of development' and that economic development that did not directly contribute to the improvement of the quality of life of the individual
human being and did not increase the capability of individual
human beings to maximise their potential was a mockery and not
worthy of the name of development."[166] The Jamaican Prime
Minister Michael Manley had some years previously publicly
written that "post-colonial societies must accomplish two things if
they are to re-establish self-confidence and re-embark upon the
process of self-discovery *that is expressed by the evolution of a
people's culture* (my emphasis). They must rediscover the validity
of their own culture at the moment of the colonial intervention
and retrace the steps that had led through history to that point.
And they must establish within a frame of reality of the culture
which colonialism imposed upon them so that this may loom neither
larger nor smaller than it deserves and suffer from none of the
distortions which can result from the ambivalence of a ruler-subject

165. *Ibid.*

166. *Sunday Gleaner,* Section A, May 15, 1977, p. 16. – being report of Budget Speech
by Hon David Coore, Minister of Finance and Deputy Prime Minister of Jamaica.

situation."[167]

By the time this was written Jamaican political leaders had made "a dramatic change toward a more West Indian cultural orientation . . . from 1962 to 1974" according to Professor Wendell Bell who did a study of Jamaican elites in 1962 and again in 1974.[168] Such a "dramatic change" was bound to facilitate the development of a political will among the political directorate to support the arts and cultural activities in general — a support which as earlier indicated, straddled political administrations between 1959 and the present. The attitude struck by those who would wish to separate arts and culture from the mundane realities of ordinary daily life was evident in the sixties and doubts as to whether there would be tolerance of rebel artists by political regimes,[169] or whether a chauvinistic Jamaican temper would permit the individual creator to detribalise himself[170] were expressed. They are questions that are bound to arise from time to time in Jamaica given the openness of the Jamaican society, the tradition of talk and cross-talk in Jamaican public and private social relations, and the strong spirit of independence manifest in the voluntary work of hundreds of cultural groups and individuals over a generation. The financial constraints of a government passing through a grave economic crisis and committed to self-reliance in the reconstruction of the economy, will in any case dictate continued reliance on voluntary work in the artistic and general cultural activities.

Yet there is room for some of the "integrated general planning" which the Exploratory Committee on the Arts conceded as necessary so as to rationalise and maximise scarce resources.

167. Manley, Michael: *The Politics of Change*, p. 146.

168. See Bell, Wendell and Robinson, Robert V.: "European Melody, African Rhythm or West Indian Harmony? Cultural Orientations of Leaders in a New State." (Unpublished article in correspondence to R. N.)

169. Burbridge, Ernest: "Patronage of the Arts," *The Arts and the Community*, Radio Education Unit, UWI, (Radio Series).

170. Vaz, Noel: "Our National Identity and the Arts," *The Arts and the Community*, Radio Education Unit, UWI, (Radio Series).

The Jamaican Government placed cultural policy after 1973 in the context of human resource development, one of the classic objectives in the framework of development strategy. Within this framework are forged the organic linkages with education and training, preparation for employment, as well as with the eternal need by man to develop source(s) of his own sense of identity (whether as "tribe" or individual), of his own glory and of the celebration of remembered life mirrored in such things as the performing arts, literature (oral and scribal), music, painting and sculpture, the cinema, architecture and historical studies.

Jamaica, in anticipation of the spirit evident in the many declarations and conventions emanating from such international cultural bodies as UNESCO and the Inter-American Council for Education, Science and Culture (CIECC) of the OAS,[171] long ago adopted the official view that there is a cultural mission of the State in the stimulation and promotion of the creative arts and intellectual creativity as well as in the exercise of tutelage and curatorship over the cultural inheritance and historical interests of the nation. In the thrust since the early 1970's into accelerated decolonisation, the country's leaders have become even more committed to cultural growth as an instrument of development policy.

There have been active instruments of such a policy with some years of experience behind them. There were between 1944 and 1962 (Independence) the Jamaica Social Welfare Commission, the Jamaica Library Service, the Jamaica Broadcasting Corporation, the University of the West Indies (with its Department of Extra Mural Studies), the voluntary groups which pursued artistic/cultural activities of national proportions, the work of the Ministry of Education in the primary and secondary schools in areas of arts and crafts and music. There was also the august Institute of Jamaica with its youth wing, a training school for painters and sculptors and the West India Reference Library (WIRL). During the first ten years of Independence there were added the Jamaica

---

171. See e.g. "Policies in Matters of Culture" in *Basic Study of FEMCIECC,* Parts 1 and 2, O.A.S. General Secretariat, Washington D.C. 1976.

Festival Commission, a Craft Development Agency with an outlet in Things Jamaican Ltd., the burgeoning of more firmly based voluntary groups like the National Dance Theatre Company and an energetic thrust in development of popular music starting with the "ska" which was officially projected on the international market and ending up with the well established "reggae", while work within the Institute of Jamaica was enhanced with the publication of *Jamaica Journal* and the collaborative work (with the National Trust Commission) on the underwater excavation work at Port Royal. From 1972 the accelerated decolonisation process ensured the continuity of what went before and focussed attention on the rationalisation of all these institutions of cultural action against the background of deliberate social change. Emphasis was placed on training facilities to benefit from the multiplier effect of schools of training which were brought together in a cultural training complex. Personnel and budget allocations were in the process redeployed for greater efficiency. For a generation all the above-named instruments of cultural action together and separately have served to (a) preserve the country's assets (b) promote interest in culture among the varied segments of the population (c) stimulate and disseminate literary and artistic expressions of the creative imagination (d) encourage and lay foundations for serious education and training in the different branches of the arts and their related disciplines. By 1977 Jamaica could genuinely refer to a cultural policy that has an identifiable mechanism of implementation (in practice an aggregation of interlocking institutions and procedures) which if properly worked can help lead the nation towards a socially just and humane society.

Investment in Education and Training in Arts and Culture

There is an ancient Chinese proverb which reads:

"If your vision is one year, plant rice
If your vision is ten years, plant trees
If your vision is one hundred years, train people"

Education and training in the widest sense are seen by both official and private cultural leaders as vital means through which the preservation and development of cultural values could take place. The Ministry of Education had long employed Education Officers of Music, Arts and Crafts and later of Dance (which was subsumed under Physical Education). In May 1977, the Jamaican Minister of Education in outlining his Five Year plan for education lauded the virtues of the "Total School" concept to which his Government was committed. In naming the five essentials of the concept he listed among them "creative and cultural expression" alongside involvement in the wider political process, manual work, economic production and community life.[172]

The formal and informal institutions of learning would therefore have to be equipped with expertise to transmit not only skills and the craft that underlie artistic expressions but bring to the overall learning process cultural sensibilities that could presumably stimulate the young to greater interest in their academic work at school. The separation of cultural experience rooted in collective tradition from the process of formal education is part of the alienation and schizophrenia that grip the nation in its search for identity. The preparation of expertise to transmit artistic skills co-curricularly and integrally as part of the learning process was therefore seen as a first priority; so following on the Exploratory Committee's recommendation a Cultural Training Centre was established in 1976 "to provide adequate facilities for the training of teaching, creative and performing talents in art, music, dance and theatre."[173] The location of the training schools at a cultural centre was not seen merely as a matter of economy. It fulfilled the earlier vision (of a stretch of public property devoted to cultural pursuits) with the construction of the headquarters of the Jamaica Library Service and its Kingston and St. Andrew branch as well as the theatre built by the Little Theatre Movement on lands which were to house a Rehearsal Room used by voluntary drama groups and private dance studios as well as the National Dance Theatre

---

172. See *Five Year Education Plan (1978-1983)*, Draft Two, Ministry of Education, Jamaica, December 1977, especially Chapter 1.

173. *Report of Exploratory Committee*, p. 15.

Company and its fledgeling School of Dance and the LTM's own School of Drama. The juxtaposition of all the national schools signified more, *viz* the crossfertilisation necessary for a vigorous development of the arts and cultural sensibilities was seen as being best served by this arrangement.

It is important here to record that the construction of a 2.6 million dollar cultural training complex in 1976 came years after the schools which it houses had been functioning. The Schools of Drama and Dance, the two youngest of the four schools, had been functioning for six years previously under the guidance of their founding organisations — the Little Theatre Movement in the case of the Drama School and the National Dance Theatre Company in the case of the Dance School. The Drama School had been in receipt of a very small grant out of public funds from its inception. Both the Drama and Dance Schools operated out of makeshift sheds on property belonging to the LTM or (in the case of the Dance School) out of premises rented from the Institute of Jamaica at nominal cost. The School of Music had been established in 1962 by the Jamaican musician, Vera Moodie, whose private initiative attracted matching Government funds which became permanent grants for recurrent expenses for rented premises as well as for teaching staff and administrative costs. The oldest school was the Jamaica School of Art which emerged our of the art classes started by Edna Manley twenty-five years before at the Institute of Jamaica. By the time the Training Centre was built, the Jamaica School of Art, operating on the basis of public funds from the Institute of Jamaica's budget, had developed a well-tried curriculum for the training of artists and art teachers of painting, sculpture and ceramics as well as a national and regional reputation and a vital responsiveness to new needs as is evidenced in the introduction later of jewelcraft, graphics, textile and work on native dyes.

But what is most important is the fact that the School of Art operated within an environment of practising artists — of 'masters' who actually had an organic relationship with the growth and development of the school and the art it serves. The pioneer teachers were Edna Manley, Albert Huie and Cecil Baugh. A great many of Jamaica's major artists have either taught at the School or have been trained there. This development within an environment shared by native Jamaican practitioners of excellence has given the Jamaica School of Art a special sense of purpose in the cultural development process without the would-be effect of a stifling parochialism. On the contrary, activity in the visual arts has been greatly stimulated by this phenomenon for even the artists returning from abroad have been goaded to greater effort by the fact of this vitality. Exhibitions of painting and sculpture are, as a result, frequent and of usually a high standard.

This development within an environment shared by practitioners of excellence is not true of the Jamaica School of Music, the second oldest school, which up to 1974 functioned in virtual isolation from the vibrant creativity that was evident among the popular creators of music from the late fifties and throughout the sixties. The almost total surrender to the canons of the European classical tradition robbed the school of the vitality which existed outside of its walls. There was the attempt to salvage it from a threatening irrelevancy by the establishment of the Folk Music Research Unit in 1965. But while the Unit collected and through the Jamaica Folk Singers projected Jamaican folksongs following the practice of individuals and groups that preceded it, little by way of in-depth analysis and cross-cultural testing of findings for transmission to the School's students of music was done. Seemingly there was not enough encouragement of this in practice though the Folk Singers had visible impact on groups in the wider community. For the emphasis continued to be on the production of performers rather than on primary creators — i.e. composers and arrangers. Even so, the tendency was still to send abroad the most talented of the young practitioners in the European classics who continued to emerge from the private studios run by dedicated London-trained music teachers in the capital city. It was not until the latter half of the seventies that realistic questions were asked as to whether the limited resources of the country were not best spent on training large numbers of much-needed teachers for work in schools and popular musicians who could become active in music locally, rather than the one or two executants who could operate only on an international level, at great expense and with little return to the country. In fact the past history of sending young music students abroad at public expense to train as performers had brought less than satisfactory results. By 1975 it was clear that there was danger in some of them returning but with what could be described as a narrow elitist attitude that was more alienating than enlightening. One "student" gained something of an international reputation but was lost to a provincial town of a European country. Others doing less than good in metropolitan countries have been invited back home sometimes misguidedly as "celebrities". One music scholar has since 1975 returned giving hope in that his interests and talents as composer, arranger, producer and conductor are already pointing directions to his likely future substantive contribution to the development of music in the country. Still, the country is yet to experience the services of a Jamaican-born trained musicologist "capable of interpreting Jamaican culture in disciplined terms, from a Jamaican standpoint". The training of skilled musicologists is crucial. The field of Music Education is also in need of extra thrust and depth and no doubt the School of Music will give the foundation to native Jamaicans who can pursue advanced work in this field in different parts of the world (including Europe) for work back in their own country. The Principal of the School is hard-nosed about the choice before the country. "It is time we got away from the 'performer' syndrome, no matter how glamorous it appears", she said, "and start coming to grips with music at home on a much deeper, more informed and broader level than we have done in the past".[174] Perhaps the assistance sometimes offered by European governments in the field of music could be geared towards training outstanding young performers in the classical field in the appropriate environment where there exist the facilities and the international competitiveness which are necessary for training top class performers in the field of classical music.

The erection of the new School of Music in the Cultural Training Complex was to give fresh impetus to the restructuring and re-orientation of the School's programme of activities which

174.   O'Gorman, Pamela: Correspondence with R.N.

had begun at Government's request in 1974. Planned were the introduction of a programme for popular musicians, the development of a course for teachers of music in primary and secondary schools which all have a rich tradition of choral music and the addition of a department of African-American Music covering the world of musical forms to be found in Africa and Plantation America (the USA, Latin America and the Caribbean) where 'Africa has met Europe' in the now legendary process of attraction/repulsion and rejection/acceptance. The strong presence of Jazz, African drumming and traditional/ancestral and contemporary music of Jamaica and the Caribbean alongside the wealth of European classical musical expression and the music of other lands will undoubtedly make a difference to the creative musical output of the generation of Jamaicans to come. In the meantime the School must make itself part and parcel of the vital world of music-making that actually exists outside its walls within Jamaican society and the outer reaches of the Caribbean, not only in the contemporary pop forms but in the on-going and revived traditional folkforms.

In this, the School of Dance has been more fortunate. Training and experiment in Jamaican dance forms have taken place against the background of the development of dance as an art which consciously draws on the Jamaican traditional/ancestral experience as the prime source of energy as well as on indigenous contemporary Jamaican life experience for experiments in dance-drama and movement design as can be seen in the work of the National Dance Theatre Company over a period of fifteen years. The Jamaica School of Dance was brought together by the NDTC out of the classes run by three of its principal dancers Sheila Barnett, Barbara Requa and Bert Rose. Quite apart from reflecting the philosophy of the Jamaican dance company in its effort to discover an artistic expression faithfully reflecting the movement patterns and dance aesthetic of Jamaica and the Caribbean, they were each to bring to the exercise of training their own particular gifts drawn from their varied backgrounds of educational dance, dance as a performing art and dance composition. These serve the School well in the varied approaches that are offered students while a single vision of evolving something truly Jamaican/Caribbean is maintained. The above-named were later to be joined by other principals of the NDTC like Dorothy Fraser who had danced with the London Festival Ballet in the classical ballet tradition, Yvonne daCosta, the longtime dancer and balletmistress of the NDTC as well as Barry Moncrieffe and Patsy Ricketts, highly acclaimed dancers whose commitment to the work of dance in Jamaica brought them, as it had done Bert Rose, back from the United States where they had done some of their studies and performed while still members of the Jamaican company. By 1976 when the School was fully absorbed into the Institute of Jamaica and supported from public funds, Cheryl Ryman, another NDTC dancer from her position as Research Fellow in the African-Caribbean Institute of Jamaica, could bring her skills in dance research studied in West Africa, to the curriculum offered future teachers of the dance.

The NDTC's activities had long found wider spread and cohesion in the work done by another of its founding members Joyce Campbell, Dance Officer in the Festival Commission working under the chairmanship of the NDTC Artistic Director while Sheila Barnett's work in the training colleges and later in the Ministry of Education enriched the output in Festival and helped spread the popularity of dance in primary and secondary schools. The three-pronged outreach inspired from the same source and with constant reference to the traditional/ancestral roots plus the development of a visible disciplined corps of dedicated dancers, singers, musicians and creative technicians presenting a varied repertoire in regular seasons at home and highly successful tours abroad, served as stimulus for other groups. It also set the stage for the formal national school which had had its earlier counterpart in the training classes given for years by the NDTC's artistic director and company members to studios like the Ivy Baxter Creative Dance Group and the Eddy Thomas Dance Workshop which continues to operate under its founder Eddy Thomas, a former co-director of the NDTC. Another important forebear was the series of summer schools organised by the University of the West Indies (Department of Extra Mural Studies) and later by the NDTC with visiting tutors from Haiti, the United States and Trinidad and Tobago.[175]

Today the national School of Dance is the beneficiary of this organic growth and is part of that environment shared by dancers and dance creators of proven excellence. The danger of unrelieved imitation and replication must be met by creative leadership, artistic honesty and by the fact that the source of energy with which Jamaican life provides the dance is itself multi-faceted and exposure to it will bring challenges to serious students of the dance whose training (whether as teachers or performers) demands, judging from the curriculum, not only exposure to the field realities of this cultural activity but also creative analysis and use of such sources in the exercise of the creative imagination. What is more a danger is the perpetuation of myths about the studio techniques that have come out of the hard work of Europe and America and supported by philosophies, lifestyles, psychological attitudes rooted in the specific experience of those parts of the world. The Martha Graham technique,[176] for example, without the soul and intellectual sophistication of Miss Graham herself is likely to be an indulgence in sterility – a fact which was not lost on the early critics of the Jamaican dance company.[177] The genuine discoveries made over the past quarter of a century in the realm of Jamaican dance and dance-theatre plus the rich lore of movement, music and customs that exist throughout Plantation America (especially the Caribbean) must provide the source of energy for future invention.

175. Visiting tutors came primarily from the United States but among the Caribbean oriented tutors were Beryl McBurnie (Trinidad & Tobago), Lavinia Williams (Haiti), Jean-Leon Destine (Haiti), Neville Black (Jamaican). Ms Williams taught several summer schools before going to Guyana in 1972 and Bahamas in 1977 on long-term contracts.

176. Many of the principals of the Jamaica National Dance Theatre Company have pursued studies at the Martha Graham School of Contemporary Dance in New York. The Jamaican Company is *not* however a Caribbean version of this great New York company and unlike the Cuban modern dance theatre does not draw primarily on that technique for the Jamaican company. The principal choreographer and second choreographer of the NDTC whose works have flourished since 1965, did not study at the Graham school. The quest for a Caribbean dance aesthetic is still the Company's goal.

177. Nettleford, Rex: *Roots and Rhythms, the Story of the Jamaican Dance Theatre* (illustrated by Maria LaYacona), Andre Deutsch, London 1969.

The School of Drama may be said to be facing challenges of a similar kind. For the need to foster an environment conducive to the daring and adventure that creative action in the theatre arts imply is going to be a major responsibility of the school. It is this spirit that it is hoped will inform the teachers of drama who must be produced to help staff the hundreds of schools throughout the country which as "total schools" will be in need of teachers of drama not merely as aids to academic learning but as source of self-discovery and self-discipline among the young. Dr Carroll Dawes, a former Director of the School of Drama while it was still under the aegis of its founder, the Little Theatre Movement, drew attention to the "intense activity" that had gripped the Kingston theatrical scene between 1973 and 1976 only to conclude that "perhaps we are in a merry-go-round which is not really leading anywhere although it seems to be".[178] Her own imaginative and controversial productions had brought new dimensions to theatre life and excitement to many of the students in the School of Drama. She, however, abhorred the virtual abandonment of the "search for quality" and the surrender to a formula of well-tried theatre successes. She therefore saw the Government's investment in the arts through the training programme as an excellent opportunity to restore to the theatre a pristine sense of adventure and as she said, quoting Stanislavski, the two reasons which really mattered, *viz* "knowledge of the subject and excellence in the art".[179] For these reasons the arts (and especially the theatre) she said should be left to artists to take decisions rather than to "middlemen" – presumably such non-artists who are promoters and impresarios. If the "parable" thus spoken referred to the Drama School's founding organisation, the Little Theatre Movement, which has been run by non-artists, then it raises the arguable point of whether artists are the best equipped people to run all cultural institutions though their right to determine policy in their own interest is impatient of debate.

That the cultural institutions in the performing and so-

---

178.   Dawes, Carroll: "Whose Caribbean Theatre?" *Arts Review,* Creative Arts Centre, UWI, Vol. I, No. 3, Christmas Term 1976.

179.   *Ibid.*

called fine arts should be in the hands of creative artists, is a good and sound proposition as long as artists themselves fully appreciate that different kinds of skills are needed in the totality of that process which is artistic creation-execution-projection-development. The production of a play depends on the interaction and collaboration of a playwright, a creative director (who may indeed turn out to be a "middleman" between author and audience), actors, technicians, front-of-house managers and the like. In fact, a vibrant theatre depends on the simultaneous functioning of good playwrights and creative directors working together to stimulate fine actors who together will attract interested audiences as Trevor Rhone of Jamaica demonstrated with his Barn Theatre in Kingston in the late sixties and early seventies and Derek Walcott (playwright-poet-director-theatre manager) did in Port-of-Spain, Trinidad. The collaboration of Dennis Scott and that director of daring, Carroll Dawes, gave a glimpse of what could be done but the collaboration has not been sufficiently sustained to bring to the Jamaican Theatre all that Scott's "Echo in the Bone" promised. The quiescence of Sam Hillary who promised hope in the fifties can be explained by the absence of a creative director willing or sufficiently inspired to strike up a collaboration. The existence of an "international" repertoire of plays in English from Shakespeare to Pinter is possibly a deterrent to grappling with the challenges of building an indigenous 'legitimate' theatre though the Secondary Schools Drama Festival throws up commendable efforts among the young from time to time. Creative directors by themselves do not give rise to a vibrant theatre and even though the talented playwright is central to all this, he needs the creative director who in turn needs others. The theatre, whether it be drama or dance, teaches or rather *dramatises* the inescapable interdependence of humanity to make life whole. Ironically it is the "tribe", the "collective" in inspired collaboration that makes the most effective theatre. It is this knowledge and the acceptance of it which makes possible that sense of equality so eloquently invoked by Dr Dawes in appropriate reference to the Jamaican Government's pledge to egalitarianism. In the performing arts the inputs of all operatives from "star" to stagehand becomes important to a given production. Exaggerated claims cannot be justified for the artist over and above what can be claimed for the carpenter, the plumber, the farmer, the factory worker or skilled professional. Like the theatre artist all the above-named desire the "business of a master-servant relationship", which Dr. Dawes said plagued the theatre artist, to disappear. They also need what is further demanded for the creative artist, *viz:* ". . . time . . . quiet . . . peace . . . solitude [though not at the expense of learning to work co-operatively with others] and . . . friendship".[180]

The theatre artist who wishes, and should indeed insist, that he has "access to decision-making processes and, if he is able, to fashion and guide and direct his own progress", needs to face the practical realities of autonomy in operating cultural institutions like Schools of Drama and of Dance in a developing country like Jamaica. Such realities relate to the serious financial constraints even in situations where governments say they are fully committed to official support of cultural activities. The competition for scarce money resources will frequently be resolved in favour of the hungry, the underhoused and the unemployed and no representation on the argument of the threat of 'spiritual hunger' will change that. Then there is the day-to-day drudgery of administrative chores in the field of cultural management. Buildings must be maintained; meetings have to be held and one must learn to communicate with people who are not artists; budgets must be planned and expenditure made to relate to estimates; the mundane industrial relations needs of unionised workers arguing about conditions of work, working hours, uniforms, lunchrooms, etc. must be attended to and with the full realisation that the current play or dance-show or exhibition of paintings to be mounted is likely to be less important to these workers than getting their grievances heard. Long hours, low salaries, the frustrating discovery that the world of public affairs does not revolve around the choreographer, playwright, or play director, however talented, are all part of the reality of participation and control by artists of the world of management. Again,

180. *Ibid.*

in that situation of scarce money resources, artist-administrators and decision-takers must be prepared to work twice as hard as they probably would on the "developed professional" circuit and must be prepared to do so without the luxury of metropolitan material facilities or adequate support expertise. What is needed is a resolute will to overcome the greatest odds including a possible lack of understanding on the part of the very patron-Government that provides what funds are available as well as on the part of friends and foes alike.

What many people and their governments in developing countries are not likely to understand (or tolerate) is the self-indulgent individualism of the artist; and the Jamaican society is no exception in this. Yet this is no excuse for the deliberate stifling of cultural growth by an imposed cultural bureaucracy. The Jamaican approach betrays a full understanding of the challenge the country has to ensure that expenditure of public funds on art and culture will have to show returns to the benefit of the mass of the population and not just to the few. But there is the compensatory sensitivity to that other challenge — *viz:* the need for the society to facilitate the free creative growth and expression of its citizens individually as well as collectively! The contradictions and tensions emanating from these two separate considerations can be particularly hard on a young country eager to make its mark but they are the source of a certain dynamic in the Jamaican approach to cultural planning and the development process.

In this the perception and orientation of the cultural training schools is instructive. They are designed among other things, to produce "graduates" who are able to enter the job market — a very important factor in a country plagued with 25 percent unemployment and an even higher figure among the 18-25 age group. Performers will also be trained but with the full realisation that employment possibilities in the area of the performing arts are likely to be limited in view of the small population base to support it. The School of Art is better circumstanced since beside producing teachers, it can supply the nation's needs for designers to feed the fields of manufacturing, handicraft, textiles and fashion, publications, television, not to speak of the graphic artists, potters, ceramicists, and jewellers many of whom can be self-employed. The School of Art is therefore a proven "useful" (and productive) cultural instrument in development.

It is this sense of 'usefulness' and, more appropriately, of purpose within the totality of an integrated social process that will rid Jamaica of its threatening pockets of alienated souls. The easel painter or studio sculptor who cannot 'market' his products to make a living is not likely to be supportive of a society that in his view leaves him 'to starve'. But not all who have a hand for the brush and palette will necessarily wish to make a living *exclusively* from his painting. His pursuit of training and practice may be simply to satisfy a personal need or may present him with "something productive and pleasing" to fill his leisure time pleasurably and/or meaningfully; and this presents another kind of need for which public facilities may be provided, if only for (a) the continuing education of a citizenry that may, from boredom, find more destructive alternatives and (b) for the enrichment of the lives of the various communities that cultural training can bring to the country. In fact sports (especially cricket) have played this role since colonial times. The performing arts themselves have long been amateur in status though professional in standards, making the pursuit and practice of them an integral part of the daily living of those who are engaged in them and bringing real cultural dividends to the society as a whole.[181]

The Jamaican approach to the arts, then, has been in the tradition of a hobby-to-income progression. In the process the values of discipline, dedication, sustained application and systematic study have been nurtured among many, even where there is no guarantee of the reward of a "job" in the foreseeable future. The advantage of a "developing" state is that the capacity for innovation and continuing discovery once people obtain the opportunity, is seemingly unlimited. It was the dedication, disciplined application, even reckless adventure of hundreds of "amateurs" over a generation that inspired leadership and cultural achievement which

---

181.   e.g. Village, parish and county festivals, Opportunity Hours and Variety Concerts, Craft fairs, Schools drama festivals, LTM, NDTC, JFS, etc.

laid the foundation for what can now be termed a rational cultural development policy, articulated by the Jamaican elected representatives with the coming of Independence. It was, in some instances, only left for provision to be made for the sharpening and refining of the instruments of cultural training.

One such instrument is the Jamaica School of Dance which may not be seen to be as "useful" as the other Schools teaching Art, Music or Drama.[182] It can bear some brief discussion. That it can produce skilled performers and clever choreographers to provide ornamentation for theatrical spectacles, there is no doubt. But the dance can do and actually does more than that for Jamaicans who are a people to most of whom movement of the body denotes a ready eloquence of cultural significance and for whom movement is a decisive complement of, if not substitute for, verbal communication in daily social intercourse as in formal ritual worship. Movement of the body, like musical sound or the intellectual/emotional appeal to "higher science" (God or Satan), is by nature immune to the master's or oppressor's influence or interference. All oppressed people know this! Coupled with the sound of music *in* religious ritual such movement becomes what is called *dance* which can be an excellent vehicle of liberation and self-actualisation and not of escape or sublimation as some more literary-minded Caribbean progressives would probably claim. A society in search of itself on its own terms may find the art of the dance among the most effective instruments for developing and teaching endurance, stamina, dedication, a sense of process and self-confidence as the field of sports (especially athletics and cricket) has done for generations of Jamaican and other Anglophone Caribbean people. Such virtues or values do no harm to the development process. On the contrary, they have been the social indicators for

182. Music and Painting have had a longer history as part of the education process in Jamaica, what with the Royal School of Music examinations and Art as an offering in the old Cambridge Certificate examinations and the more recent 'O' and 'A' level examinations. The Classification Division of the Jamaican Ministry of the Public Service not surprisingly found difficulty in assessing the curriculum content of the Dance course in the Jamaica School of Dance for the purpose of classifying the tutors and instructors of the School.

persons involved in artistic endeavours, like dance and dance-theatre, for some thirty years; and it was such evidence that helped to convince succeeding Jamaican governments that public support to such efforts in the interest of both cultural and overall national development is desirable.

So the Jamaican Schools of Dance, Art, Music and Drama are not private studios, nor are they to be seen as conventional teacher training colleges, secondary schools or primary schools. In fact, the attempt is to develop in the entire Cultural Training Centre the type of institutions that will give to the teacher-in-training all the exposure to the aesthetic sensibilities of the creative artist as well as give to the trainee-artist the sense of discipline and seriousness of approach in pursuing systematic and structured courses. While the teacher will and must be given special attention and courses must be tailor-made to suit his/her profession, it is hoped that the ambience of each school and of all of them together will provide the product (sc. teacher) with a special dimension that will add to the development of the Jamaican child other than through the established methods and approaches used in teaching such 'academic' subjects as Maths, English or Chemistry.

For none of the Schools should end up being factories turning out barely competent technicians rather than growing into a rich and fervent bed of creativity and invention. This is why it is important that the fulltime members of the teaching staffs must be prepared to meet not only the needs of the teacher *qua* teacher (in the sense of transmitter of knowledge) but also the needs of the teacher as an innovative motivator and inspirer of creative talent.

The Diploma (or Certificate) courses, though separate, must not be held to be mutually exclusive of the performers', choreographers' or easel painters' courses though those in pursuit of each will eventually go their separate ways. Classes in basic technique, background studies and related subjects should be offered to everybody.

The School of Dance, for example, is expected to continue to be the centre of experimentation in shaping a movement vocabulary faithful to the realities of Jamaican and Caribbean life without closure on the rich mine of established dance techniques to be found elsewhere, universal body language, national dances of other lands, and the role of the dance in human civilisation. It must therefore assume the functions of a Research Institute in good time with the experiments of the Tutors being the basis of analysis and testing and eventual codification for use by dancers and teachers of dance in the generation to come. The Folk Music Research Unit is already located in the School of Music and there is work in progress on native dyes in the School of Art.

The national Schools of Dance, of Drama, of Music and of Art, have obligations, then, to a variety of clients:- to the national educational system (in the case of all the schools); to dance theatre (in the case of dance and sometimes art); to musical theatre (in the case of music, dance, drama and sometimes art) and to theatre generally (in all cases); to community youth and adult groups (in the case of dance, music and drama) and to the Festival movement (in all cases); to cabaret and entertainment in the tourist industry (in the case of music and dance and in some cases speech and drama); to radio (in the case of music and drama); to television (in all cases); to choral groups (in the case of music) and to instrumentalists (in the case of music); to business and commerce (in the case of art) and finally to the entire cultural ambience of Jamaica (in the case of all the Schools) through the availability of sufficient numbers of trained 'cultural agents' for work throughout Jamaica especially outside the Corporate area. A variety of training must therefore be provided.

The field then is broad and this explains the locus of the four Schools for national cultural training. Teacher-training is one aspect; the production of professional or semiprofessional performers and creative artists another; the preparation of a cadre of designers and technicians for industry and the theatre yet another. There is also the supply of 'cultural agents' for work among community groups; the facilities for exposure to those who will need it for nothing more than for personal enrichment and refinement of the spirit is another equally important aspect. In view of the limited funds available it is important that plans are made to meet all these requirements to the best of the nation's ability. For in terms of development of human resources for gainful employment and creative living, the investment by the country in such cultural activities is as positive an approach to national development as growing food.

Institutional Rationalisation: Transformation of the Institute of Jamaica

Much of the above indicates a national response to the need to bring to the activity of cultural development greater institutional rationalisation and sophistication so that the instruments of cultural action could be better mobilised and be more responsive to the sensibilities of the Jamaican people in a changing society. Among such cultural instruments must be numbered the cultural training institutions, libraries and archives, museums, exhibition facilities such as theatres and galleries, research facilities, dissemination mechanisms such as publications, festivals, colloquia and extensive use of radio and television. Such institutional rationalisation serves not only the demands of relevance but also is prudent response to the serious constraints of scarce financial and administrative personnel resources. It says something for their society that, despite the serious economic problems attendant on world recession and the hiking of oil, wheat and soyabean prices in 1973, Jamaican taxpayers allowed their government to continue with the thrust in cultural development as part of national development between 1973 and 1977. During this time the four national training schools were built in a cultural training complex at a cost of 2.6 million dollars (Jamaica) and provision of funds was made for the community cultural programmes both through the Festival Commission and the Ministry of Youth. In 1977 a Minister of State with responsibility for Information and Culture was appointed and located in the Prime Minister's Office, itself an indication of the importance attached to the subject.

At the centre of this rationalisation of the institutional infra-structure and mobilisation of the instruments of cultural action is the transformation of the old and revered Institute of Jamaica, into a more serviceable and responsive instrument of implementation of contemporary Jamaican cultural policy. The old Institute was founded in 1879 by a colonial Governor "for the encouragement of Literature, Science and Art." Whose literature, whose science, whose art, one might ask; and one might get the answer "Mankind's literature, science and art." But in actual fact it was the art, science and literature of the ruling British (or the English to be exact). Neville Dawes, the new Institute's executive director, himself a novelist, is coldly realistic about it. "Cultural control was an essential part of colonial policy and it is a perfectly understandable thing: if you *have* to administer colonies, you had better make certain that the cultural standards of that colony are your own and *not* indigenous . . ." he once said.[183] Admittedly the interest in indigenous (i.e. Jamaican creolised) forms increased with the cry for self-government and the advent of Independence. But up to the 1960's the valuable work done by the Institute in laying foundations was not generally known or, if known, not generally regarded as being of relevance to Jamaican realities. Since the early seventies what has been demanded of the political and economic institutions and processes has also been demanded of the country's foremost formal cultural institution — and that is to operate in the interest of the vast majority of the Jamaican people and to reflect the potentialities of a proven resourceful people. A total dismantling of the Institute, as some would have it, was deemed to be no more practical or sensible than it would be to destroy the inherited national political and economic institutions overnight. There may, indeed, be times when reaction is revolutionary and revolution reactionary. After all, excellent work had been done in natural history under the guidance of Bernard Lewis and in the stimulation of Jamaican cultural sensibilities — thanks to the vision of past Institute officials like Frank Cundall and Philip Sherlock. But Cundall did not live long into the era of the new awakening among nationalist Jamaicans and Philip Sherlock spent from the late forties into the early seventies giving form and purpose to yet

183. Dawes, Neville: Address to Lions Club, Montego Bay on May 2, 1975. Note also that even in West Africa where the doctrine of Indirect Rule held sway cultural domination and the Anglicisation of the West African were part of the apparatus of British colonial hegemony in those colonies.

another great instrument of cultural action, serving the entire Anglophone Caribbean — the University of the West Indies from which he retired as Vice-Chancellor.[184] So despite the record of achievement the Institute could not rid itself of its Eurocentric and colonial image — an image fostered by the archaic bureaucratic procedures which girded its operations and the seeming resistance to the sort of change the wider society was undergoing starting from the late fifties. The sixties brought significant change to the Institute under the chairmanship of Frank Hill who had emerged from the political and social "revolution" of the late thirties and early forties. The emphasis on "Jamaicanisation" by the then political Administration was reflected in the work of the Institute. New blood drawn from the post-1938 generation was introduced on to the Board of Governors (the policy-making body) and into the Institute's Administration.[185] By 1973 when accelerated decolonisation became the commitment of the new political Administration the Institute's role as an over-arching national institution for cultural development was settled but on the under-standing that it restructured and re-ordered its priorities.

The addition of three national schools of training (the Art School was already operating under the old Institute) was a major development since it brought a greater number of Jamaicans drawn from varied walks of life within the ambit of the institution's services. Another important addition reflecting an important aspect of the new Jamaica, was the *African-Caribbean Institute of Jamaica*

---

184. Philip (now Sir Philip) Sherlock is a Jamaican man of letters, educator, historian, poet. After a distinguished career in education and the arts he joined the newly established University College of the West Indies as Vice-Principal and Director of Extra Mural Studies, later becoming Vice-Chancellor of the independent UWI. On retirement he became Secretary-General of the Association of Universities and Colleges throughout Latin America and the Caribbean (UNICA).

185. e.g. Sylvia Wynter (academic and novelist), John Maxwell (journalist), Rex Nettle-ford (academic, political scientist, creative arts), John Hearne (academic, novelist, journalist) on the Board of Governors; Neville Dawes (academic, novelist) in the Administration. The trend was to be followed by addition of Dahlia Mills-Repole (science teacher), Jean D'Costa (academic, authoress) as well as Bruce Golding, Neville Gallimore, Francis Tulloch (politicians) to the Board. The operational areas of the Institute are now peopled by young Jamaican graduates and talented artists.

(ACIJ) designed to carry out research into the African heritage in Jamaica and the Caribbean as well as into the counterparts or sources of those African continuities in West Africa. The formal association with the Institute of African Studies of the University of Ghana registers the scope and nature of the exercise. Languages, dance and archaeology have been the initial areas of activity but there are plans for extension of the work to religions, diet, family life and structure, and political and philosophical systems. Music which had had a start in the work of the Folk Music Research Unit will no doubt be incorporated into the ACIJ programme. The Unit's collection (based largely on the work of Olive Lewin) and the private collections of individuals like Louise Bennett and Edward Seaga (Jamaicans) as well as of Alan Lòmax, the American whose vast collection is the property of the University of the West Indies, now need to be properly analysed and the findings as well as some of the original material made available to scholars, teachers of music and creative artists (especially composers, arrangers and choreographers). The ACIJ's interest in Rastafarian culture is a new dimension of its work and the discography project designed to collate and codify the rich repertoire of popular music dating from the late 1950's to the late 1970's is underway. All these projects betray new and significant departures from the work of the old Institute as it operated before Independence.

The collection of Jamaican paintings and sculpture acquired over the past half-century were rationalised into a *National Gallery* which was officially opened in 1975. The Gallery is intended to operate less as a museum of decorative national treasures and more as a living dynamic institution to celebrate such national treasures and train the aesthetic sensibilities and cultural awareness of the adult and the massive youth population of Jamaica. The collection has the added effect of providing some interest for the thousands of foreign visitors to Jamaica each year. But not all the country's art treasures are housed in the National Gallery. Many are to be found in the Jamaican embassies and consulates overseas as well as in public buildings at home in Jamaica. The Government in 1973 agreed that up to 2 percent of the cost of new public buildings will be spent on art work. The public display of such works of art is regarded as a guarantee for strengthening the Jamaican cultural identity among a wide cross-section of the Jamaican people at home and abroad. A programme of reproductions through prints and slides and photographs is planned waiting on the proverbial "available funds" to give it the action and impact it could have on schools, youth clubs and adult community groups.

Other divisions of the new Institute of Jamaica reflect the retention of long-established activities initiated by the old Institute but which were modified and further developed during the first decade of Independence. They were to be the main targets of overhauling and reorientation during what has been referred to as the period of "accelerated decolonisation" i.e. since 1973. Such divisions are the *Community Cultural Centres,* developing out of the old Junior Centres, *Museums and Archaeology, Publications* including *Jamaica Journal* and the Cultural Heritage Series which was introduced in the 1962-70 period, the *West India Reference Library* (WIRL) projected as the basis for a National Library and *Natural History* which has flourished under the direction of natural scientist C. Bernard Lewis, a longtime director of the old Institute of Jamaica.

The Community Cultural Centre programme has antecedents of real significance for it was the Junior Centres of the old Institute, established in 1941 by Philip Sherlock the then Secretary of the Institute and developed by Robert Verity and his wife Carmen (nee Lawrence), that opened up to thousands of Jamaican children the programme of the Institute in its pursuit of arts, literature and science. The Junior Centres were to spawn the work in music education carried out later from the Ministry of Education.[186] The work done there was also the forerunner of the reading and activity sessions carried out today by the Junior libraries of the excellently organised island-wide Jamaica Library Services. The Community Cultural Centres which now include the Tivoli Gardens Centre in the heartland of the country's most famous

---

186. The work in music was done largely via the radio and latterly educational telecasts have been added. The chief influence here is one Lloyd Hall, a highly accomplished choirmaster and music educator.

ghetto and the Franklin Town Centre in East Kingston will in time develop into training centres for the kind of leaders (voluntary and partly paid) who can be deployed out into the wider society for work centres catering to young people all over the country. The Ministry of Youth has since 1974 run a cultural programme through its Social Development Commission all over the country and therefore fulfills a need which the old Junior Centres intended to but had little or no resources to fill.

The Division in charge of *Museums and Archaeology* discovers and preserves the material culture of the nation. Arawak middens unfold the lifestyle of the country's aboriginal peoples, 'digs' on the Old King's House site reveal artifacts from a plantocratic and colonial upper class life as well as the life of African slaves whose work in the earthenware clay pottery (yabbas) was for use by different segments of the population in the slave period. Documentation, analysis through careful and painstaking scholarship and display, take this work into museums. Today the Institute is wellknown for its museums located in different parts of the country — the Historical Gallery (in Kingston), the Portrait Gallery (in Kingston), the Arawak Museum (in Central Village), the Museum of Folk Art and Technology (in Spanish Town, the old capital), the African Museum (in Kingston and operated as part of the ACIJ), the Military Museum (in Kingston at Up Park Camp) recalling the decades of British military and naval presence when the Caribbean was a major battlefield for European imperial rivalry. Together they give an overview, albeit inadequate, of the chequered history of Jamaican life over the past four centuries. The preservation of monuments and historical sites from the Spanish era down to the turn of the twentieth century is placed under the jurisdiction of the *National Trust Commission* which under the new Institute Law becomes an integral part of the Institute of Jamaica. In any case the extensive work done on the underwater exploration of the treasures of Port Royal, the 17th century Jamaican capital and haunt of pirates was done under the joint management of the National Trust Commission and the Institute of Jamaica throughout the sixties.[187] In preparation is a museum of artifacts many of which have already been displayed all over Jamaica and have been the basis of reproductions in such items as pewter utensils (jugs, mugs, knives, forks, spoons, plates) — a significant tourist attraction since the late sixties when international cultural concerns focussed on what was known as "cultural tourism." The Jamaica Tourist Board's department of Domestic Marketing in 1976 erected "points-of-interest" signs all over Jamaica. Today Jamaicans are able to identify rivers and historic locations at a glance which in its own way is a marked improvement over the colonial experience which produced generations of highly literate Jamaicans who knew a great deal about British monuments, coalfields and historical sites from reading but knew little or nothing about their own Jamaican environment. The Tourist Board has also published the texts of short radio thumbnail sketches of historical events, personages and places, a useful hand-out for a population which has grown increasingly scribal and literate since the late fifties when educational opportunities were extended.

The *Publications Division* is another division of the Institute. It is still in its embryonic form but can draw on a history of "Institute publications" dating back to the works of Frank Cundall who edited and authored several of the early publications.[188] Volumes that came later were pace-setters in such fields as Jamaican history, natural history and the study of Jamaica's indigenous tongue.[189] In the 1960's the *Jamaica Journal* was

187. Marx, Robert: *Port Royal Rediscovered,* Pub. Garden City, New York, Doubleday 1973. It is only fair to say that the former Director of the Institute of Jamaica disputes much of what is in this book by Marx.

See also *Pirate Port — Story of the Sunken City of Port Royal,* Pub. Cleveland, New York World Publishing Co., 1967.

See Mimeograph "Brass and Copper Items Recovered from the Sunken City of Port Royal" (May 1966 — March 1968) Pub. Kingston, Jamaica National Trust Commission, 1958.

188. e.g. Cundall, Frank: *Bibliographia Jamaicensis,* Institute of Jamaica, 1902. A Supplement was published in 1908. In 1909 *Bibliography of the West Indies* (excluding Jamaica) was published by the Institute of Jamaica.

189. e.g. Cundall's *Jamaica Under the Spaniards* being an abridged and edited version of the documents discovered in 1916-17 by a Miss I. A. Wright in the Archivo de

established to disseminate factual information and stimulate critical writing on literature, art and science — the Institute's main areas of concern. Soon afterwards were added to the list of Institute publications (a) the Cultural Heritage Series with titles dealing with colonial administration, social history from slavery to the introduction of crown colony government, biography of a nineteenth century Jamaican martyr and patriot, (b) Jamaicans of Distinction Series covering the life and achievement of great Jamaican sportsmen and others, (c) creative writing in the form of novels and collections of poetry, and (d) occasional papers — essays and lectures — on a wide range of topics dealing with Jamaican cultural life, thought and history. To all these can be added the divisional publications currently emanating from the ACIJ (Research findings, capsule histories of nations of Africa south of the Sahara), the National Gallery, the Natural History Division and those that will no doubt come from the National Training Schools. The production of audiotapes and phonograph recordings of cultural information for wider dissemination in keeping with the realities of the last quarter of the 20th century is naturally considered an appropriate activity of the Institute's Publications Division, the problem of foreign exchange earnings notwithstanding. The recording of the nation's written treasures is one thing, the systematic deposit and storage of them for easy retrieval is another. The West India Reference Library was placed at the centre of the old Institute's activities for this very reason.

The West India Reference Library is undoubtedly one of the greatest and most valuable treasures not only of Jamaica but of the entire insular Caribbean (West Indies). It is a place where the history of the country and region can come to life if users know where to find the information and are directed to it. No major piece of research into Jamaica and Caribbean history can be done without reference to the WIRL which houses the finest collection of rare books, documents, maps, newspapers, private

Indias at Seville, which were transcribed for the Institute, translated by Joseph L. Pietersz and published by the Institute of Jamaica in 1919 and *Jamaica Talk* by F. Cassidy (1971).

papers, manuscripts of life and work in the insular Caribbean over three centuries. The credit goes to the Librarian/Secretary of the old Institute, Frank Cundall, who over 46 years collected books on West Indian history and affairs dating back to the Spanish period. As such the WIRL anticipated the concept of a National Library for Jamaica. Mandatory deposit of all publications (print and electronic) found support among advocates for a new Copyright Law but even without this many Jamaicans have sent their publications to the august Institution. Still, many important publications are missed. Today its greatest problem is that of conserving and restoring to manageable shape the rich mine of information which is in danger of being lost to Jamaican and West Indian civilisation. For the past is indeed the prologue to the future. Between 1966 and 1973 the readership in the Reference Library soared from 900 to 9000.[190] It is a source of vital information for school children, scholars (local and foreign), government officials, businessmen, journalists and documentalists. The WIRL is a national collection but not yet a National Library. The implications for its rapid modernisation, rationalisation and transformation are not lost on the Jamaican government in its strategy to provide the Jamaican people with efficient and serviceable means of providing information vital to the development of the country and its people.[191]

The express political will awaits positive action by way of budgetary allocation. Such an allocation has long been needed and is immediately pressing for the conservation programme that is vital for the saving of the invaluable material in the West India Reference Library. To retard or arrest the deterioration that has set in, money needs to be allocated to improve shelving techniques, to store manuscripts, maps, and similar material in acid-free file folders and storage boxes, to store photographic prints in acid-free envelopes. The training of binders in the latest techniques of binding, the microfilming of material which are about to disappear in

190.   "Talks on the Institute of Jamaica", Section on the WIRL by J. Richards. (Unpublished paper).

191.   See *Report of Exploratory Committee on the Arts;* also see Report on *Plan for a National Information System (NATIS) for Jamaica,* Kingston, Jamaica, April, 1977.

dust and the training of a conservator, are some of the pressing demands if this aspect of the nation's patrimony which the West India Reference Library houses, is to be saved. Such is the urgent call from an expert from the Preservation department of the United States Library of Congress.[192] This expert listed among the problems of the WIRL the very building in which the collection is housed. "The Library — whether it continues to function as the West India Reference Library or is redesignated the Jamaican National Library — cannot function effectively in the present physical structure. Poorly laid out in terms of library functions and convenience for users; the building lacks adequate space for staff, sufficient space for the collection, and even the most rudimentary elements of environmental control."[193]

That the nation's commitment to nurturing its national identity and protecting its national heritage must be reflected in the proper care and preservation of the invaluable records of the past, there can be no doubt. That the West India Reference Library has suffered from years of administrative lethargy (a Chief Librarian's post has had "acting incumbents" for some twenty years), poor preventive conservation practice of a basic nature, and a misguided exclusivity (free of developments, say, at the University of the West Indies and the excellent Jamaica Library Services), there can be no question. In fact the Government's earlier decision to make it the basis of a National Library was born of appreciation for its central importance to the world of scholarship and the preservation of the heritage. In the hands of highly trained professional librarians of vision and intellectual sophistication the future of the West India Reference Library will be able to take its appropriate place of priority among the many other priorities with respect to the preservation of the national heritage. Not least among them is the development of human resources which has attracted the attention of succeeding administrations since Independence as evidenced in the heavily subsidised literacy programme, the development of

192.   Poole, Frazer, G.: *Report on Conservation Problems of the West India Reference Library*, Kingston, Jamaica — a Report with Recommendations, 1977.

193.   *Ibid* p. 4.

the facilities for increased readership among the populace throughout the island, the establishment of cultural training institutions,
and the development of the mass media which have been important
and effective transmitters of information about the national heritage
to the large mass of the Jamaican people. The West India Reference
Library's role in this urgent matter now needs to be made clear to
"those who stand in the only position to take effective action" —
the political directorate; and they must be made to understand that
it is there, not for the exclusive use of a narrow group of privileged
Jamaicans but for the service of all Jamaica. A change in philosophy
as to what libraries do and what they are for is not the least of
changes needed among those who guide Jamaica's future in the field
of cultural development.

The Division of Natural History originally pledged to
systematic study of all natural objects, animals, vegetables and
minerals is known largely for its extensive collection and documentation of Jamaican and Caribbean flora (taxonomy) and insects
(entomology). The study-material on every type of animal in
Jamaica however remains in storage. All together they are intended
to meet the four objectives of the Division *viz:* collection, preservation, education and research according to its director George
Proctor.[194]

His work and that of C. Bernard Lewis over some thirty
years of sustained research has gained for the Institute of Jamaica
(old and new) an international reputation for the expertly docu-
mented information that exists on the flora of Jamaica and the
Caribbean. The advent of a Faculty of Natural Science in the
University of the West Indies in the early 1950's and the establishment of the Scientific Research Council at the end of that decade
provided a welcome division of labour in the field of science, as
did the setting up of a national zoo in Kingston in the 1960's.

Still, the Division's work carries far-reaching implications
for agriculture (in the rehabilitation of strip-mined bauxite lands
which by law must be restored), commerce (the preparation and
marketing of weedkillers), pharmacology (with respect to the

194. See "Talks on the Institute of Jamaica", Section on Natural History Division by
George Proctor. (Unpublished Paper).

medicinal properties of bushes extensively used as folkcures by the country's extensive rural population), academic research (in the chemical studies of plant alcolydes at the UWI), ecological balance and environmental control as well as for the wider world of scientific scholarship. The Division's continuing role in education through displays, consultant practice and seminars received more vigorous planning under the guidance of Dahlia Repole, a natural science teacher and Vice-Chairman of the Institute, since it must be seen as an important aspect of that deeper commitment which the country must have to science and technology as part of its national development strategies.

All the "cultural activities" outlined above betrayed the wide range of needs to be met and the diverse nature of the functions to be performed. It is the full appreciation of the nature of this phenomenon that, in rationalising the official institutional infrastructure, the Jamaicans have opted for structural diversity in a network system of interrelated cultural institutions. Besides satisfying the dictates of a persistent cultural pluralism, this no doubt provides the creative tension so necessary for the cultural process as every conscious artist and cultural agent in the exercise of his duties or the indulgence of his individual vision will aver. The radical tradition in a climate of change would expect no less since cultural expression is seen as a means of protest as much as an instrument of constructing identity. The multiplicity of institutions is itself a guarantee against bureaucratic sclerosis which is death to cultural dynamism. Needless to say, the entire process of "rationalising" the country's cultural institutions has been a source of confusion to those Jamaicans who would prefer the clarity of monolithic hierarchies.

In effect the new Institute of Jamaica, while being the over-arching national cultural institution working directly with and under the Office of the Prime Minister, is an umbrella rather than an iron-grid. It has a permanent Council of the Arts charged with "the encouragement and development of Literature, Science, the Arts and Culture, the pursuit of history, the preservation of monuments for the public benefit . . ."[195] But that Council is composed of persons drawn primarily from the Boards of Management (in practice the Chairman) of each constituent unit of the Institute. The principle of autonomy in the areas of action is here invoked and the participation of a wide cross-section of voluntary workers as well as paid employees and artists is ensured through membership on the Boards of Management. Artists of repute, persons with proven interest in cultural development, educators, and community service leaders are among others appointed to the Institute's Council. Rural youth and urban mass representation are included in the Boards of Management — a genuine departure from past practice in the appointments to the old Institute's Boards of Governors which the Arts Council replaces. Statutory provision is made for ex-officio membership on the Council of representatives from the *Jamaica Festival Commission* and the *National Trust Commission.* Both of these institutions which date back to the 1960's in practice operate as parallel national institutions with direct access to the nation's policy-determiners through the Ministry for Culture, as do private individuals. They work in close collaboration with the related divisions of the new Institute and all work in collaboration with the media (radio and television) which are important vehicles of transmission. This is facilitated by the fact that the media fall under the same Ministry as the above-named cultural institutions.

The *National Trust Commission* which was created in 1958 with responsibility for the preservation of the country's historic sites and monuments continues to work in practice in close collaboration with the Institute's division of museums and archaeology, of Publications (in the production of popular historical studies) and of African-Caribbean research.

The Jamaica Festival Commission

The *Jamaica Festival Commission* collaborates with the national schools of training which are expected to provide long and some short-term training for cultural officers for work in the

195.   See Act to "change the name of the Board of Governors of the Institute of Jamaica; to extend the functions and alter the constitution thereof; to amend the Institute

rural communities. Part of this complex of activities is the cultural programme run by the Social Development Commission (SDC) attached to the Ministry of Youth and doing for youth groups organised by the Social Development Comission what the Festival Commission does for the entire nation. This gives further institutional texture to the arrangements and provides the necessary creative tension already referred to. But it is the Festival Commission which since Independence has monitored and organised the annual festival of arts and crafts and has provided a showcase for cultural expression throughout the country. It has stimulated renewed interest among the rural and urban populations in traditional culture and contemporary creative artistic expression. More than any single official cultural institution the Festival Commission has been able to mobilise more Jamaicans from all over the country and from all classes and age-groups, around to a lively awareness of the country's indigenous artistic/cultural potential whether it be culinary arts, fashion design, drama, music, dance, arts and crafts, or grand spectacle.

Popular participation through voluntary effort was worked into the organisational and operational structure of the Commission from the beginning. The paid officials of the Commission are perceived as "servants" of the people they serve and they stand guided by the fourteen parish committees and a variety of subject area advisers, many of whom take their involvement seriously enough to challenge headquarters on decisions not to their taste and are not afraid to take the initiative in determining the rules that must govern their participation in the exercise. It is this spirit, sometimes combative, that has saved the entire festival movement from becoming what popular culture has so often become i.e. a victim of official manipulation and imposition from above. That vigilance is never absent from the work of the Commission is evident from the annual public and private controversies

of Jamaica Act; and for connected purposes . . ." Also *Institute of Jamaica Act of 1978*, "– debated in the Jamaican House of Representatives on Tuesday, February 28, 1978 and taken through all its stages in one sitting. Hon. Arnold Bertram introduced the Bill on behalf of the Government. Mr Edward Seaga, Leader of the Opposition, led the Debate from the Other side of the House."

over such matters as the procedures and substance of the Festival Song Contest, the adjudication methods employed in the assessment of works offered in different branches of the performing arts, and the national row some years back as to whether the Festival should continue its involvement in the "Miss Jamaica" beauty contest. The Festival is more of a movement rather than an event.

Voluntary contribution in the cultural dynamics

The voluntary participation in the Jamaica Festival movement has the ring of authenticity since it reflects a long tradition of voluntary individual and community collaboration for the public good. This had formed part of the immediate post-slavery rehabilitation exercise in the setting up of Free Villages, and was later utilised through Jamaica Welfare Limited, founded by Norman Manley as a means of mobilising people around to the new national spirit in the late 1930's, already referred to.

The harsh fact of the lack of adequate funds, if for no other reason, will dictate the continuing involvement on a voluntary basis of large numbers of Jamaican individuals and groups in the country's cultural development. In any case, the nature of the cultural process would tolerate no less. And if political rhetoric is to be taken seriously, the declared thrust of the popularly elected government since 1972 towards "social justice, equality and participatory democracy" should guarantee the preservation of this tradition. Wide participation in the process of social and cultural change must clearly be reflected in the operational procedures of institutions set up to facilitate this change though *with the full understanding that the values of (a) knowledge of the subject (b) excellence in execution, and (c) disciplined application are as vital to cultural development as they are to agriculture and manufacturing.* So those who volunteer must be prepared to work hard and not mistake the status of committee membership for the effectiveness of their contribution. The history of voluntary work in cultural activity in Jamaica is not without its blatant examples of such errors. But there are more examples of genuine contribution through hard sustained and serious work. What has emerged is the possibility of fruitful relationship between voluntary workers and official functionaries in cultural planning and action. The Tivoli Gardens Centre in West Kingston is also part of the West Kingston Trust but operates in part as a cultural centre of the Institute of Jamaica. Other such centres will be added no doubt to the Festival Commission as the agency responsible for community cultural activity. The Jamaican Georgian Society works with the Museum and Archaeology Division, the Jamaica Historical Society with the National Trust Commission, the Association of Science Teachers with the Natural History Division, the Bolivarian Society with the Executive Director's office, the Count Ossie Rastafarian Centre with the ACIJ, the Jamaica Artists and Craftsmen Guild and the Olympia International Art Centre which is funded and operated privately by A. D. Scott with the National Gallery and School of Art, the Jamaica Federation of Musicians with the Festival Commission and the School of Music, the Jamaica Folk Singers with the Folk Research Unit of which they were the virtual progenitors, the National Dance Theatre Company with its offspring the Jamaica School of Dance and the Little Theatre Movement with the School of Drama, which it founded. Outside of these institutions the work of the teachers and parents in the annual Festival adds up to a great deal of invaluable human effort while the energy of creative activity in the field of popular music over a span of some twenty years has received ready, enthusiastic and proprietory embrace from the authorities and general populace alike.

But while the majority of Jamaicans must be made to feel that what they create is worthy of recognition in the building of their civilisation in answer to the centuries of denial of just this, it will do the country and its succeeding political directorates no harm if the temptation of equating mass culture with democracy is studiously avoided. For the equation has its inherent dangers. Not least among these is the capacity of mass culture with the help of the electronic media to breed political totalitarianism, the spirit of which has resided for long enough in the plantation life and colonialism of most of modern Jamaican history. In fact, it is the fearless defiance of all attempts to perpetuate this which gives to Jamaican popular culture in its most original manifestations, the special force it has at this time of Jamaican history. It may well be argued that to transform it into instruments of conformity or resignation is to rob it of its historical mission as well as its essence. However, this is not to argue for that crass individualism which is associated with Eurocentric notions of high culture. Rather, it is an argument for the preservation of the human being's capacity for expression in a spirit that can be the basis of his fundamental equality with every other being and at the same time the occasion of his dignity and sense of self-worth. It is a position that neither chauvinistic reformers nor vulgar Marxists of the region may wish to agree with but it is a position that carries a telling correspondence with the realities of Caribbean life evident everywhere — as much in the socialist Cuba of José Martí and Nicolás Guillén as it is in liberal nationalist Trinidad and Tobago of Dr Eric Williams and the Mighty Sparrow.

Communications Media, Information and Cultural Policy

The building of cultural institutions devised to advance the cultural dimension of development and to facilitate cultural action cannot, however, be done in isolation of the sort of activity that will address itself positively to the danger that confronts the cultural identities of a developing nation. The reference here is to "the mass-produced outpourings of commercial broadcasting"[196] of the North Atlantic (particularly the United States) and to the domination of the entire world information system by some five giant news agencies, all of which are transnational organisations and none of which are situated in the Third World. Jamaica and the Caribbean, therefore, are the victims of the effects of cultural domination and dependence fostered by most of the prevailing information patterns said to be "much more penetrating than those of purely economic domination and dependence."[197] As with economic power, so with this aspect of cultural power. The

---

196.   Hosein, Everold: "The Problem of Imported Television Content in the Common-wealth Caribbean" *Caribbean Quarterly*, Vol. 22, No. 4, December 1976, p. 8.

197.   *Ibid.*

battle for liberation will be a fierce one since it will "be all the harder for those who need and want change." In this the press, the most vociferous in the cry for freedom, is regarded as "the tool and principal exemplification of [information] subservience."[198]

For Jamaica which for two years had been the target of misreporting and misrepresentation in the North American press,[199] the place of information sciences in overall national development assumes a sense of urgency. As part of all this, a lively press freedom controversy has been raging furiously and frequently throughout the Commonwealth Caribbean. As Dorcas White in an insightful article pointed out, the colonial legal heritage has bequeathed to the Commonwealth Caribbean nations political constitutions guaranteeing the right to free expression. Many governmental leaders are not "satisfied that the actions of the media are subject [merely] to the laws of libel. They are asserting that the press is under duty bound to commit itself to the *support of national development goals* whether they are planned within the context of existing capitalistic structure or a projected socialist undertaking."[200] The same spirit that informs the individualism of the creative artist who insists on the inviolability of the creative imagination and the autonomy of the cultural process is the same that informs the claims to press freedom. It stems from the notion of individual rights being central to the culture of democratic politics.

198.   "Moving Towards a New International Information Order", *Development Dialogue* 1976: 2, p. 10, Dag Hammarskjold Foundation, Sweden.

199.   Lord Laro, the Trinidadian calypsonian who is a resident of Jamaica, puts it thus:
   "They trying their best, to stop our progress
   With bad propaganda, I think it's the foreign press
   But things are blown out of proportion, and spread all around
   But the good things of the island, they will never mention.

   Chorus: Like our scholars sit and pass their test
         There's nothing mention 'bout that in the foreign press
         You know our music is rated among the best
         There's nothing 'bout that in the foreign press
         But if a man steal a mango or breeze blow up a woman's dress
         Bet your life it will make headline in the foreign press."

200.   White, Dorcas: "Legal Constraints and the Role of the Mass Media in a Caribbean in Transition" *Caribbean Quarterly*, Vol. 22, No. 4, December 1976, p. 28.

White indicates, significantly, that the debate is keenest in those "territories where national goals are based on socialist policies which seem to run counter to capitalistic goals."[201] Jamaica is certainly one of the former and the debate has indeed been acrimonious. Public denunciations by some politicians against the "indiscretions" of a leading daily newspaper known for its Establishment advocacy and which has attracted to it ardent and consistent critics of the democratic socialist party in power, have been made in the wider context of the challenge to new values supportive of fundamental change from dependency to economic, political and cultural independence.

As has been said elsewhere[202] "many advocates of fundamental change in the Caribbean would share the view that the call for a new information order is not intended to replace the monopoly of the transnationals with a monopoly by the national governments, however well-intentioned the latter might be. The advocacy, in other words, is not for a more restricted press but for a freer one — one that will meet the need to inform and be informed." The Government of Jamaica, as if to retain the sensibilities of their declared democratic mission, spoke of "people control" of a commercial radio station on the announcement of a possible takeover from the private and foreign owners. The rationale is that the control and ownership by communities of citizens would guarantee the sort of output that is culturally responsive to the needs of the general mass of the people as well as being accurate and credible in the dissemination of information.[203]

If the debate over the freedom of the press is strong, the debate over the exploitation of the electronic media for the continuing cultural subjugation of the Jamaican and Caribbean people is even stronger. The fact that television services in the most populous

201.   *Ibid.*

202.   Editorial, *Caribbean Quarterly*, Vol. 22, No. 4.

203.   Hence the announcement of Government's intention to transform the commercially run Radio Jamaica and Rediffusion (RJR) radio station accordingly. The radio enterprise was finally taken over by the Jamaican Government in September, 1977.

territories (i.e. Jamaica, Trinidad and Tobago, Barbados)[204] are
government-owned, offers little solution for what is clearly the
major problem – *viz* programme content which is largely imported.
Jamaica's weekly programme-schedule until mid-1977 depended
on 73 percent imported programmes, which reached some 30 percent of the homes of the country with a set count of 110,000.[205]
The Jamaica Broadcasting Corporation which started first as a
Jamaican BBC-type radio station and later expanded to offer
television services, is up to now conceived as a service which will
faithfully reflect the cultural and social complexity of the nation
while at the same time remaining a viable economic proposition.
Economic viability has depended primarily on advertising revenue
as the major source of income. In a society which seeks to bring
competition in marketable commodities to non-exploitative proportions, there can hardly be an advertising industry to produce
the kind of revenue that can provide the financial resource base
for a commercial station such as the JBC is and has been. Part of
the development strategy must therefore turn on budgetary provision of ample subsidy out of the public purse for the production
of output that is responsive to the cultural and information needs
of the society. The JBC, like its sister institutions throughout the
region, has a responsibility which indeed extends beyond the borders of mirroring the society. It has also to help create new tastes
and lead the society towards reconciling social conflicts and interests through well informed discussion and the propagation of ideas
according to Gloria Lannaman, a writer, historian and broadcaster.
For the output must inform, educate and entertain.

Needless to say, those directly concerned with output or
programme content, from News and Programme Directors to
announcers and producer-directors, professionalism must be
informed by a good basic education, a sound knowledge of the
society's political, cultural, social and economic mechanisms, a

---

204.   The TV services in St. Kitts-Nevis and Antigua are also government-owned.

205.   Cp. 15% in St. Kitts-Nevis (2000 sets); 50% in Antigua (8000 sets); 70% in Barbados
(40,000 sets); 50% Trinidad and Tobago (110,000 sets). See Hosein, Everold:
op cit p. 7.

responsiveness to changing trends in the society at large so that the staffer can formulate and devise outlets for the society's expression, and a strong general knowledge and awareness of the affairs of the wider world. That such a basis for professional action is conspicuously absent among far too many who are now called upon to take decisions as to what goes out over the air or on the television screen, is part of the problem of development. American-style disc-jockeying transforms substance into froth and renders to trivia disproportionate exposure, though the frequency of Jamaican popular music in transmission is due to the zeal of the disc-jockeys. The preparation or upgrading of skills in this particular and especially in providing a frame of reference consonant with the history and experience of the Caribbean and the wider world, is already part of the in-service training programme of the Jamaica Broadcasting Corporation[206] and of the newly established diploma in Mass Communication at the University of the West Indies, pursued by media employees from all over the region since 1974.[207]

A former director of that programme, Dr Everold Hosein, is less concerned with the reported bad effects of the imported content of television programmes and more perturbed by the abridgement of what he calls "a national right." "The public needs to be given back its television medium, its broadcast time, simply because it is theirs," he says. "Content expressive of the people's lives would make the medium theirs. It is on this principle that television policies should be based," he advises, "and not on exaggerated fears of culture change resulting from imported television."[208]

Will Caribbean governments heed this advice? The constraint of costs is frequently invoked by station-managers who are

206. Instituted by the General Manager, Wycliffe Bennett in collaboration with the UWI's Department of Extra Mural Studies.

207. The syllabus of the Diploma in Mass Communication reads as follows: History, Politics and Culture of the Caribbean; Principles of Sociology and Economics; Communication Principles; Media and Language; Communication Techniques (Radio, Television, Film, Print).

208. Hosein, Everold: *op cit* p. 12.

required to make profits through advertising revenue. This is in itself limited and could not cover the costs of local programmes which run five to ten times the cost of the imported material. The vicious circle is completed with the inadequacy of production facilities, staff and high level talent – at least this is what Caribbean Information Ministers are told. Hosein gives tentative endorsement but adds his own observed constraints such as (i) the lack of programming will, through inertia on the part of television staffs, (ii) the Eurocentric perception of "good quality" programme in the sense that Hollywood gloss and glamour are the constant criteria of assessment, (iii) the restriction of producing opportunities to fulltime station staffers when many able outsiders in the wider community could participate effectively, (iv) the idea that good programmes need large sums of money (a view which according to Hosein inhibits creativity) and (v) the insularity of the Caribbean territories which "deter effective regional collaboration." Dr Hosein's recommendations for action, some eighteen in all, should be required reading for all Ministries of Culture and/or Information throughout the Caribbean region.

Jamaica's declared intention to set up a national body on Media policy to advise the Government on media development in the context of overall national development is clearly a step in the right direction. In the meantime the existing communications media institutions will have to address themselves to the challenges of internal change generally in the light of national development and specifically in the context of cultural change. Without cutting off the nation's populace from the wealth of information about the wider world, the focus on matters that will relate the Jamaican experience meaningfully to a world-view and give to each Jamaican of whatever social origin an opportunity for a positive point of contact with his society, is a cultural responsibility that the media cannot avoid. The projection of esoteric games over and above the sports known to and enjoyed by the large mass of the people, the domination of the news headlines (print, radio and television) by foreign trivia over and above happenings of genuine importance to the Jamaican and Caribbean people, the domination of the television screens by foreign soap operas, situation comedies out of alien situations which push values born of other experiences, the advertising campaigns showing "actors and actresses" few or none of whom are representative of the majority ethnic types to be found in the Caribbean, the failure to help the Caribbean people themselves to put a value on their own creative output and experience — all these past and present sins of the colonial and Eurocentric media now need to be expiated as part of that process of psychological transformation which is crucial to the mobilisation of the Caribbean populace for Caribbean development.

That this is easier said than done is obvious to the most casual observer. The problem is not one of political will. The Minister of State in charge of Culture and Information draws attention to the influence of the metropolitan North Atlantic on the mass media in the Caribbean region. The 73 percent foreign content on Caribbean television programmes is seen to constitute a"danger that cannot be overstated, for no matter how innocuous and socially meaningless an imperialist (sic) play, movie or cartoon may seem to us, it produces a cultural stream of influence that contradicts the stated goals of national liberation."[209] As with the electronic media, so with the press. "The dominant one-way flow of the press propaganda from the metropolitan countries to the Caribbean," asserts the Minister, "and our inability, so far, to use radio as an effective medium of education and orientation, raises grave doubts as to *our capacity to protect our cultural integrity*" (my emphasis).[210] "The doubts", he concluded, "had to do particularly with means — *viz* technology, equipment and training." A scholarly commentator thinks they have to do with advertising policy since the advertising industry is a "key supporting role of these primary activities of the communications media in Jamaica."[211] The young Minister of Youth and Sports showed how the advertising industry brings harm to cultural integrity. He is

209. Bertram, A. B.: *op cit* p. 5.

210. *Ibid.*

211. Brown, Aggrey: "The Mass Media of Communications and Socialist Change in the Caribbean: A Case Study of Jamaica" *Caribbean Quarterly* Vol. 22, No. 4, December 1976, p. 48.

quoted as saying that "Everytime an advertisement comes over the television that portrays beauty being European and elegant as involving non-Negroid hair, it is indoctrination because it is building a particular doctrine about beauty and culture which cannot be attained by the masses." He goes on to make the significant point that "despite this cultural distortion that goes on in the news media, we have had the rising consciousness of the people" – a fact that is the occasion, cause and effect of the dynamics of cultural growth since the late thirties in Jamaica. Yet the work is nowhere complete since there are still "some people who have been led astray by the indoctrination of the mass media by the constant showing [of material] that comes out of North American television studios. This has had the effect of alienating some of the young people's minds against themselves, and pride in their country."[212]

Some would probably accuse the young Minister of conscious exaggeration since with only 30 percent of Jamaican homes using television sets, at least 70 percent of the households escape the worst consequences of foreign domination. But this would be to ignore the all pervasive influence of radio in the age of transistor-radio. Some 76 percent of the adult population listen to the radio each day in Jamaica according to a 1973 radio survey.[213] In analysing the allocation of what time to what content, Aggrey Brown states that only 5.1 percent of weekly broadcast time is given to public affairs programming; 5.9 percent of broadcast time however goes to religious programming – meaning *Christian* religious programmes. 80 percent goes to entertainment which consists of "soap operas [local ones in the conspicuous minority], quizzes, North American style disc jockey programmes, etc."[214] It must be admitted that a good deal of local musical compositions are played on the two radio stations (to the chagrin of many among the Eurocentric

212. Interview of Hon. Hugh Small, Minister of Youth and Sports by Ian Boyne in *Jamaica Daily News*, Sunday, June 12, 1977.

213. *Jamaica Radio Survey*, Market Research Jamaica Ltd., March 1974, Kingston (Revised edition).

214. Brown, Aggrey: *op cit* p. 47.

middle strata) but as Brown points out these are mere links to the string of advertisements based on Madison-Avenue-type copy.

The heavy weighting given advertising, not always in the economic or cultural interest of the nation, is repeated in the print media as well. The prestigious and austere *Daily Gleaner* which dates back to 1834 and the newer *Jamaica Daily News,* a more popular-type tabloid depend on advertising for survival. The fact that they are owned by "private economic interests" whose objectives would not always be compatible with the masses is a point that is worthy of debate. But it has not prevented them promoting for popular consumption many of the cultural expressions that in fact belong to the people. The *Daily Gleaner's* conscious policy in the sixties to give increasing exposure to the pop musicians and their achievements was a significant departure from the emphasis on the manifestations of "high art" in the decades before that. Some will say it was good for business, as the pushing of reggae and ska records undoubtedly were for Radio Jamaica and Rediffusion, but the exposure by these two media to the products of the popular creative imagination did much to disseminate such products and help with the development of confidence and a self-perception more attuned to reality.

Why then does Brown insist that "any government desiring to transform social and economic relationships in the society will have to contend with the inevitable counter-propaganda effects of the entrenched media in Jamaica, notably the *Daily Gleaner* and *RJR*"?[215] It is clear that the factor of private economic interests in the spirit of free enterprise is a major consideration in these cases. The *Daily Gleaner,* an intensely *Jamaican* institution, therefore finds throughout its history frequently moving against the popular spirit from the time of Emancipation, through the period advocating the advent of self-government, up to the present time when the cry is for fundamental reconstruction of the society in terms of its economic, class and cultural structures. A brief content analysis by Marlene Cuthbert of sample issues of the *Daily Gleaner* since the Jamaican Government's declaration of

---

215.   Brown, Aggrey: *op cit* p. 49, i.e. RJR before it went under public ownership.

democratic socialism reveals strong editorial bias against this brand
of social and cultural transformation and the evidence lies in the
frequency with which the newspaper reprints adverse articles
written by foreign journalists in foreign newspapers discrediting
the country's efforts to transform itself. That "as others see us"
continues to matter more than how the Jamaicans see *themselves*
is borne out by the *Daily Gleaner's* preoccupation with reprinting
such articles even when the articles are known to contain a "mis-
leading juxtaposition of certain facts, a series of inaccuracies and
exaggerations, and an obvious malicious intent."[216] The fight
against the philosophical position of a party in power is one thing;
the cultural consequences of such a fight whereby some of the
worst cultural values of a degrading past are perpetuated, albeit
unintentionally, is a dilemma that a newspaper like the *Daily
Gleaner* now faces in the challenge of serious and fundamental
change. The support of the fight against communism by the
prominence given to articles against that creed, suggests a lack of
faith in the wisdom of the Jamaican people to choose for themselves, and misleads them in respect of the country's real need to
realise that independent choice of one's friends is a right that must
not be given up lightly or that the right to place a value on one's
natural resources in the face of crass foreign exploitation is not a
crime or an act of plunder. While arrogance and foolhardiness must
be abhorred, slavish obedience to mighty powers and a continuing
satellisation cannot be encouraged if a country, however small,
expects to be taken seriously. Waste of columns of valuable editorial
space chiding the nation for not giving heavy celebratory weight to
the Silver Jubilee of Elizabeth, the Queen, is hardly appropriate to
the cultural realities of modern Jamaica. Cuthbert would probably
argue that the country's most influential newspaper is culturally
irresponsible in Jamaican and Caribbean terms, by refusing to
subscribe to the Caribbean News Agency (CANA) because it fears
"political control" of the agency while depending on syndicated

216. Cuthbert, Marlene: "Some Observations on the Role of the Mass Media in the
Recent Socio-political Development of Jamaica", *Caribbean Quarterly*, Vol. 22,
No. 4, December 1976, pp. 50-58.

material of the metropolitan news agencies, the control of which is not less "political."[217]

Whether the *Daily Gleaner,* the most "Jamaican" of Jamaican institutions, will follow in its historical role of first objecting to dominant trends of change and then appropriating them once these changes become reality, is left to be seen. But the inherent contradictions of its posture as "a forum of opinion rather than as a newspaper" continue to be harshly tested in these times of fundamental and serious change. The editorial page is still able to carry articles from the most colonial/Eurocentric to the most progressive though the choice of Letters to the Editor gives a clear picture as to what kind of change is endorsed and which is not. The evening newspaper *The Star* owned by the Gleaner syndicate satisfies a middle of the road perspective and catches the popular cultural trends with commendable frequency. It is clear that the future national identity is not tied up with silver jubilees of British monarchs even if they continue to carry the title of King or Queen of Jamaica for constitutional convenience. Nor can the cultural identity be made possible if a sovereign Jamaica continues to be the target of wanton economic exploitation, political/military control or cultural subjugation by the North Atlantic powers. The *Daily Gleaner,* like all other media units, cannot be considered to be supportive of the quest for cultural identity and national coherence if it operates in a way or disseminates information which seeks to "reproduce the structure of domination/subordination which elsewhere characterises the system."[218]

The need then, for a strong media policy as part of the developmental process, is a major responsibility for any Administration in a developing region like the Caribbean. The credibility of Government-owned media agencies is not the least of the problem. For the "counter-propaganda" against the "reactionary press" must be rooted in facts and in truth. There is enough in Jamaican and Caribbean history and contemporary experience to feed the

217.   Cuthbert, Marlene: *op cit* p. 51.

218.   Hall, Stuart: "The Structured Communication of Events" in *Getting the Message Across,* Paris UNESCO Press, 1975, p. 143, (quoted in Cuthbert *op cit* p. 55).

Government-owned media with the sort of information that could mobilise the popular imagination to productive activity and to the consciousness of confidence in shaping a national and cultural identity. The arrogance of the private-owned media cannot be emulated by the functionaries in the Government-owned media though this may be a temptation. Operatives in public information agencies, such as the Jamaica Agency for Public Information (API) must be properly equipped for the work they are called upon to do. Journalists who have never *read* and studied any of the great texts of socialism can hardly be expected to be effective communicators of that great tradition of philosophical reflection and political programmatic strategy. Worse still, if such persons know nothing about the history, socio-economic and cultural development of Plantation America. And much of the humbug throughout the media (private and public) in Jamaica and other parts of the Caribbean turns precisely on the phenomenal ignorance among those called upon to feed the public with information about Caribbean life and development.

No training for work in the communications media in the Caribbean can therefore ignore this central factor. The decolonisation of the journalist, broadcaster, and media policy determiner and their liberation from the cultural entrapment in a solidly Eurocentric (including the Anglo-American) and colonialist frame of reference is a prerequisite for any meaningful exercise of judgement in the selection, projection of news, information, and whatever else the communications media transmit to the populace at large. With this the exercise of discrimination in the choice and projection of information drawn from human experience anywhere and at different times of man's history will come with cultural ease and no likely harm to a people who know they cannot block out the sun but have had little chance in a state of domination to discover means of preventing harm from over-exposure to its rays.

Central to a national media policy must be provision for a national information system. Out of the Exploratory Committee on the Arts, appointed in 1972 came a recommendation for the establishment of a National Library of Jamaica, to co-ordinate the major libraries of Jamaica, the collections to be found in many

Government Ministries and statutory bodies, and libraries of private sector organisations. In 1973 the Prime Minister appointed the National Council on Libraries, Archives and Documentation Services to advise the Jamaican Government on a national plan for the development of libraries, archives and documentation centres, covering upgrading needs, type of legislation needed, and the establishment of a National Deposit Library. In September 1974, the Jamaican Cabinet "accepted as policy the pursuance of activities which will lead to the effective provision or improvement of national information systems which can be accommodated within the national budget."[219] A series of follow-up discussions with UNESCO resulted in proposals by a UNESCO consultant (Dr. Dorothy Collings) who had acted as consultant to the West India Reference Library earlier and was responsible for setting up the Library School at the University of the West Indies. Familiarity with the territory and the conditions therefore gives to her recommendations a welcome authority which it would be unwise of the Jamaican Government to ignore.

Top priority is understandably given to the establishment of the National Library of Jamaica "as the storehouse of our culture and traditions, the guardian of our history and heritage, and the wellspring of inspiration for our cultural and economic future."[220] In keeping with an earlier policy decision, the National Library based on the restructured West India Reference Library of the Institute of Jamaica, is to serve as the legal repository, and the national reference source for all print and non-print materials issued in Jamaica, about Jamaica and by Jamaicans issued elsewhere."[221]

Not all in the dedicated and hardworking community of professional librarians in Jamaica are comfortable with the prospect of a National Library based on the West India Reference Library as part of a restructured Institute of Jamaica. One visiting librarian

219.   Cabinet Submission No. 365/ME – 26; Decision 37/34 dated September 19, 1974.

220.   Fowler, Henry: Letter of Transmission of *Report on Plan for a National Information System (NATIS) for Jamaica* Kingston, Jamaica, April 1977.

221.   *Ibid.*

caught the local mood accurately when he wondered whether "the Jamaican people will be best served by permitting the new Jamaican National Library to remain attached to the Institute of Jamaica or whether it should be made a true national library by being established as a separate entity so that it can receive its support and guidance *directly from the Government."* "A good case can be made," he emphasised, "that for so long as it remains a subordinate unit under the Institute of Jamaica, the library can never achieve its full potential. One can only hope that those who make the final decision will give this problem the most careful thought."[222]

   That the constraint of lack of funds first prompted the authorities to contemplate utilising and maximising existing resources, is a well-known approach of the Jamaican government at this time. That this is not always most acceptable to parties affected is equally well known. The pressing conservation demands of the existing collection in the West India Reference Library, though not mutually exclusive with the other duties of a National Library, may well force the Government of Jamaica to a position that would meet the wishes of many in the profession, *viz* an independent National Library charged with "the co-ordination of all types of libraries, archives and documentation services and their planned development on a phased basis, aimed at providing the information services and materials needed by all sectors of the society with maximum effectiveness and economy."[223] Such a system would embrace (i) the National Library of Jamaica (ii) the Jamaica Archives and Records Centre, (iii) the JAMAL Foundation (with its new literates), (iv) the Jamaica Library Service (a most accomplished agency servicing all Jamaica since 1948 through public libraries, school libraries, bookmobiles and branch libraries), (v) teachers' college libraries, (vi) Government and special libraries and (vii) University of the West Indies libraries. The report with inputs from leading members of the Jamaican community of professional librarians gives excellent guidelines for implementation. It is for

222.   Poole, F.: *op cit* p. 3.

223.   *Plan for a National Information System for Jamaica,* p. 5.

the Government of Jamaica to address itself seriously to this important matter of information systems bearing in mind that he who is in possession of information and is master of the Information systems *owns* an important means of production. *The need to take decisions on the basis of factual data rather than on the basis of guesswork is an inescapable responsibility of Third World leaders who are plagued with scarce resources that have to be mobilised to meet excessive demands.* A development strategy without an information policy is doomed to failure. Matters are not helped when resistance is encountered from a people who have been taught to regard their history as a history of severance. For having achieved nothing, there is nothing to record, preserve or explore. The inferiority complex of a colonial experience sends its tentacles into every crevice of the human psyche and has a way of acting as effective deterrent to action. The importance of keeping records is yet to be appreciated as a cultural as well as an economic necessity in post-colonial societies.

This is no doubt part of the justifiable call for "scientific" approaches to public policy (ideological programming) by the progressive elements in the movement for change.

The Financing of Cultural Policy

The need to maximise scarce money resources by careful management of budgetary allocations through the strategic deployment of such funds as are available is a commonplace one in the exercise of cultural financing in Jamaica.

For the year 1977-78 the budget allocations to "cultural activities" provided out of the public purse were as follows:

Ja. Movement for the Advancement of Literacy Ltd. (JAMAL)	$7,282,740
Office of the Prime Minister (Central Administration)	66,696
Jamaica Festival Commission	538,070
Institute of Jamaica	1,471,711
Jamaica School of Music	263,375
Jamaica National Trust Commission	367,800
National Council on Libraries, Archives & Documentation	51,280
Jamaica National Gallery	187,000
Jamaica Broadcasting Corporation	1,000,000
Social Development Commission	150,000

Public Libraries	1,163,075
Schools Library Service	815,000
Ministry of Education	50,000
Total	$ 13,406,747

With the passage of the new Institute of Jamaica Law, the allocations for the Jamaica School of Music and the Jamaica National Gallery fall under the overall Institute budget as a matter of course. The Divisional Subventions for 1975-77 give a picture of funding for the different areas:

	1975	*1976*	*1977*
Administration	$ 192,496	249,616	337,406
West India Reference Library	213,895	246,651	297,211
Natural History Division	83,780	100,335	103,125
Museums and Archaeology	61,257	58,415	63,951
African-Caribbean Institute	101,695	116,028	100,750
Cultural Projection &			
Junior Centres	95,154	78,954	97,074
Publications	75,556	94,909	101,947
Jamaica School of Art	116,991	139,760	202,191
Jamaica School of Dance	–	49,145	68,605
Jamaica School of Drama	–	68,200	93,451
Total	$ 940,824	1,202,013	1,465,711

In addition, there have been allocations for Special Development Projects for 1977 in the amounts of $20,000 (for the West India Reference Library); $3,200 (for the Natural History Division); $1,000 (for Museums); $12,000 (for the African-Caribbean Institute); $5,300 (for Junior Centres and the Cultural Projection Programme); $38,000 (for Publications); $13,000 (for the Jamaica School of Art); $1,000 (for the Jamaica School of Dance) and $5,400 (for the Jamaica School of Drama). Such allocations have been made over the past three years on the basis of felt needs. The allocation for the Central Administration of the Institute which forms approximately 18 percent of the Institute's budget is to finance the co-ordinating functions performed by the Institute headed by an Executive Director aided by a full-time staff of some 200 "of whom 70 are professionals and 130 are technical and support staff."[224]

The largest single grant of over $7 million goes to JAMAL for the development of literacy, an activity which many regard as an inescapable infrastructural necessity for any meaningful cultural programme. The grand total of just over $13 million being the visible amount spent on cultural activities, is only a fraction of the amounts actually spent since a good deal of this comes from voluntary and other contributions to many of the agencies listed above as well as the large number of voluntary cultural groups of national and local significance. The University's Creative Arts Centre at Mona, Jamaica, operates on a recurrent grant of $84,720, 48% of which comes from the Jamaican public purse.

The Festival Commission receives anything up to $100,000 as sponsorship contributions by private business firms to specific areas of Festival each year.[225] Private benefactions in money and kind are also made to the Institute of Jamaica and its constituent divisions especially the National Gallery, and the West India Reference Library from private sources. The JAMAL Foundation is also the recipient of money benefactions from similar sources.

The Little Theatre Movement as a community theatre movement has survived for nearly forty years largely on the voluntary service and donations of private individuals and firms and continues so to do, despite strategic assistance by way of a loan from the Government of Jamaica. The National Dance Theatre Company has also developed without the advantage of a Government subsidy but with the unremunerated service of its members (dancers, singers, musicians, technicians) and the "advertising and sponsorship fees" it receives from private firms each year in the commissioning of works or the publication of an annual brochure.

---

224.   Dawes, Neville: *Cultural Policy in Jamaica* – paper for UNESCO, Institute of Jamaica, 1977.

225.   The amounts from private sponsorship have decreased since 1973-74 which experienced a high of $100,000. In 1974-75 it declined to $70,000, in 1975-76 to $39,000 and in 1977-78 to $20,000 (Festival Commission Records). There is no doubt that the abandonment of the Miss Jamaica Contest was responsible in the early years for the decrease in private funds. The 1976 and 1977 figures betray the economic crisis in the country at large.

Like the Little Theatre, revenue from gate receipts has become crucial to the Jamaica National Dance Theatre Company. Its many overseas tours are self-liquidating, at times with the help of the national airline and foreign carriers. The Jamaican Folk Singers have also depended on voluntary service, public goodwill, sponsorship, contributions from private firms and gate receipts. The role of private voluntary funding of the arts (whether in money or in service) has been vital to the development of a cultural policy in the territory. In the light of scarce money resources in the area of public financing, this particular type of funding will no doubt continue to be necessary in the foreseeable future. This suggests an appropriate funding model for art-and-culture groups in poor developing nations.

The importance of craft development to the turn-around of an ailing economy following on the world economic crisis of the mid-seventies led the Jamaican government to place the development of craft as one of the main areas of action in the Production Plan of 1977. Commenting on an end-of-year report on the performance of this Plan, a Jamaican economist wrote as follows: "The Plan had expected an extra 2,000 persons to be employed in the area of textiles and craft to offset the downturn in manufacturing. No figures are given, but it is quite clear that the extra $11 million worth of output was not achieved nor were the extra 2,000 persons employed. Three factories did begin operation under the aegis of the SDC [Social Development Commission], however, employing some 300 people mostly in Westmoreland and St. Elizabeth [parishes known for their exquisite work in straw and woodcarving]." The report also announces that 'Things Jamaican Limited' after years of being neither fish nor flesh, will be merged into the National Institute of Craft and will receive additional financing of $1.17 million. It is expected to employ some 200 people, and produce $1½ million worth of goods.[226]

International funding plays an important role. Again,

226. See article "Production Plan: shortfalls in most areas" by an Economic Analyst in *Sunday Gleaner,* January 8, 1978 (Public Affairs) p. 10.
See also Report on Emergency Production Plan.

JAMAL has been a significant beneficiary[227] and the help of UNESCO and the OAS in preparing feasibility studies for cultural projects has become a staple of cultural activity in Jamaica since the late sixties.[228] An American Development Foundation recently funded the Jamaica School of Dance's research project designed to collate and codify dance material for dissemination in schools and to discover methodologies of transmission as part of the regular learning process in primary and secondary schools.[229] It was a Portuguese Foundation (Gulbenkian) operating out of London which provided the major portion of the capital funding for the construction of the University's Creative Arts Centre and a Canadian Foundation which provided it with funds for recurrent expenses in the early days.[230]

Despite this, sources of international funding had all but dried up by the end of the sixties. Out of the Cultural and Conservation Conference jointly sponsored by the Government of Jamaica, UNESCO and the University of the West Indies in 1970, came a resolution that "steps should be taken towards the creation of a Cultural and Conservation Bank as an arm of UNESCO, to give inspiration and encouragement for the identification and preservation of the cultural heritage and the protection of the environment of developing countries on a basis similar to the encouragement and assistance given for economic development." It was the brainchild

---

227.   e.g. UNDP/UNESCO gave an early grant of $365,000. UNESCO later granted $8,200 for a Mobile unit and gift coupons in the amount of $2,000. Other donors have been World Literacy of Canada ($43,000) and the Government of New Zealand ($59,000) – JAMAL Records.

228.   See UNESCO studies on (a) *Conservation and Development of Sites and Monuments* (Sept. 1968 – April 1969) by C. Tunnard & J. C. Pollaco, (b) *Conservation of Objects Recorded from Submarine Excavations,* (Oct. 1967 to July 1968) by G. Thomson. (c) *National Information System for Jamaica (op cit* 1977) by Dorothy Collings.

229.   Grant of $142,000 (US) by the Inter-American Foundation based in Washington D.C. for a period of two years (1977-79).

230.   The Gulbenkian Foundation was the principal donor of the capital grant to the UWI for the erection of the Creative Arts Centre. A grant for recurrent expenses came later from the Old Dominion Foundation.

of the then Jamaican Minister of Finance (Edward Seaga) who also had responsibility for cultural affairs. It was submitted to the Venice Conference in August/September of that year and accepted in principle. After a number of conferences and technical meetings on the matter, an International Fund for the Promotion of Culture was established by the eighteenth session of the General Conference and subsequent meetings of the Fund's Administrative Council and Executive Committee refined the objectives of the Fund and the procedures to be followed in the administration of the Fund. The original Jamaican proposer now sits on that Council. When the Fund becomes operative it could make a significant difference to places like Jamaica, where the "provision of resources is still extremely slender in relation to needs . . . whether in respect of State budgets, of loans or technical assistance supplied by development banks, or even of the availability of bank credit facilities for artists and craftsmen."[231]

The access to strategic funds is not the least of the problems of cultural growth in the Caribbean. But for the problem to be solved or even decently approached legislators and electors must see the reinforcement of the cultural process as a developmental imperative alongside population and health, agriculture, food and nutrition, the transfer of technology, and the rationalisation of information systems. In fact there is the view that the development process is itself a cultural process — as value-loaded as it is the result and substance of scientific objective data. For "each society relies first on its own strengths and resources and defines its personalised vision of the future."[232] That the Caribbean people sometimes forget this basic fact of the developmental dialectic is a function of the cultural diaspora that many find themselves to be in, whether as alienated labouring class or deracinated transplants "uprooted" from Africa or isolated from Europe, India, China or the Levantine Coast. That the conscious address to the specifics of

231.   See UNESCO pamphlet – *International Fund for the Promotion of Culture.* (Background and General Characteristics), UNESCO, Paris.

232.   Raymont, Henry: Paper, "The Regional Program for the Cultural Development of the Organisation of the American States" (OAS, Washington, 1977).

one's own concrete experiences must have priority over spurious claims to "universality" is too frequently ignored in the face of a stifling self-contempt or lack of confidence in the region's creative potential. Yet, it is the nurturing of this self-confidence that is the greatest challenge and hope for the cultural process in praxis. And the fact of "struggle" is by no means the exclusive prerogative of the political and economic processes. Indeed, the achievement of such self-confidence and creative courage may very well be the occasion of, if not the necessary basis for, the realisation of such ideals as equality, power, social justice and cultural authenticity.

INSTITUTE OF JAMAICA
*founded 1879, restructured
under Law of 1978*

West India Reference Library
Natural History Division

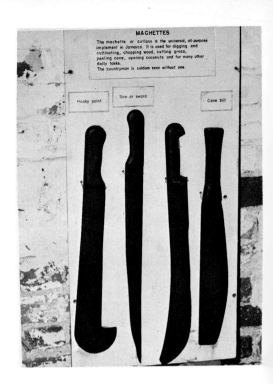

Folk Museum (artifact)
Arawak Museum (artifact)
Folk Museum, Spanish Town

THE NATIONAL GALLERY
(Institute of Jamaica)

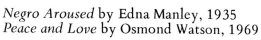

Negro Aroused by Edna Manley, 1935
Peace and Love by Osmond Watson, 1969

Ras Smoke I
by Karl Parboosingh, 1972

Grande Finale of the Tea Party by Carl Abrahams, 1955
Old Richmond by Kapo, 1972
National Gallery of Jamaica

Male Figure for Norman Manley Monument by Christopher Gonzalez, 1976

Girl Surprised by David Miller, 1949
National Gallery of Jamaica

Banana Plantation
by John Dunkley
National Gallery of Jamaica

Portrait of Edna Manley
by Albert Huie, 1940
National Gallery of Jamaica

CULTURAL TRAINING CENTRE
(Institute of Jamaica)

THE JAMAICA SCHOOL OF ART
founded by Edna Manley

THE JAMAICA SCHOOL OF MUSIC
founded by Vera Moodie

THE JAMAICA SCHOOL OF DANCE
founded by the National Dance Theatre Company

THE JAMAICA NATIONAL SCHOOL OF DRAMA
founded by the Little Theatre Movement

THE JAMAICA NATIONAL TRUST COMMISSION
Court House, Morant Bay
Old King Street, Kingston ca. 1844

THE JAMAICA FESTIVAL
established in 1963

Festival Song Winner
Costume Queen

Traditional Ritual (Kumina)
Popular Dance
Community Drama

POPULAR ENTERTAINMENT

Cabaret
Vaudeville (Gun Court Affair)

Fife & Grater
Bruckin Party (Manchioneal)

Rastafarian
Revival
Jonkonnu

POPULAR CRAFT

Wickercraft, Pottery
Crochet & Embroidery
Woodcarving, Drummaking

Calabash Carving
Basket Weaving
Gemcraft

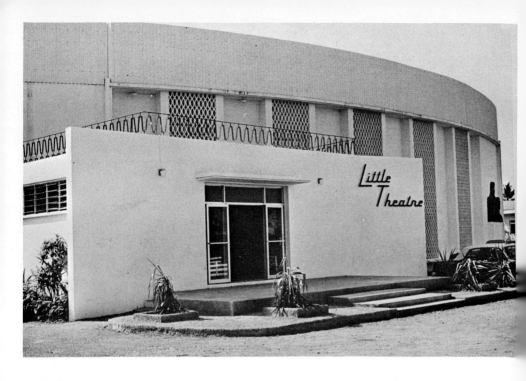

LITTLE THEATRE
built by LTM
led by Greta &
Henry Fowler

WARD THEATRE
a bequest to the
people of Kingsto
Jamaica

THE LTM NATIONAL PANTOMIME
with Louise Bennett & Ranny Williams
The pantomime is an annual theatrical
event and now a 'national institution'
in Jamaica. It was first staged on
December 26, 1940

THE JAMAICA FOLKSINGERS
led by Olive Lewin

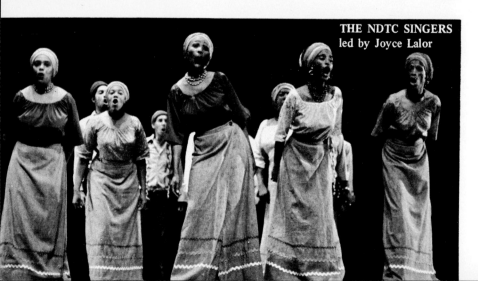

THE NDTC SINGERS
led by Joyce Lalor

REGGAE ARTISTS

Bob Marley
Jimmy Cliff
Big Yout'

Toots Hibbert
Peter Tosh
Desmond Dekker
Judy Mowatt

NDTC

National Dance Theatre Company of Jamaica

Myal

The Crossing

*Ch*oreographers

*Re*x Nettleford
*Sh*eila Barnett
Bert Rose
*Pat*sy Ricketts

NDTC

Ni-Woman of Desti

The Crossing

I Not I

Dialogue For Three

The Brothers

Ebb-Flow

West Indian drama
Shakespearean drama
Jamaican revue theatre

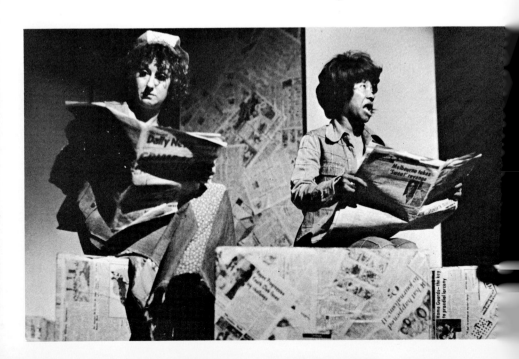

UNIVERSITY OF THE WEST INDIES (UWI)

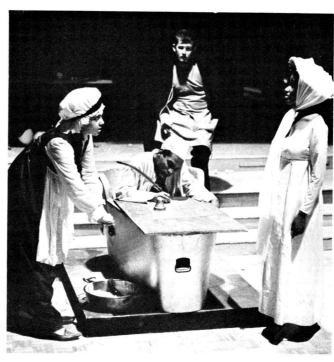

Marat Sade (production by Noel Vaz)
Carnival on the Mona campus
Creative Arts Centre

Ancestor,

Progeny

Part IV

**CULTURAL INTEGRATION
AND CO-OPERATION IN
THE WIDER CARIBBEAN
AND LATIN AMERICA**

CULTURAL INTEGRATION AND CO-OPERATION IN THE WIDER CARIBBEAN AND LATIN AMERICA

The common history of domination and the struggle for political freedom, economic viability and cultural identity and, within that framework, the common experiences in the process of creolisation offer a logical basis for ease of communication between the different communities of what is sometimes referred to as a 'sub-region' (i.e. the insular Caribbean) or a 'region' (i.e. Continental Latin America and the insular Caribbean combined). Yet there are divisive forces rooted in that very history that keep the territories culturally apart. There are, as well, the realities of geography evident in the wide expanses of water and mountain ranges, forests and rivers which separate community from community. The dominant European colonising forces have also bequeathed imprints of language, religion and other cultural forms to their different spheres of influence, placing Caracas nearer to Madrid than to Port-of-Spain and Kingston nearer to London than to Havana, Cuba, St. John's, Antigua, or Bridgetown, Barbados.

The fact is underscored by the poignant presence of distinctive culture spheres known severally as (i) Plantation America, brutalised and ravaged and for that reason endemically rebellious, (ii) Meso-America, valiantly resistant to the onslaughts of European 'discovery' and correspondingly majestic in its ancestral certitude, and (iii) Euro-America, still the active and often assertive purveyor of the ideas and technology of the Conqueror-forebears and therefore reflective of that ambivalence with which any thrust towards regional co-operation must contend.[233]

233. All the Commonwealth Caribbean, Haiti, Cuba, Santo Domingo as well as the Eastern littoral of the American continent from Nova Scotia to Northern Uruguay are good examples of Plantation America where Europe has met Africa on foreign soil; Meso-America is represented best by the evolving cultural ethos of places like Mexico, Peru and Guatemala; Euro-America is represented by Argentina, Chile and the greater United States and Canada. In many of these territories there are manifestations of all three culture spheres though one may be the most dominant in each case.

These particular differences do underscore a sense of separateness. Yet within some territories all three culture spheres are known to co-exist sometimes in pluralist uneasiness and dynamic counterpoint struggle. The entire region possesses this sense of struggle and there are those Caribbean and Latin American persons who entertain a romantic vision of the sea as a connecting link though it in fact breaks up the string of rocks which form the Caribbean archipelago and merely washes the littoral of some Latin American nations. "Mare nostrum" was a popular phrase with the Cuban patriot, José Martí. It is echoed by compatriots like Guillén. Geo-political realities run parallel with cultural sensibilities. Cuba now sees herself as a "Caribbean nation" and the Cubans as "Afro-Latins." The common heritage of slavery, imperial domination and struggle has made the Caribbean archipelago one "communal yard."[234] The decision by the four independent countries of the Commonwealth Caribbean to extend full diplomatic recognition to Cuba in 1973 opened up a new era in regional co-operation that has forged greater links between Anglophone and Hispanic Caribbean in unprecedented ways and, in the case of the Jamaica-Cuba link, has even created problems for some who thrive on traditional Cold War Hemispheric geo-political assumptions. The implications for cultural co-operation in the strictly artistic sense manifest themselves in the exchange of cultural groups, individual artists and the signing of cultural agreements but they extend, as well, to the deeper issues of social and economic organisation that progressives in territories like Jamaica and Guyana feel will free a post-colonial people from fear, want, ignorance and disease. The now legendary achievements of revolutionary Cuba in the areas of agriculture, self-reliance, education and literacy as well as community health care are frequently cited as models for emulation; and the economic and political system that supports such achievement is correspondingly invoked in support of the advocacy for closer neighbourly links.[235]

234. Guillén, Nicolás: Acceptance speech on the Award of the Musgrave Gold Medal of Jamaica. *Jamaica Journal*, Vol. 9, No. 1, p. 26.

235. Cultural exchanges between Cuba and Jamaica have been as follows: 1973 – delegation of artists and writers to Cuba; 1974 – Cuban Folkloric Ballet to Jamaica, Exhibition of Cuban paintings in Jamaica, visit of Jamaica National Dance Theatre to Cuba, visit of Jamaican musical group (Light of Saba) to Cuba; 1975 – Visit of

But this idea is contingent on the cultural realities too. For the constraining commitment to the idea-system(s) of the colonial past presumably prevents political leaders throughout the region from taking bold decisions for programmes leading to fundamental change. The resolution in ideological terms throws up new problems depending on what government is in power: Guyana and Jamaica which now commit themselves to a "socialist solution" in politico-economic terms may find difficulty relating ideologically to the twin-island state of Trinidad and Tobago or with Barbados — a state of affairs reminiscent of countries of Latin America which have in the past found difficulty accommodating each other in the Organisation of American States (OAS).

New developments in the OAS itself since the mid-seventies are significant enough. For one thing Cuba is no longer the anathema she once was to all the members of the Organisation. For another, the countries of the Commonwealth Caribbean now regard themselves as part of the Inter-American System and have decided to become members of the OAS, though they do not cherish the idea of their being tacked on to Latin America for administrative convenience in some of the councils of the wider world. The frank speaking by the Caribbean novitiates adds a new dimension to the Hemispheric dialogue. Moreover due emphasis on the rationalisation and optimum use of the technical and professional services of the hemispheric club will no doubt assume greater priority over the now well-known geo-political apprehensions about the might and power of the United States of America, the richest and biggest member of the club. Back in the Caribbean itself, strong common cultural roots at times exercise the sensibilities of the new Caribbean man far more vigorously than certain geo-political considerations and throw up rank shoots of yearning for greater co-operation.

Cuban writers to Jamaica, visit of Jamaican cultural administrators to Cuba; 1976 — Cuban pop music bands, Cuban Modern Dance Company to Jamaica (Carifesta), Jamaica reggae band to Cuba, Exhibition of Jamaican Primitive painters in Havana, Exhibition of Cuban Primitive painters in Jamaica; 1977 — Cuban artistic delegation to Jamaica, Cuban Ballet Nacional (dir. Alicia Alonso) to Jamaica, Jamaican artistic delegation to Cuba (with Minister for Information and Culture).

The idea of *regional festivals of arts* comes to mind most readily. As means to cultural co-operation they can be plausibly justified as a way of investing historical tendencies with positive force and as a device to forge the solidarity of the Caribbean collective consciousness. The Caribbean Festivals of Arts (Carifesta) held first in Guyana in 1972 and in Jamaica four years later certainly made strong claims to such aspirations. It was one of the many "dreams" of Forbes Burnham, Prime Minster of Guyana, that there should be a "Caribbean Arts Festival, featuring Guyanese and Caribbean artists whose work in poetry, painting and sculpture project our dreams and visions and help to foster and develop a Caribbean personality . . ."[236] Such dreams had in fact been dreamt before and realised in part as far back as 1952 when the first extensive *Caribbean* Festival of Arts was held in San Juan, Puerto Rico.[237] The Haitians and the Puerto Ricans were in bold attendance as were the Trinidadians and the Jamaicans, then still under British colonialism. With the launching in 1958 of the West Indian Federation (involving territories under British rule), a parallel Festival of Arts spearheaded by the University's Extra Mural Department with the support of the government of Trinidad and Tobago, was held and all the constituent territories of the new federal state participated. A revival of the idea of a regional arts festival gained new currency with the Guyanese Prime Minister's initiative on the occasions of Guyana's Independence and Republic celebrations in 1966 and 1970 respectively when the Guyanese government extended personal invitations to leading Caribbean writers and artists. Bacchanalian indulgences did nothing to prevent the seriousness of approach to the forging of regional cultural links

236. Burnham, Forbes: in Address to Caribbean Writers and Artists Conference held in Guyana, May, 1966.

237. Mapletoft Poulle, the Jamaican orchestra leader who participated along with the Ivy Baxter Dance Group, the Frats Quintet (singers) and a number of Jamaican painters and sculptors in the 1952 (Puerto Rican) Festival, reminds readers of such Caribbean-wide festivals predating Carifesta I. See his letter to the editor of the *Daily Gleaner,* September 22, 1972. For Reports on the 1952 Festival see *Public Opinion,* August 9, 1952 and *Daily Gleaner* August 10 and 18, 1952. See also Baxter, Ivy: *op cit* p. 301.

and the idea was kept alive by enthusiastic advocates so much so that one of the main recommendations of the Cultural and Conservation Conference held in 1970 in Jamaica under the joint auspices of UNESCO, the University of the West Indies and the Government of Jamaica read as follows: "Governments of the territories of the Caribbean be asked to support any action that might be initiated especially *periodical inter-Caribbean Festivals including films, art, and tourist promotion in the region . . .*"[238] Besides the Anglophone Caribbean, the Netherlands Antilles and Surinam, Mexico, Cuba, Puerto Rico, Haiti, Venezuela and even Canada and the United States were represented. Such broad-based participation was to reflect itself in the first Carifesta which had participants from Brazil as well. The second Carifesta held in Jamaica attracted a group from Martinique, despite its organic administrative attachment to metropolitan France. It was Aimé Césaire, the Martiniquan-born mayor of Fort-de-France who took the initiative and raised funds for a contingent to participate in Carifesta '76 despite an apparent coolness on the part of the metropolitan government. But then this great founding spirit of the Negritude movement had always identified with the Caribbean and had even encouraged the appearance of the Jamaican Folk Singers in Martinique before the Carifesta event in Kingston.

The aims and objectives of the 1976 Carifesta were outlined as follows: (1) to expose the people of the region to each other's culture through creative activity, thus deepening their knowledge and awareness of the native aspirations of their neighbours; (2) to forge through cultural participation closer relations between peoples of the region; (3) to demonstrate the importance of the arts as a unifying force in building a wholesome society; and (4) to develop the content of our regional culture as well as its aesthetic forms.[239] Objectives (3) and (4) echoed the call for an "educational" dimension by the Cultural and Conservation conferees in 1970. For the "deterioration" of the Carifesta exercise

238. *Report of the Cultural and Conservation Conference,* July 29 to August 2, 1970 (mimeographed).

239. Souvenir Programme, Carifesta (Jamaica) '76, p. 5.

into mere minstrelsy or self-indulgent ostentation is feared by a good enough number of Caribbean people who may be regarded as too solemn in their approach to cultural development but who are, in fairness, well aware of the historical trap of substituting instantaneous "effervescence" for sustained meaningful work. The organisers of the second Carifesta felt it was important to state that "Carifesta '76 continues to demonstrate the positive connection between cultural expression and the struggle for political and economic self-determination."[240] Forbes Burnham in his earlier addresses to the Caribbean writers and artists had himself pointedly stressed the importance of grass-roots participation in any Caribbean Festival of Arts and the Guyanese exercise in 1972 fulfilled that aim beyond any doubt.

Despite such exhortations and declarations, not all are enthused by the idea of Caribbean Festivals. Derek Walcott, whose artistic credentials are unquestionable, is skeptical about the paroxysmic carousings that such Festivals frequently promote. Such transient diversions should give way to more lasting commitments, he seems to feel. What is the society "doing to house the artist, to make him feel he should remain? Why should he go and jump up and down three times and meet somebody and have a Scotch?" Walcott asks. He is also of the view that Governments merely "require the visible evidence of the artist" when they wish to host other countries or "at a convenient time to show that there is art in the Caribbean, then as fools we will all go together, jump up and down three times and go home . . . to nothing."[241] It is this fear of going home "to nothing" after the noise and din of celebration, which invites a skepticism about grand spectacle being mistaken for serious cultural achievement. It is significant that the most successful offerings in the first Carifesta came from countries like Jamaica and Cuba which had something to go home to in the sense of an on-going home-grown movement in cultural expression The Trinidadians whose own phenomenal Carnival has long become

240. *Ibid*, p. 9.

241. *Jamaica Daily News* (Xaymaca, Sunday Magazine) Dec. 7, 1975. Interview with Derek Walcott, written by Ric Mentus.

more than an annual show were not substantively represented in this sense though their influence through the steel-pan music was everywhere evident. Guyana herself was to learn from Carifesta and the country's National Council of History and Culture soon after embarked on a rational programme of cultural development involving the encouragement and official promotion of training in the arts as well as the systematic conservation of the Guyanese heritage.[242]

The point that needs to be explicitly made with regard to the foregoing discussion is that individual territories of the region must commit themselves to the building up of capabilities to encourage cultural growth within their borders as a priority rather than indulge the glamour of regional spectacles, however beneficially cathartic or politically convenient these may be seen to be. That the two are not mutually exclusive can, no doubt, be plausibly argued but the constraint of inadequate funds forces on governments of the region who are serious about development, inescapable choices — a factor not always appreciated by international organisations which may find it more satisfying to list in their annual reports large numbers of Caribbean and Latin American countries as having participated in this or that "festival." What is more, the evaluation of the effect of such arts festivals on meaningful cultural development is seldom undertaken though there is evidence enough of continuing contact between individual artists and cultural planners from all over the region after an initial meeting at these festivals.

One salutary development has been the inclusion in these Arts Festivals of colloquia, symposia, workshops and seminars all designed to come to grips with the deep issues of Caribbean history, literature, media, and cultural development. This was facilitated in the 1976 Carifesta by the presence of the University of the West Indies and the availability of scholars

---

242. Lynette Dolphin, Frank Pilgrim, A. J. Seymour who had all figured in the organisation of the first Carifesta were to be the administrative anchors of the Guyanese National Council.

and researchers who could give advice on, as well as participate in the planning and operation of such exercises. This at once directs attention to crucial points of institutional contact for effective regional collaboration.

The University of the West Indies complemented by the younger University of Guyana, represents one such point of contact. No effort at cultural integration and co-operation in the Caribbean region can be fulfillingly pursued without positive reference to such institutions and particularly the *University of the West Indies* which has served the Anglo-phone territories since 1948 and has a strong track record in the field of cultural studies and cultural action. Its presence has indeed made a significant difference to the quality of cultural and intellectual life in the Commonwealth Caribbean as part of the decolonising process. The teaching departments, research institutes, and the outreach (extramural) activities have together produced a network of activities which facilitate the sharing of new and old knowledge and have inspired new perspectives about Caribbean society and development despite the much articulated complaint by political leaders from some of the contributing territories that the manpower supply from the institution is inadequate if not all but useless. The West Indian University, admittedly, is also vulnerable on the question of its unspectacular display of intellectual daring in terms of the early restructuring of curricula and a bold and immediate thrust in new areas of inquiry contingent on third world developmental needs. But for all its 'Oxbridge' orienta-tion and certain clear Eurocentric biases, the University of the West Indies has been a major instrument of indigenous
cultural change in the region, raising levels of consciousness among its graduates and teachers — an achievement which has in turn fed not only rivers of rhetoric but also programmes of action in vital areas of the region's life.[243]

243. See *Beginnings,* a 16mm documentary film directed by Lennie Littlewhite of Mediamix, Jamaica. Also, the polemics of the New World group which operated out of the Faculty of Social Sciences during the mid-Sixties stimulated much discussion and interest in such topics as multinational economics and regional

In the field of creative artistic endeavour, the University has led the way in laying foundations for serious cultural co-operation, if not integration. It has encouraged Caribbean-wide activity in the creative arts through its summer schools, workshops, seminars and symposia.[244] It has encouraged research into and the wider dissemination of Caribbean folklore and folkculture.[245] It has created opportunities for individual artists and performing groups to express themselves in the fields of their special aptitude and interest through regular classes in many territories, through grants for study outside of the region, through grants to summer schools with visiting tutors, through training in the Jamaica School of Art for example, (Extra Mural Resident Tutors sometimes see themselves as scouts for talent) and through assistance in kind or money to dancers and actors. It has housed and nurtured leading Caribbean artists and cultural animateurs, innovators and planners either as students or as members of its academic staff.[246] The services of its academic employees have been liberally

economic integration. Community health and health care delivery have also developed out of the work throughout the region by the UWI's Department of Social and Preventive Medicine. Important research into food, nutrition and agriculture continue apace with not insignificant results.

244. See Annual Reports of the Staff Tutor in Drama and Resident Tutors for Jamaica, Trinidad and Tobago, Belize, St. Lucia, Antigua, Grenada and Montserrat especially.

245. e.g. the early research work into the folklore of Trinidad and elsewhere. See "A Rada Community in Trinidad" by Andrew T. Carr, *Caribbean Quarterly,* Vol. 3, No. 1 (1954) pp. 36-54 "Form and Style in a Bahamian Folktale" by Daniel J. Crowley in *Caribbean Quarterly,* Vol. 3, No. 4 (1954), pp. 218-234 also his "Festival of the Calendar in St. Lucia" in *Caribbean Quarterly,* Vol. 4, No. 2 (1955), pp. 97-121. Numbers 3 and 4 of the same Volume 4 was devoted to the Trinidad Carnival and among the contributors were Andrew Pearse, Daniel Crowley and Andrew Carr all of whom received early support from Philip Sherlock in the Extra Mural Department.

246. Outstanding examples are the St. Lucian Derek Walcott, the Guyanese Slade Hopkinson and the Jamaican Dennis Scott — all of whom are poet-playwrights and were students at UWI, Jamaican Carroll Dawes, a creative director of plays. Members of the academic staff who have worked in the cultural field from the campuses of the University are Errol Hill and Noel Vaz (dramatists), Edward Brathwaite (poet and animateur), Mervyn Morris (poet), John Hearne (novelist), Sylvia Wynter (critic and playwright), Gordon Rohlehr (critic), Rex Nettleford (choreographer

utilised by the governments of the respective supporting territories and significant aspects of artistic cultural life in many such territories depend on the University presence for their sustenance. The annual Festival of Arts of Belize operates out of the UWI Resident Tutor's office which liaises with the Department of Extra Mural Studies head office in Jamaica for provision of adjudicators and trainers. The St. Lucia art movement was for a decade part of the UWI's Extra Mural programme in that territory. The Leeward Islands Arts Festival of the late fifties was organised by the UWI tutor stationed in Antigua and the Resident Tutor currently located there is herself a moving spirit behind the Antigua arts movement as is the tutor in Montserrat in respect of the Montserrat creative arts programme. Carnival does belong to the people of Trinidad but the University's Engineering department is doing serious research on the steel-pan. The Extra Mural Department runs well attended annual summer schools in the creative arts on the St. Augustine campus, Trinidad.

In Jamaica the University's first Director of Extra Mural Studies who was also the Vice-Principal of the then University College and later the Vice-Chancellor of an independent UWI[247] was a poet and historian as well as a former advocate of cultural development throughout the region. He was to employ the Department of Extra Mural Studies as a base of operation for cultural research, the promotion of literature and the performing arts, as well as for the dissemination of material on Caribbean cultural life through the journal *Caribbean Quarterly*. The present incumbent[248] continues in this tradition. He not only creates dance works for what is regarded as a major dance-theatre company in the Commonwealth Caribbean, he also advises the Jamaican government on cultural policy and follows through in the operational areas as

and animateur). The dramatist and playwright Errol Hill who teaches in a New England college took leave of absence from the University to pursue Fine Arts courses in the United States leading to the doctoral degree. His thesis was on the Trinidad Carnival.

247. i.e. Philip Sherlock. See footnote 184 above.

248. i.e. the author of this essay who is now Professor of Extra Mural Studies.

Chairman of the Institute of Jamaica which is charged with the implementation of cultural development programmes in the territory. These include the areas of cultural education offered largely through the national schools of training. The fact is that it is his employment in the University which makes most of this "public service" possible, and his headship of the Extra Mural Department facilitates frequent contact with others involved in cultural development in the region and therefore widens his influence and the quality of its impact.

The early work of the Creative Arts Centre on the Mona campus has already been discussed. A historian employed to the University[249] was founder of the Caribbean Artists Movement (CAM) the short-lived active life of which has been survived by a stimulating periodical, *Savacou,* which publishes essays on cultural and historical matters. In addition, many cultural bodies throughout the Commonwealth Caribbean draw on the University for some of their most active members and leaders. The University has even provided a vibrant forum for philosophical debate on the nature, direction and scope of Caribbean cultural authenticity as well as a Caribbean aesthetic.[250] The summer and other vacation courses offered in the creative arts from one end of the region to the next have served to help sharpen the skills and develop the craft of teachers in the school system and to guide gifted amateurs to professional standards. Today the creative arts continue to be one of the main pillars of the University's outreach programme of activities. Their importance is reflected in a recommendation of an Inter-Governmental Committee on Caribbean University Education which called for a Staff Tutor in creative arts to serve the entire Eastern Caribbean.[251]

---

249. i.e. Edward Brathwaite, the poet who is also editor of *Savacou,* lectures extensively in the Caribbean and North America on African-Caribbean literature and history and was once slated to be director of cultural programmes in his native Barbados.

250. See above footnote 91 for fuller discussion of the student occupation of the Creative Arts Centre on the West Indies University campus in 1970.

251. *Second Report of the Inter-Governmental Committee on Caribbean University Education* by William E. Demas, p. 46, para. 119 (g).

In the wider cultural field, the University has spearheaded much that has gone by the name of 'citizenship education' designed to prepare the citizenry of the Commonwealth Caribbean now for self-government, now for Federation, now for Independence, now for nation-building which rests on the conviction that Caribbean peoples themselves can be creators of their own destiny. Many a practising politician was to receive his continuing education through such University "extra mural" classes.[252]

But probably the greatest and most telling effort of the University's presence in respect of raising the consciousness of the first post-1938 generation around to its creative potential as "first persons" in the region was the release of a stream of graduates steeped in new knowledge of the history and social studies of the Caribbean. Much of this took place in the fifties primarily through the Department of History; and the names of Elsa Goveia, Roy Augier, John Parry, and later Douglas Hall were to invest the exercise of teaching and research with a revolutionary dimension, the force of which is easy to underestimate simply because it revealed itself in the realm of sound and solid scholarship rather than in the heady fervour of rhetoric and polemics which were later to characterise the protest movements emanating from the campuses in the late sixties and early seventies.[253] History as an academic discipline has been introduced from 1950. Teaching in the Social Sciences, another important academic area of cultural importance was not introduced until 1959. But before that the Institute of Social and Economic Research had offered an excellent vehicle for scholars like M.G. Smith and Lloyd Braithwaite whose contribution to Caribbean self-perception cannot be overemphasised. Between

252.   Long-serving politicians like Forbes Burnham and Dr Cheddi Jagan of Guyana and George Price of Belize were regular attendants at public lecture series offered by the Extra Mural Department in the early fifties.

253.   Dr Elsa Goveia was to become Professor of West Indian History, Dr Roy Augier, Pro-Vice Chancellor on the Mona Campus; Professor John Parry at the time of writing held a chair at Harvard University after heading a university in Nigeria and another in Wales while Dr Hall, a former Extra Mural Resident Tutor, was to become Professor of History based at Mona, Jamaica. The 'protest movements of the sixties' refer to the Black Power and Student Power movements which flourished from 1968 on.

these historians and social scientists[254] aided and abetted by others like Shirley Gordon and John Figueroa in Education and Philip Sherlock, as cultural historian and university administrator, a wide range of subjects came within the purview of intellectual inquiry throwing up a corpus of knowledge which was to be tapped by a later generation of evolved Caribbean peoples who had learnt to take political self-government as given, if not for granted. Slavery and its consequences, plantation societies and their persistent features, colonialism and decolonisation, the creolisation process, neo-colonialism with all its economic, social, political and cultural manifestations, race and ethnicity, peasant life and culture, Caribbean literature and creative arts — all these have become areas of deep study and concern for a long list· of Caribbean historians, social scientists, and cultural anthropologists operating out of the University of the West Indies and even the United States.

The UWI, then, as a viable instrument of regional collaboration in cultural development has to be taken into account. Like universities and research institutes anywhere, the UWI is indeed "uniquely suited to foster and advancé co-operation, since [it exists] primarily to add to mankind's store of knowledge, to disseminate knowledge and to enlarge understanding." It is Philip Sherlock who asserts with conviction that "no government nor combination of governments, no commerical nor trading organisations, no common markets nor free trade areas can fulfill what are university functions, the search for knowledge by means of objective and free enquiry and the sharing of that knowledge."[255] The moral of this statement is that the building up of indigenous research capabilities in the Caribbean region is best done by its universities.

---

254. Professor M. G. Smith (later Professor of Social Anthropology at Kings College London) is the father of Caribbean pluralism (see footnote 1 above). He was to become a special adviser to the Government of Jamaica from 1972 and has academic engagements in Nigeria (where he has done extensive research on the emirates) and Yale. Lloyd Brathwaite is one of the region's pioneer sociologists whose work on racial stratification in Trinidad remains a significant seminal study. He was to become Pro-Vice Chancellor and Principal of the St. Augustine campus of the UWI.

255. Sherlock, Philip: *Report of the Secretary General — Association of Caribbean Research Institutes,* UNICA, 1972, p. 3.

But such scientific inquiry has become expensive and this in turn according to Sherlock means that "in regions like the Caribbean, where resources are limited and where there is always the possibility of the finest minds being attracted away to larger countries, *university co-operation* is an important way of narrowing the gap in the world of scholarship between the 'haves' and the 'have-nots.' "[256]

Such university co-operation has expressed itself in the establishment of the *Association of Caribbean Universities and Research Institutes* or UNICA. This came out of a meeting of a number of Caribbean universities and research institutes held at the University of Puerto Rico, San Juan on November 28th, 1968. The conference articulated the aims and objective of UNICA as follows: "To foster contact between member universities and institutes, (a) through conferences and meetings of a general or specific nature, (b) through the circulation of information . . . about enrollment, development, plans, staffing . . . scholarships and fellowships, admission requirements, building programmes, etc. (c) through collaboration between groups of research institutes and professional faculties such as Medicine, Engineering, Agriculture, Education and Social Sciences, (d) through facilitating co-operation and the pooling of institutional resources in research . . . to promote increased efficiency and to expedite the attainment of results, (e) through studies of the systems of higher education in the region, through seminars, surveys, research papers, publications, (f) through serving as a point of contact between other international and national university associations and (g) through encouraging the exchange of staff and students particularly at the graduate level."[257]

Out of this were to emerge plans for action programmes which placed emphasis on studies into agriculture, health, education, science and technology and the social sciences. The developmental orientation of such programmes gave to UNICA a certain credibility, modernity and relevance which have attracted to it a wide membership covering universities and research institutes from

256. *Ibid.*

257. *Ibid.*

Florida through the islands of the Caribbean (Anglophone, Francophone and Hispanic) to the Netherlands Antilles, Venezuela and Colombia. It need hardly be stressed that the capacity for collaboration and effective co-operation has been greatly affected by the constraints of inadequate funding, a communication gap which is the legacy of a language barrier, and by competing priorities between the group and the constituent members each of which serves a separate political jurisdiction which may at any given time desire specific outputs from its institution of higher learning. Such constraints notwithstanding, an association of Caribbean and Latin American universities is potentially a powerful instrument of cultural cohesion in the region that shares a common process of renewal and growth as well as the Third World anxieties of giving form and purpose to a habitually dependent and underdeveloped situation.

International funding agencies will no doubt find difficulty deciding between the competing claims of a University of the West Indies or a University of Guyana on the one hand and the association of universities of which either university is a part. It is for the Caribbean and Latin American universities to get their own spheres of activity clearly defined in terms of what areas are under autonomous jurisdiction and what are co-ordinate. One thing is certain; the wealth of specialist knowledge that exists among Caribbean scholars about the circumstances and conditions of the region need to be shared between each other to help defeat the persistent tendencies of dependency on outside (usually metropolitan) expertise and to build up cultural confidence as aid to regional development. The well tested device of conferences and colloquia, inviting both Commonwealth Caribbean and Latin American writers, scholars or artists, needs to be promoted as an accepted means of sharing knowledge and experience. It is prudent to emphasise that the universities in the region are not the only agencies capable of promoting or organising such meetings.[258] For lurking behind all

258. Cp. the work of the Institute of Jamaica, or the Centro de Estudios Afro-Colombianos which organised its first Conference on negro culture in August 1977 for Latin America and the Caribbean.

this is the likely shadow of doubt that universities are by nature exclusive and cannot therefore meet all the cultural needs of the region. The argument usually invokes the dangers of the ivory-tower nature of academia and the elitist orientation of the Caribbean university institutions. But this is to ignore the realities of the process which requires of all civilisations the capacity to plough deep into their own experiences and isolate by systematic selection and analysis the principles which regulate and guide such experiences so that life can be enriched and more fully grasped. This is sometimes done in relatively solitary confinement and at other times in the humdrum of everyday activity. Part detachment and part involvement are after all stocks in the academic trade besides being the contradictory omens of any meaningful learning process.

The advancement of knowledge has rested on just this phenomenon and the mastery of the methods of intellectual inquiry as well as the understanding of their application are part of the cultural responsibility of any civilisation worthy of the name. The mistake is often made in assuming that such a process resides exclusively in "universities". But the concentration of the activity of intellectual enquiry in a university merely focusses rather than monopolises what is fundamentally a common enough human activity necessary to the development of all mankind. The investment by Caribbean university institutions in programmes which are designed to foster cultural growth is therefore a sound one. And the study of the creative output of the vast majority of the Caribbean people is a proper job for such institutions. It would be a pity if the capacity to *think* is dismissed as too elitist an indulgence for the people of the Caribbean simply because they have come to be seen as 'naturals' in such seemingly 'less complex' forms of human activity as movement, song, or theatrical mimicry.

For the region needs its universities and research institutes to do the work of building up a corpus of that specialist knowledge required for the greater understanding of man and society, including Caribbean man and his society as well as the processes through which he works for self-actualisation and self-expression. The 'disciplines' which have led man towards this greater knowledge of self are varied and have indeed expanded over the past century from the conventional arts and humanities to the social sciences. The discovery of self and the articulation of cultural identities need the service of the *social sciences* but it is well to remember that these "sciences" form "a group of disciplines which have highly diversified intellectual traditions, methodological foundations and theoretical orientations and which . . . have undergone very considerable modification both in scope and focus."[259] Exaggerated claims by empiricists attempting to give scientific legitimacy to palpably unquantifiable variables of human behaviour have battled with scholarly intuition sometimes reinforced by 'poetic' insights of writers and the bold speculative eye of philosopher-types. Together they are nevertheless able to throw some light on the realities of existence and for the Caribbean, as for elsewhere, "if the social sciences are to perform their legitimate and indispensable function in development as regards both problem-illumination and problem-solving, it is necessary to achieve better balance between disciplines."[260]

At least one cultural regional body is echoing this view. The new Director of the Regional Programme for Cultural Development of the *Organisation of American States* sees "culture" as the "science of man — a discipline which deals with the data of anthropology, psychology, theology, mythology, sociology, economics and art as far as they are relevant to the understanding of man."[261] Following the lead from many member states, the OAS seems prepared to be responsive to what is deemed to be "a clear mandate for a far-reaching imaginative programme." Such a programme must indeed "strengthen the national institutions, incorporating

259. *Man at the Centre of the Problem,* Chap. III. Objective 3, 3 UNESCO, Paris.

260. *Ibid.* The body of literature that has come out of the efforts of Caribbean political scientists, sociologists, cultural anthropologists, historians, economists, novelists, poets, art critics, folklorists together give an excellent picture of the inner dynamics of Caribbean development over the past century and more. A Caribbean Studies course which fails to take into account all these different "disciplines" through which Caribbean society has been analysed is not likely to serve its purpose of giving full understanding of the region to those who pursue it.

261. See Henry Raymont in position paper on the Regional Program for Cultural Development of the OAS (mimeographed) dated March 22, 1977.

culture within the general framework of the economic and social, educational and scientific technological development of the countries."[262] The declarations have been many, sonorous and well-intentioned but budgetary constraints constantly thwart the translation of declaration into action. So the area of science and technology can boast a target of $15 million for foreseeable biennia and some $10 million for education but *culture* (the last to be considered) has been set $1 million and makes do with an actual operational budget of half a million dollars for the entire Latin America and the Caribbean.[263]

Yet in these matters absolute financial amounts do not definitively determine the development or otherwise of cultural affairs. The careful and strategic deployment of the available funds is what is more important and the need for the cultural committee (CIDEC) of the Inter-American Council for Education, Science and Culture to identify national subregional "cultural institutions" as well as projects likely to have a multiplier effect nationally and regionally is far more important than being able to dispense largesse from ostensibly limitless funds. A thorough on-going study, codification and classification of cultural institutions throughout Latin America and the Caribbean would be of more than archival interest: it could provide a firm basis on which to give the kind of assistance that can in turn form the basis for cultural action regionally, subregionally and in the individual territories themselves. What is not needed is a regional bureaucracy designed to swallow up scarce resources in over-extensive travelling by 'experts' whose job may be merely to outline procedures of meetings and conferences when such resources ought to be spent in the actual programme areas of cultural action. The collaborative work with universities, profes-

262. *Ibid.* See also the *Bahia Standards,* Final Report of the Sixth Meeting of CIDEC held in May 1973 in Salvador (Bahia) Brazil — OAS Ser J/XII CIDEC doc. 31, p. 8; also the *Cuenca Standards* in Final Report of the Eighth Meeting of CIDEC held in Cuenca and Quito, May 31, 1974, p. 13 — OAS Ser J/XII CIDEC doc. 40.

263. Raymont, Henry: *op cit.* The Carter Administration in 1977 decided to match the $500,000 level of the OAS culture grant so that by 1978 the total allocation for culture could reach the $1 million goal set by the Sixth Meeting of the Inter-American Council for Education, Science and Culture (Mexico, January 1975).

sional associations and other national, regional or international bodies should be further complemented by direct assistance to voluntary groups of enterprising persons of proven creative talent within the region. The building of people must in some places take precedence over the conservation of ruins.[264] The encouragement of genuine creativity rising out of the textured life and experience of the region should be taken far more seriously than hitherto even if it means placing less emphasis on the promotion of competent Caribbean and Latin American versions of established European art-expressions.

More precisely, bodies like the OAS cultural committee which can be a co-ordinating agency for Caribbean and Latin American cultural activity will have to be more aggressively committed to the cultural expressions that come out of the actual experience of Latin America and the Caribbean and be prepared to give less support to the products of a lingering desire to be facsimiles of European high culture. Even in giving the Caribbean and Latin American citizens of African descent the dignity of human existence, it is important that the pursuit of "African continuities" in all aspects of the African's development in the Diaspora be seen in terms of the process of re-ordering, rejection, renewal and innovation. The assumption that other comers to the Americas have not undergone a similar process is to be discouraged for besides being a blatant falsehood it deprives the region of the dynamic of its intrinsic creative potential and fails to recognise its capacities to produce creators and original creative work of its own. Indeed, it is this process of cultural growth which links the entire region together and offers a common purpose to the peoples of Latin America and the Caribbean as progenies from the cultural and biological mixtures between the original indigenous Americans and the 'newcomers'

264. The year 1978 was declared "Ano de la Recuperacion del Patrimonio Monumental de America" by the OAS. This author pleaded with the CIDEC committee that the literal translation, "monumental heritage", be not construed to mean the restoration or recovery of just pyramids, sugarmills, old churches and the like but also of the ancestral spirit of the Americas as is evident in other areas of cultural expression as the performing and plastic arts, oral literature, handicrafts, folklore and history.

since the fifteenth century from across the Atlantic on the one hand, and these later newcomers drawn from a variety of continents, on the other. If efforts at cultural integration and co-operation did nothing more than get Latin American and Caribbean neighbours to understand the nature of and common sharing in this process, the chasm which now exists between these ex-colonial spheres through the elements of language, geography, ethnic exclusivity and even ideological biases would be narrowed if not totally obliterated. Institutions, mechanisms and funding patterns for cultural co-operation in the region ignore this at their peril.

There is a grave responsibility awaiting the administrators of the proposed Inter-American Fund for cultural development (FIDEC) which is a clear carbon copy of UNESCO's International Fund for the Promotion of Culture.[265] It is to be implemented by the Pan American Development Foundation (PADF). The penultimate paragraph of a draft describing the fund reads as follows: "Resources from the Fund's activities shall be used preferentially to support and strengthen the cultural development program prepared and being implemented by the Department of Cultural Affairs, pursuant to the objectives established in Article 100 of the Charter of the OAS . . ."[266] Article 100 of the OAS Charter reads as follows: "The purpose of the Inter-American Council for Education, Science and Culture is to promote friendly relations and mutual understanding between the peoples of the Americas through educational, scientific, and cultural co-operation and exchange between Member States, in order to raise the cultural level of the peoples, reaffirm their dignity as individuals, prepare them fully for the tasks of progress, and strengthen the devotion to peace, democracy and social justice that has characterised their evolution".

The language of the Article is appropriately replete with noble intentions. It will no doubt prove perfectly palatable to Carib-

---

265. FIDEC came out of the Declaration of Arequipa which was approved by the XII regular meeting of CIDEC on July 14, 1976 and later approved by CEPCIECC — i.e. the Executive Committee.

266. Draft Paper on Inter-American Fund for the Development of Culture; OAS, Washington D.C.

bean cultural directorates; but only as long as a misguided missionary zeal does not in practice send regional experts raising "the cultural levels of people" who may be seen as being culturally deprived for not having built the equivalents of the Arc de Triomphe, the Pyramids, the leaning Tower of Pisa or the Eiffel Tower or for not having had Conservatoires of Music, Symphony Orchestras, Opera Houses or Fine Art Galleries. Just as bad would be the other position, usually prompted by a quaint inverted snobbery, which sees virtue and purpose in the preservation of some primordial primitive innocence among "the people", no doubt in an effort "to re-affirm their dignity as individuals." These two deadly sins are not restricted to do-gooders and humbugs from outside the Caribbean and Latin America, one might add: they are frequently to be found among opposing camps of culture-determiners deep in the heart of the region itself.

In all this the implications for funding or aid agencies (whether external or intra-regional) are far-reaching. It is true that development funding in the past had benefited largely privileged minorities throughout the Third World but it is equally dangerous for funding agencies or even intra-regional policy-determiners to now rush indiscriminately into a breathless search of the "grassroots" and "rural folk" as exclusive objects for "development." It is significant that the grassroot voters of the Caribbean very seldom display a taste for a political leadership which is illiterate, ignorant or unable to perceive the complexities of modern society. Further, the romantic musings on the virtues of the peasant and his mystical attachment to the soil often come from intellectuals and sentimental folklore researchers as well as from writers and cultural commentators who are usually safely distanced from the more blatant inconveniences of rural poverty and sometimes insulated in the cosiness of campus comforts. Many are frequently enjoying the modern amenities and social excitement of metropolitan urban centres. The grassroot folk of the Caribbean half-acre plots and the more recent urban ghettos display no contentment with being deprived of domestic comforts associated with the scientific achievements of the 20th century. What is more, they expect from their different Caribbean communities and those who assume political leadership the fruits of advanced technology in such areas as nutrition and food supply, health care delivery and housing, education and the accessibility to such modern means of information-giving as radio and television. This positive demand by the Caribbean masses to share in mankind's twentieth century progress is itself an important cultural phenomenon and the cogency of the demand is not often lost on those who periodically face their clients with a promise of political deliverance. Therefore any approach that would seek to patronise the poor with talk of bringing what may well be their own "culture" to them or making·accessible the cultural products exclusively identified with the privileged few within and outside Third World communities is likely to invite the cynicism of those who may feel that the metropole still desires to keep the ex-colonial periphery as hewers of wood and drawers of water rather than as rich source for thinkers and innovators. It was, after all, part of the logic of colonialism that the Caribbean people should be more of the former and not much of the latter. 'Culture' as an all-pervading feature of human civilisation and development cannot escape the imperatives of a change of this status. Nor can the artistic manifestations which are but one index of culture. What policy-determiners and cultural directorates do with such data once they are grasped is another matter.

What much of the preceding discussion attempts to emphasise is that international organisations like the *OAS* and *UNESCO* which are concerned with culture and development in the Caribbean and Latin American region now need to place greater emphasis on effecting delivery systems for the promotion of cultural integration in the region. The hundreds of thousands of words expressed annually in declaration after declaration do reveal a grasp, on the part of such organisations, of the imperatives of cultural development.[267] Now, appropriate programmes need to be forged to effect cultural action on all levels of operation.

267. e.g. *Declaration of Principles on International Cultural Co-operation* UNESCO, Paris 1966. See also Resolutions by Caribbean countries made to UNESCO at the Intergovernmental Conference on Cultural Policies for Latin America and the Caribbean held in Bogota, Colombia, January 10-20, 1978.

Already there is co-operation on some levels of operation. The Caribbean will have experienced Latin American empathy in meetings of UNCTAD and the North-South dialogue as well as in some of the special organisations of the United Nations. But as H.C.F. Mansilla asserts, "while Latin American co-operation with the Third World in this area can be viewed as particularly meaningful, participation in predominantly political organisations, whether in the UN General Assembly or meetings of the Non-Aligned Nations is rather modest. Apparently there is a limit to the degree of co-operation between the New World and the rest of the Third World; a limit which in the long run could hinder co-operation with the Afro-Asian nations in other areas and probably also in economic and development policies." That cultural factors are a determinant in this situation Mansilla makes clear. He concluded as follows — "the cultural and language ties to Western Europe, the older and relatively firm tradition of sovereign statehood and not least, the ever-present Western development model *will prove a hindrance, in the long run, to a strengthening of the Third World movement,* including its socialist-Marxist variations." (my emphasis).[268]

Such, indeed, was the concern of the Intergovernmental Conference on cultural policies for Latin America and the Caribbean sponsored by UNESCO and held in Bogota, Colombia between January 10 and 20, 1978. Decisions at this historic meeting will no doubt be expected to have a lasting effect on the promotion of cultural development in the Commonwealth Caribbean and Latin America as well as on the flow of resources between Latin America and the Caribbean in the service of such development. The points of emphasis of each Delegation merely articulated the diversity in the region in terms of the Euro-, Meso- and Plantation American culture spheres. The geopolitical pre-occupations of Cuba still in search of acceptance of its own ideological commitment and of Panama seeking allies in its struggle for self-determination and the

---

268. Mansilla, H.C.F.: "Latin America and the Third World: Similarities and Differences in Development Concepts." *Vierteljahres-berichte,* No. 68, June 1977, Forschungs-institut der Friedrich-Ebert Stiftung, Bonn pp. 124-5.

decolonisation of the Canal Zone, were added dimensions. The Commonwealth Caribbean was well represented with delegations attending from Barbados, Grenada, Guyana, Jamaica and Trinidad and Tobago. They all addressed the process of synthesising a Caribbean aesthetic out of disparate elements with the Guyanese emphasising the energising power of Marxism-Leninism in *their* quest. The Jamaicans called on UNESCO to commit itself to aiding Jamaica and the Caribbean in the "revolutionary process of decolonisation and in their efforts at constructing a new society which will be free of the indignity of poverty and ignorance, the psychological paralysis of dependency, and the cultural marginality that is the lot of the vast majority of their people."[269]

In this UNESCO has a ready-made task to assist in ridding the Caribbean region of an overbearing Eurocentric cultural domination, by decentralising its own activities and transforming Paris, its present headquarters, into just *one* of many centres in the diverse world it is supposed to serve. The world organisation also needs to discredit any tradition of thought which views 'culture' as an elitist expression by a privileged few within nations and internationally. There were, indeed, more than glimpses of this lingering perception in the presentations of some delegations as they lauded the civilising power of the Great Tradition of metropolitan culture. UNESCO and the OAS could well encourage and promote the view of culture as a dynamic cyclical process of growth in human development – a process in which the rich textured experience of the mass of the people forms the source of energy for cultural expressions in both classic and popular modes, making cultural products the result of organic interaction between all classes and manner of people. For Latin American-Caribbean co-operation in the field of culture depends firstly on the disappearance of colonial notions which transform native peoples into anthropological specimens to be civilised into a master culture and, secondly, on the

269. Speech to UNESCO Bogota Conference by author as leader of the Jamaican delegation. Other members of the Jamaican delegation were Jean Smith, chief civil servant in the cultural division of the Minister of State (Culture and Information) in the Office of the Prime Minister and Lloyd Barrett, Jamaica's Ambassador to Colombia.

recognition that there is a common meeting ground in the shared experience of a creolisation process. In fact, UNESCO and the OAS will have to be prepared to address themselves increasingly and specifically to the *processes* of cultural development rather than to the *products* so as to (i) facilitate the work they do in areas of intra-regional and inter-national cultural co-operation and exchange and (ii) avoid the perpetuation of one unfortunate aspect of Caribbean experience whereby things metropolitan are placed high in some hierarchy of cultural values while things produced by the colonised and formerly colonised peoples are dismissed as subordinate. *A new international cultural order is no less needed than a new international economic order.*

Priority ought to be given to; (a) programmes aimed at promoting *the cultural forms native to the region,* through exhibition and study. The declaration that "each culture has a dignity and value that must be respected and preserved,"[270] is yet to gain the sort of practical force which can overcome the Eurocentric bias of the post-colonial Caribbean which tends still to measure its cultural achievements by European norms; (b) the strengthening of existing cultural institutions within the region by way of upgrading them to serve regional needs. The idea of "multinational centres" is already operative in the OAS system; (c) specific support to the region's universities and research institutes especially in the opening of new areas of knowledge relating to the "science of man" and to the totality of the region's developmental needs. Every people, indeed, has the right and duty to develop its own culture, knowing that all cultures do form part of the common heritage that belongs to all mankind; (d) the encouragement of cultural activities which are fully integrated into the economic and social life of the vast majority of the region's populations – e.g. handicrafts for domestic use, culinary arts with emphasis on aesthetic

270. This is one of the standards and principles established by the Declaration cited above. Some of these principles were to be studied in depth at the Intergovernmental Conference on Institutional, Administrative and Financial Aspects of Cultural Policies, held in Venice in August/September 1970. It was at that Conference that the Jamaica delegation presented the case for an international "culture bank."

presentation of locally prepared foods selected for their nutritional value, and all other creative endeavours that are likely to foster individual and collective self-reliance. Here the idea of "culture as a leisure activity" needs to be seriously re-thought; (e) the concentration of support on efforts to integrate into the overall educational process the content and methodologies of cultural education of the kind that will instill in the young self-discipline, early habits of relating actual experience to the learning process, a sense of self-worth through first-hand experience in creative activity, and the habit of sustained application in the systematic study and eventual mastery of a specific craft (e.g. music, dance, ceramics, painting, weaving, etc.); (f) the facilitating of greater dissemination of cultural information and products through assisting the region to decrease its dependency on metropolitan publishing and printing facilities, or on metropolitan-based news agencies servicing the region's electronic media. In this the work on the building up of communication skills within the region and the capabilities of refining techniques within the context of developing conditions is crucial; (g) building up the central funds for cultural development established by both UNESCO and OAS with all speed and activating such funds to assist Caribbean and Latin American member states substantively in their programme-development and institution-building; (h) the dynamic evaluation of cultural programmes in the light of declared principles, utilising not only a metropolitan-based corps of "experts" but cultural activists recruited from the region itself whose "authority" is rooted in proven achievements, knowledge and appreciation of all the nuances of the Caribbean and Latin American conditions.

The charges laid out above must also be addressed to such regional or sub-regional organisations which purport to have cultural policies. In the case of the Caribbean, the *Caribbean Community* (CARICOM) comes to mind. Caricom is a regional grouping of twelve Commonwealth Caribbean countries.[271] It is concerned with economic co-operation through the Caribbean Common

271.   i.e. Antigua, Barbados, Belize, Dominica, Grenada, Guyana, Jamaica, Montserrat, St. Kitts-Nevis, St. Lucia, St. Vincent, Trinidad and Tobago.

Market, co-ordination of foreign policy among the independent
Member States and common services and co-operation in functional
matters such as health, education and *culture,* communications
and industrial relations. It was at the Seventh Heads of Government
Conference held in October 1972, that it was decided that a
Cultural Officer should be based at the Regional Secretariat to
work in close liaison with the Education Desk in the promotion of
cultural activities in the Caribbean. Inspired somewhat by the
success of the Caribbean Festival of Arts (Carifesta) held in Guyana
in August 1972, the "cultural desk" which was established at
Caricom is yet to develop a dynamic programme of cultural interaction. The first incumbent, a Guyanese cultural administrator,
communicator and playwright[272] carries within his person the sort
of gifts that made him the chief organiser of the first Carifesta and
a consultant to the African Festival of Arts (Festac — 1977) but in
the absence of proper facilities he has seemingly not been able to
function as the effective regional facilitator that a Caricom function-
ary such as he should be. The development of guidelines to cultural
planning working in collaboration with international agencies and
the cultural institutions of member states is still in the future. The
compilation and analysis of cultural statistics for the Commonwealth Caribbean would be a welcome activity and the activation
and the monitoring of certain joint projects (study of say the
employment potential for artists, education for cultural action,
management of cultural policy, economics of cultural action,
cultural development policies in member states, etc.) await the
support from Caricom's Secretaries-General, Commonwealth
Caribbean governments and their Ministers of Culture and/or
Education for further conceptualization and implementation,
using Caricom as co-ordinator and clearing house.

Caricom's Standing Conference of Ministers responsible
for Education has been established to ensure co-operation between
the territories on education. The local production and distribution
of textbooks, curricula development, educational planning and

272. Frank Pilgrim who has also done a great deal to revive interest in Guyanese folk-
    lore.

education *inter alia* are on the agenda of concern.[273] But regional co-operation will depend on the effective collaboration between members of the profession of educators. The Caribbean Union of Teachers is reported to be dissatisfied with the educational system in the entire Commonwealth Caribbean region for being "geared to producing under-achievers", for being elitist and irrelevant to the developmental needs of the region and for being ill-prepared for its tasks in terms of understaffed schools and inadequate physical facilities.[274]

This is merely an up-to-date echo of a cry that dates back virtually to the late thirties and early forties when the movement for self-government got into full gear. In fact, much that has developed in Caribbean education for over a generation or so has been an attempt to decolonise the system. The firm grip of colonial mores on the populace has, however, thwarted the thrust for change — what with the hold of the Christian religion, the greater accessibility to the metropolitan based school-leaving examinations and the increased influence of the communications media controlled from the centres of imperial power. Yet, probably because of the continuing threat of cultural subjugation, native counterpoise forces have continued to develop. There have been frequent meetings of Eastern Caribbean teachers and their on-going concerns have had to do with educational development to serve the region's needs. The indigenisation of the Caribbean school-leaving examinations to replace the old Cambridge, Oxford and London University general certificates has been regarded as a highly significant advance though it has not failed to attract criticisms for its alleged Eurocentric vestiges. The development and expansion plans of the Trinidad and Jamaican governments reveal a vibrant responsiveness to the demands of educational change in terms of new needs for a more democratised polity as well as a more culturally aware populace. Isolated innovative experiments by farsighted educators all

273. *Caribbean Community — A Guide* p. 54.

274. *Daily Gleaner,* Tuesday, August 16, 1977 — frontpage report of the Caribbean Union of Teachers' Conference in Barbados in article "W.I. Education System under Fire".

over the region have long pointed directions to possibilities of effective change but not enough of these have been the subject of regional exchange, discussion or formal analysis.[275]

The Caribbean universities have been responsive to some of these needs through their Schools and Departments of Education but the total restructuring of a colonial educational system continues to demand of educators and planners the sense of daring and adventure which, though evident among individual pace-setters, is yet to find wider expression on a regional basis. The tasks for regional co-operation are clearly enough defined, then, in this area of cultural endeavour.

The integration of cultural disciplines (narrowly defined in terms of the creative arts) into the wider education system has received widespread lip-service. A regional thrust is needed at getting to the young through a learning process that links them organically to the realities of their own environment and to the potential of their creative capacities. The implications for international cultural bodies such as UNESCO and the OAS (CIDEC), and indeed for Caribbean Ministers of Culture, are far-reaching. Projects reaching their committees in search of funding or expert guidance should reflect a responsiveness to such a need as outlined above. For the cultural liberation of both the present and future generations is fundamental to the development of the region. That the changes in the educational system represent something of an over-arching challenge in the pursuit of the task is generally accepted. That the will to act is frequently weaker than the readiness to indulge the rhetoric is fully enough demonstrated in the actual experience of the region. Regional co-operation may very well be measured by the extent to which collective programmes are able to match action with declared intentions. The ease with which nations have been able to organise two-week Festivals must now be matched by a genius and energy to produce sustaining mechanisms within and

275. In Jamaica the experimental work of Wesley Powell with Excelsior High School and the Excelsior continuing education project (EXED), also that of Lewis Davidson with the 'total school' concept of Knox College and of Simon Clarke at the Green Island Secondary School stand out as progressive breakthroughs in educational planning and development in the island.

between Caribbean territories and to engage in on-going dynamic processes for a deeper cultural thrust as means to achieving greater self-confidence and sense of purpose among the peoples of the region. For there may be something in the view that the establishment and strengthening of national identity through cultural action is a prerequisite for economic and social progress in post-colonial situations.[276] Whether so or not the cultural dimension of that sort of progress is an inescapable variable of the equation of change. The case of Jamaica, like that of all the Caribbean and post-colonial Latin America, could be the acid test for this challenge of change and development in preparation for the twenty-first century.

Are there signs of this readiness in the Caribbean? And are such signs, if they exist, the substance of that inevitable revolutionary process which any society on the move must undergo if it is not to perish?

---

276.   *Final Report of Inter-governmental Conference on Institutional Administrative and Financial Aspects of Cultural Policies,* Venice 1970. Number 29, cited in Basic Study of FEMCIECC (Par. 11) OAS (Gen. Secretariat) Washington D.C. 1976, p. 135.

Epilogue

CULTURAL ACTION
&
SOCIAL CHANGE

" . . . to question our culture is to question our
human reality itself, and thus to be willing to
take a stand in favour of our irremediable
colonial condition since it suggests that we
would be but a distorted echo of what occurs
elsewhere."

Roberto   Fernandez   Retamar

EPILOGUE

There is a revolution apace in Jamaica and the Caribbean and we who live and have our being in the archipelago need
no ghost to tell us so. Some of us would sooner have the ghosts of
History know that not only are we the inventors of this revolution:
the world would actually cease revolving but for us and our consciousness. Such misplaced arrogance and heady conceit are
common enough human indulgences and may be nothing more
than handy props for the postures of re-assurance which we affect
from time to time in our anguished encounters with that cyclical
process of change and decay, of disintegration and rebirth. For the
revolution constitutes a continuing dynamic revolt against external
political and economic domination, against internal exploitation
reinforced by the ascriptions of class/colour differentiation, against
the dehumanizing evils of poverty and joblessness, disease and
ignorance and in defiance of all that would conspire to perpetuate
among us a state of dependency and self-repudiation — in short a
process of decolonisation of self and society by the conscious
demolition of old images and the deliberate explosion of colonial
myths about power, status and the production process. The revolution constitutes, at the same time, the constructive act of articulation of the collective self in terms of the variety of experience that
is the inheritance of a vibrant, resilient, though still bombarded,
people who have had to come to terms with a hostile environment
in which they found themselves — a people who have had to take
initiatives in giving a dynamic to the agonising process of shaping a
new and serviceable mode of existence in which we might secure
for each of us a sense of place and a sense of purpose. The two-
pronged phenomenon of decolonisation and creolisation (or
indigenisation) represents that awesome process actualised in
simultaneous acts of negating and affirming, demolishing and constructing, rejecting and reshaping. The phenomenon is one of
heightened contradiction characteristic of all far-reaching change
processes and it often raises more questions than it provides answers.

So not everyone is agreed on what the pace should be and there are significant disagreements and contentious debate as to the emphases that should be given this process of change. But no one has seriously denied to that process the imperative of a cultural dimension — in other words the need for that dynamic which moves us creatively to discover the wide range of autochthonous expressions which authenticate our distinct identity not only as beings *of* the Caribbean but as fully accredited members of the human race. That this cultural dimension has its prologue in a *Caribbean* past is now generally accepted by the more secure among the serious students of Jamaican and Caribbean society. That this cultural dimension of necessity assumes greater intensity during critical times of deep-rooted social change is sufficiently understood by all sensitive souls who have lived their young adult lives through the late nineteen thirties and the early forties and more recently through the late sixties and current seventies.[277] Moreover, along with the early apostles of negritude and the advocates of constitutional surrender by mother countries as well as the later protagonists of economic self-reliance, many of us who are now engaged in cultural action recognise that the cultural dynamics of change must go hand in hand with the political and economic thrust in a tripartite assault on the enemies of freedom, independence and sovereignty.

But while political, economic and cultural strategies must be deployed together in close alliance for what is at core a common struggle, each area of action must be seen to have its own intrinsic logic, methodology and vernacular. To deny to any of them this feature of specificity is to deprive ourselves of a rich arsenal and a wide variety of tactical and strategic armaments which are crucial to all combat especially when the combat is being conducted in terrain that is ecologically diverse, unpredictable if not unknown, and unrelievingly rugged. For the struggle of which I speak is not a pitched battle designed for generals pouring

---

277. The late thirties and the early seventies can be regarded as definitive periods of social crisis in modern Jamaica and Caribbean history — the one with respect to the ending of colonialism, the other with respect to the socio-economic transformation of the society.

out of stately military academies. It is the sort of struggle that requires the swampland genius and bush intelligence as well as the studied cunning and sophistication of the guerilla warrior. But enough of metaphor! Those of us who see cultural action as a conscious agent of over-all national development in the real world view creative expression not simply as reflecting life. We see it more as a dynamic flow emerging out of a continuing dialogue between the creator and the people to whom he speaks. He is seen to speak in the context of the realities of social struggle, using such tools of communication as are at hand but which tools in turn undergo dynamic change in a symbiotic interaction between tool and the substance worked upon. So the creative acts of our people forged collectively over time or by individual protagonists with our people as witness, have thrown up classic expressions which have in turn become prime sources of energy for that vital quest for cultural certitude.

The Jamaica ring-games and story-telling for play and recreation, the rituals and dances for worship and expiation, the poems, proverbs and action-music which have recorded the memories and collective wit and wisdom of generations, the masquerades which have masked reality by the use of irony to transmit poignant coded messages of deep social significance – all such expressions emanating from social interaction now serve as the living archives of our patrimony as well as the testament of a valid collective experience signifying the germ of a definitive civilisation. It is not by accident, then, that the performing arts which depend on dialogue and social interaction for their dynamic, are the artistic cultural expressions which tend to carry greatest conviction among Caribbean people. And where the scribal and literary arts gain currency and instant power among both the literate and the non-literate, it is frequently through the medium of the "public poet" who is none too high-brow to recite his rhythmic couplets on street-corners, in concert-halls or rumshops.[278] Readings by the novelist

278. Louise Bennett of Jamaica, Nicolás Guillén of Cuba, Robin Dobru of Surinam, Elis Juliana of Curacao are such popular poets. More literary poets who have read their work frequently are Edward Brathwaite of Barbados and Jamaica, Derek Walcott of St. Lucia and Trinidad, and Martin Carter of Guyana. A new generation of

are themselves less of a Dickensian borrowing from Europe and more a genuine Caribbean response. When the poet is also musician, as are the Trinidadian calypsonian and the Jamaican reggae-artist like his mento-singing predecessor, the vigour and power of our organic collective existence summon Caribbean people from all strata to myriad rituals in homage to the gods and demons of our ancestral inheritance. The social interaction which underlies all such cultural phenomena should not prejudice our acknowledgement of the undoubted prowess of the many specially gifted individuals who have blazed trails and displayed unique genius. But to pretend that their existence has had nothing to do with the social realities of Caribbean life and experience is to make a mockery of intelligence and to deny ourselves a sense of process. Indeed, both our exiled writers and our stay-at-home creative artists have had to engage in this dialogue with ourselves without being able to escape the mediation of the social struggle in the search for definition and purpose. This has all but transformed our creative artists into "revolutionaries" despite themselves. And in serving the process of change, all will have appealed to that which is older than revolution itself — to borrow a pointed phrase from Derek Walcott.[279] I understand by this felicitous Walcottian literary offering the psychic call to ancestral wisdom and integrity — the primal and final guarantee of triumph in a struggle against that which would seek to deny to the vast majority of our people the existence of that very ancestral wisdom and integrity.

In saying this I am not arguing a case for a romanticised ancestral mysticism. Instead, I am declaring against the continuing attempts to denigrate the proven and solid creative acts of the vast majority of the Caribbean people on whose labours the society was built over centuries of struggle, survival and further struggle.

engaged poets has emerged in Jamaica and the most exercised of them up to now is Orlando Wong.

279. Walcott, Derek: Article "Superfluous Defence of a Revolutionary — Focus on the Jamaican Dance Company" in *Trinidad Guardian* Friday, August 20, 1971. In tribute to the dance-work "Kumina" Walcott writes: "It is older than revolution, it illuminates, it moves with a separate uninsulting grace . . . it dances for itself, it is authority and celebration."

And in saying this I am not yielding to the now prevalent temptation to invest whatever comes from the ghettos or the canefields
with summary authenticity or to elevate ignorance, sloppiness and
the liabilities of material and intellectual poverty, as blessings from
the "roots." The primitive innocence that this particular vision
sometimes encourages is ever so painfully reminiscent of the noble-
savage image of genres of Enlightenment and 19th century Eurocentric literature attempting to give the transculturated Caribbean-
African his sense of place.[280] But we now know that the transculturation of that 'noble savage' (the slave and ex-slave) into a
new Caribbean man was and continues to be a complex affair. For
it took place on several levels and not on the simple two-way contact between European master and African servant. Early generations of slaves after all assumed a peculiar legitimacy, which was
punctiliously invoked when such generations came into contact
with "salt-water negroes" — the newly arrived Africans. Those salt-
water negroes had to be inducted in turn by their native-born and
native-bred Caribbean colleagues. Betwixt and between them all
there was the added necessity for adjustment and adaptation since
different tribal groups met in circumstances which forced on the
encounters a dynamic interplay of differing customs, social forces,
and compassions. All these in turn had contact with different
types of Europeans at different points of history on foreign soil
where the variables of power, domination, resistance and violence
helped to shape the new creolised cultural being who now stalks
these Caribbean lands. In many places the added dimension of the
continuing Amerindian Presence deepened the complexity and
extended the range of adaptation, adjustment and challenges. To
this must be added latter-day arrivants and the interplay that
followed on this between the established groups and the new East
Indians, Chinese, Arabs and even the more recent transitory North
American visitor. The creolising process in fact continues. We are,
in fine, the inheritors of a richly textured ancestry which in turn

---

280. See Roberto Marquéz's excellent article "Zombie to Synthesis — Notes on the
Negro in Spanish American Literature" in *Jamaica Journal*, Vol. 11, Nos. 1 & 2
1977, esp. p. 24, column 1.

determines the claims to an indigenised "Caribbean" ethos and informs the dynamics of contemporary Caribbean life.

At the height of the slave period the evidence of such texture was displayed in the fractured profile of that 'noble savage' (the slave) if we are to believe the written records left by the Europeans to whom the slave carried many faces. We hear that the slave could be treacherous and loyal, kind and cruel, passively indulgent of his master's whims and just as aggressively resentful of his master's sadism. The slave could be cowardly and courageous, humourless and witty, gentle but also bellicose.[281] In short, even when he was being denied his sense of person under the yoke of forced labour and the law, he was exhibiting the attributes of the total human being – rational, complex and threateningly unpredictable. That now in freedom, contemporary Caribbean man should still be engaged in a battle to prove the incontrovertible fact of his humanity is the burden, I contend, of much of what he does and seeks to project in the name of culture and the assertion of his cultural identity.

Yet not even this guarantees him safe harbour. For even when culture' is narrowly defined (as it often is) to mean the artistic products of the creative imagination which is virtually beyond the reach of external domination, he is relegated to the role of minstrel, buffoon, mimic. Which one of us has not shared at some time the exasperation of that Hispanic Caribbean mulatto poet who cried:

> "Are we no more than merriment?
> Are we no more than rumbas, black lust, carnivals?
> Are we no more than grimace and colour,
> grimace and colour . . .?"[282]

That the world of sports falls readily into this category of merri-

---

281. Both Bryan Edwards and Edward Long the foremost historians of the enslaved West Indies attest to this. See two very good papers on "Slave Images and Identities" by Patricia Romero ("The Slave Traders' Images of Slaves") and Emilia Viotti da Costa ("Slave Images and Realities") in *Comparative Perspectives on Slavery in New World Plantation Societies* (Vera Rubin & Arthur Tuden, eds.) Annals of N.Y. Academy of Sciences 1977, pp. 286-310.

282. Marquez, Roberto: *op cit* p. 28. Regino Pedroso is the poet.

ment, grimace and colour can be seen from the gladiatorial applause reserved for the great Caribbean "performances" by those of us who play the game of cricket, equalled only by Brazilian Black achievement in football (soccer) and the American Negro's stylish command over the fields of Boxing, Baseball and Athletics.[283] American Blacks have indeed, long sought to escape the minstrelsy syndrome by bringing to sports dimensions of political conscious-ness and social struggle.[284] This is an innovation that is matched only by the wider White society's attempts to frustrate such efforts.

In Jamaica itself the Rastafarian brethren not only shocks this outpost of Christendom by declaring Haile Selassie, the late Emperor of Ethiopia, as God and themselves (and all men of pure heart) as divine, they also cultivate a ferocious theatricality complete with 'dreadlocks' of matted braids and knitted woollen headgears as well as accessories bearing the revolutionary colours of the brightest red, green, gold and black, as if to amplify their anguish and assert a would-be denied presence through the device of programmed high visibility. Needless to say, their bold, 'dread' and defiant exterior masks an organic protest against the Carib-bean's "sufferation" from the centuries-old crimes committed against our people. But this dread exterior also conceals a firm inner commitment to peace, love and a quiet determination to guard their own and mankind's self-respect and dignity. Such basic decencies of existence have after all been kept away from them by an economically and socially unjust society which has been a place of enforced and oppressive Exile for ancestors over centuries. The Rastafarians of Jamaica represent one of Plantation America's most authentic expressions of organic revolt in appropriate, if anguished,

283. Cricket is the Anglophone Caribbean's national game and carries far-reaching psychological implications for the colonised. See *Caribbean Quarterly*, Vol. 19, Nos. 2 & 3 for M. St. Pierre's essays on "West Indian Cricket." Names like Headley, Weekes, Worrell, Walcott, Ramadin, Valentine, Kanhai and Sobers figure in the gallery of heroes among young West Indians. So do the names of Pele, the Black Brazilian soccer "superstar" and Black Americans like Jesse Owens, Joe Louis, Muhammad Ali and Sugar Ray Robinson.

284. Tommy Smith and John Carlos gave the Black Power salute on the victory podium at the 1968 Olympics held in Mexico City.

response to some of the deepset social forces that have shaped and still determine the dynamics of our Caribbean society. Small wonder that Rastafarianism now boasts great cultural clout among a groping generation of Jamaican and Commonwealth Caribbean youths in search of themselves and of a just society which they have been taught to expect but which is yet to be in their grasp. It is as though the Rasta-man is prophet, priest, and advocate — in short the society's cultural conscience.[285]

The identification of cultural action with social change is therefore seen as a development imperative in countries like those of the Caribbean. The job of the artist as a prime cultural agent is often seen to be the same as that of the priest or guru — *viz* "to guide individual life back into collective life, the personal into the universal [so as] to restore the lost unity of man"[286] or to negate the negation expressed in alienation as another tradition of analysis would put it. This mission is certainly understood by many in the Caribbean but unfortunately it sometimes leads some of us into delusions of grandeur which we often hear are good for many an individual painter, poet, dance-creator or musician. But Caribbean society which is in dire need of a sense of community and of the integration of personal awareness with collective consciousness, continues to cherish the priest and artist, perhaps because in serving themselves these functionaries must first serve their society. The large number of cultural groups organised, nurtured and developed in Jamaica on the basis of sustained voluntary service have been a major contribution to the relatively strong institutional infrastructure and tradition of goodwill supporting cultural action and policy today. As for the individual artist who weaves around himself theories of alienation-therapies and claims exclusive insights into the creative imagination, a gentle reminder that he performs a social function which is no more or less necessary than all other categories of work in society, can be beneficial to his sanity.

285. See my Introductory Essay to Joseph Owens' *Dread . . . (op cit)*; also Chapter 2 of my *Mirror, Mirror . . . (op cit)* also Leonard Barrett's *The Rastafarians*, Heinemann — Sangster 1977. Jamaica's leading pop-music artists are either declared Rastafarians or they empathise fully with the belief system of the Brethren. The notion of "dread culture", as sustained anti-Establishment protest, is Rasta-derived.

286. Tynan, Kenneth: "To Divorce Art from Money-Making" — a contribution to a symposium on culture held at the Manhattan School of Music, 1962.

And it is to this sanity that I will further address myself by reflecting on what are needed to develop in ourselves a capacity for confidence and a faith in the validity of our own creative potential and creative acts.

II

First and foremost is the need for us to recognise that rooted in our history is a Caribbean Experience that is worth being taken seriously enough to be explored.[287] The organic links of that history/experience with the history of Western Europe and West Africa, with infusions later — much later — from the Orient, the Levantine and post-War America, give to the society of which Jamaica is a prototype, tremendous texture and complexity. At worst it spells confusion, uncertainty, insecurity, helplessness. At best it signifies a richness born of the dynamism of a dialectical process in which contradictions battle to forge new synthesis. This very fact offers to the generations since 1938 a compelling summons to study, analysis, interpretation and, indeed, change, in the service of both public policy and private individual action.[288] The

287. See essay "Towards the Formulation of an O-Level Syllabus in Caribbean History" in *Curriculum Studies*, 1977, Vol. 9, No. 1, pp. 56-59: by Howard Fergus the Montserratian educator and writer. He says among other things that "Perhaps what can be claimed for history and other such seemingly luxury subjects is that as modes of intercourse they form part of certain traditions of critico-creative thought which have been achieved by the human mind. If this is true, they have educative potential which transcends localities and levels of socio-economic advancement." I concur with this view.

288. The debate over the West Indian History syllabus in the new Caribbean Examinations (CXC) referred to above (see footnote 108) had two articles by the group of West Indian History Teachers in the Jamaica *Gleaner* on October 9 and 30. To the former came a reply from Peter Ashdown of Sussex University who asked that the history syllabus be created for students and not for teachers' ideology (see *Sunday Gleaner Magazine*, December 18, 1977). He quoted Elsa Goveia's comment on Eric Williams' "British Historians and the West Indies" which reads "No one is ever educated or liberated from the past by being taught how easy it is to substitute new shibboleths for old." To avoid such a temptation Howard Fergus *(op cit)* has an answer in "A study of history does not automatically make students patriotic, democratic or good citizens by what ever criteria, though such claims are sometimes made ... However, if Caribbean citizens become critically aware of their past and the relations of that past to the present with its peculiar values, trends, problems and privations, it will be difficult for learning transactions to take place without reference to the general area of affect."

temptation to subvert this responsibility by ready surrender to the hard-earned products of other people's Experience, has long been the bane of our life, ever since mercantilist greed transplanted hordes of humanity, transformed them into mere statistical units in the production process and nurtured them into dehumanised 'zombies' in a barbarous system of forced labour. Even today in Independence where colonial hegemony has given way to the formal instruments of constitutional autonomy, the beneficiaries of the newly transferred power betray a continuing cultural self-doubt. Great systems of thought spawned by the indigenous Caribbean Experience and a developed intellectual capability are still not seen as possibilities that can emerge from the archipelago. Rational thought like melody is seen to be the exclusive property of Europe while Africa is made to evoke the atavistic intuitiveness of primitive innocence like the rhythm of the drum! The religious systems of the Orient have indeed become fads in the North Atlantic and the great philosophical systems of Japan, India and old China are instruments of spiritual renewal for a bored youth-population of affluent Western societies. But although Nyerere's ujaama as a homegrown piece of African political experiment attracts some admirers, the native thought systems of black Africa are either still regarded as fetishistic curiosities or have become subsumed under the borrowings from Europe in the name of nationalism, liberalism, Marxism and the like. That Cuba, Guyana and Jamaica are capable of developing their own patterns of social organisation independent of Europe's Communist and Liberal Democratic models, still cannot be conceived by those who are yet to release themselves from the stereotyped perception of us as child-like imitators of our betters. This is why those new Caribbean men who claim to be in the vanguard of change and development must avoid being mere mimic men and, instead, try to find not only new paths but also new ways of traversing old paths. In all this our Caribbean Experience must be a primary source of energy for the quest. But it will be so only if we are prepared to vest the Experience with the intrinsic validity of its being, and if we are courageous enough to recognise its weaknesses without self-pity and celebrate its strengths with conviction and faith.

The strengths are indicated as much in economic and political systems as in all those cultural expressions known to Man over time — language and literature, religion and philosophy, kinship patterns and modes of socialisation as well as artistic creation. And out of such Experience have come, according to a West Indian artist, "the chronicles of our history, our comfort in defeat, our protection against despair and disillusionment."[289] Such are the inner reserves which guarantee resilience and such is the nature of that internal landscape that supports the beleaguered exterior in a world that constantly threatens our very humanity. A creative process, concerned with the agony of choice in the shaping of new directions toward new forms appropriate to our needs and sensibilities, has, in fact, been at large among us for centuries in ways that have nurtured our survival and endorsed our struggle.

It is imbecilic, then, to deny to Caribbean Experience the capacity claimed by all other civilisations to throw up verities, maxims of prudence, moral guidelines — in short a philosophy of existence that can be of universal significance. The apparent weakness of the youth and recency of that Experience constitutes the very strength of its vibrancy, dynamism and responsiveness to the challenging creolising process of absorption, rejection, renewal and growth! It has, above all, the gift of a sense of process, if we as Caribbean men are sensible enough to make use of it. But it also has its own distinctiveness of which its flexibility is only one paramount trait. What it lacks, of course, is the support of great economic power, military might and, happily, the urge to dominate herds of humanity beyond its shores.[290] We are yet to decide among ourselves whether not being able to quote from Shakespeare or hum Shostakovitch should debar us from membership in the human race. There is no doubt in my mind that failure to recognise a phrase of music from the compositions of Bob Marley, or a line

---

289. Morris, Robert: "Personal Overview of the Arts in Barbados" *Manjak,* No. 3, Dec., 1973, p. 6.

290. Notwithstanding the seeming attempts at colonisation in reverse as Louise Bennett, the folklorist wittily and ironically describes the large migration to and settlement of Jamaicans in Britain, the former Mother Country.

from the poetry of Derek Walcott would not render such an "unexposed" Englishman or Russian less than whole. I certainly do not wish to make a case for blockading ourselves against the richness of Man's creative endeavours anywhere. But neither would I wish to plead a case for mistaking fertilisers for the soil, not if the soil must be our own indigenous Experience.

I regard that Experience as the stuff of Caribbean history and social studies which between them offer the objective reality challenging us to a sense of struggle in our efforts to defeat the dependency and the degradation of spirit that are the progenies of the cultural philanthropy of the European imperialist tradition. The post-war generation of the Caribbean owes much to the C. L. R. Jameses, the Eric Williamses, the M. G. Smiths, the Elsa Goveias, the Frantz Fanons and the Marcus Garveys for bringing scholarly vigour in the case of some and passionate homiletic advocacy in the case of others to that Experience.[291] We would do ourselves a great disservice if, through a lack of generosity of spirit, amnesia, intellectual arrogance or continuing entrapment in the dependency on Europe, we were to ignore them on the journey.

The turn to a more urgent radicalism is of course a dynamic of public life ever since the late sixties in Jamaica and other parts of the Caribbean. It is, we know, not the first time the need has presented itself. Issues surrounding the abolition of slavery, the revocation of Representative Government, the move to Self-Government and now the socialist transformation of the society are all responses to this need. Nor will it be the first time in our history that differences on the matter of the nature and style of the radicalism will have exhibited themselves among the protagonists of fundamental change. In the context of the socialist solution there are separate camps of progressives who now call for unity

---

291. See footnote 109 above for references on Goveia, Williams and James. M. G. Smith is the father of the pluralist school of analysis in the Caribbean. Garvey, now a National Hero in Jamaica, has left behind a rich corpus of writings on black nationalism but which are also regarded as ideologically anti-imperialist and Frantz Fanon whose *Wretched of the Earth* is a classic in the study of the Black Diaspora and colonial oppression generally, is a source of inspiration for many in the Black world.

against the very real and sometimes tactically imagined forces of reaction in the society. But the progressives are just as quick to shower abuse on each other with sobriquets drawn from the polemics of vulgar Marxism which is now blowing in the wind. 'Scientific socialists' treat with contempt the 'reformist' zeal and moral suasion of 'democratic socialists'. 'Cultural nationalists' are pitted against 'revolutionary nationalists'; 'anti-imperialists' claim to have more revolutionary pedigree than pro-Western 'reactionaries.' The attraction of Fanonian cathartic violence on the level of theory finds ready antagonism from those who advocate development by negotiation and painstaking application of skills and rational planning. The primacy of *race* and *ethnicity* in progressive intellectual analysis vies with the claims for the priority of *class* and an *economic determinism* that is said to be all-pervasive. And the entrapment in the capitalist-socialist dissensus of 19th century political economy sometimes threatens either to blur the vision or to frustrate the grasp of new categories of perception and the objective realities rooted in the Caribbean Experience. Colonialism *is* indeed a matter of economics but to vulgarly ignore the cogency of the "superstructural" factors which in turn assume independent logic and reinforce, as well as deepen and intensify the colonial strangulation is to miss excellent opportunities for further discoveries about Caribbean society. For such a society can never depend for its liberation exclusively on either the cleansing powers of revolutionary violence or the magic of an ancestral cultural mysticism, or the milk-and-honey dream of an immediate economic apocalypse devoid of poverty.

We are all, of course, caught up in this maze of competing claims to our spiritual and intellectual loyalties and though some of us know that none of these can be regarded as mutually exclusive, we are nevertheless sometimes afflicted by the passion and arrogance which are the commonplace indulgences of the committed who are steeped in self-righteousness. We so often kill the right strategy with the wrong tactics. The tendency to invest the development process with a totally predictable and one-dimensional course is a common enough weapon in the psychological warfare waged by one school of Caribbean radical progressives.

Empirical evidence disputes the practicality of this, happily, and the dogma of this or that deterministic posture in Jamaica will no doubt go the way of all the other dogmas before it — unless, of course, the monopoly of coercive power by protagonists of this or that determinism becomes a reality. Already there is concern about the matter of the totalitarian syndrome which freedom-loving ex-slaves in the Caribbean may, in any case, regard as a return to that other great totalitarian experience of Caribbean history — the Plantation. Scare tactics are, therefore, being used by some of our own people to suggest that what is in store for us in the new development thrust are: (a) the politicisation of every aspect of human life including ethics; (b) police terror; (c) state monopoly of the mass communication media; (d) a centrally controlled economy, and (e) the rule of one charismatic dictator presiding over one vanguard mass party which in turn presides over a passive, if seething, population. Such propaganda is irresponsible since there is no existing 'totalitarian society' which quite fits this description or which stands as ideal model for the engineers of Caribbean socialist transformation. Moreover, all the coercive powers employed on the old sugar plantations to maintain a *status quo* of subservient slaves and high status autocratic masters did not prevent repeated armed rebellions among the said slaves, nor the illicit sharing of conjugal beds between subordinates and their so-called superiors, nor the thwarting of the wanton use of Establishment force by the most ingenious means (other than armed resistance) invented by the oppressed.

In other words there is more to a society and to the complex network of interacting forces which shape such a society than any one strait-laced dogma could account for. And a failure by anyone to understand this would-be simple fact of life disqualifies such a person (or persons) from giving leadership to the preparation of the Caribbean people for their engagement in the sort of revolutionary struggle needed to bring about fundamental change.

This is why with the 'socialist solution' now boldly on our development agenda, an imported Marxian dialectic which provides an intellectual base for a good many among us, must be expected to accommodate variables as are dictated by the realities of Caribbean history and experience — a demand which the great Karl Marx would have had very little difficulty endorsing. There is, after all, some point to the Russians having their own phenomenal efforts reflected in the gospel of Marx according to *Lenin* and the Chinese their version according to *Mao*. The Cubans notably date their revolution from 1868 (before Marxism propagated itself beyond Europe) and make José Martí, the *Cuban* patriot, the prophet of their movement. Yugoslavia gives the credit to their own Tito and North Vietnam is serious about Ho Chi Minh. Surely this is saying something which we in the Caribbean ought not to ignore unless we have decided to succumb to intellectual indolence and to remain the perpetual victims of a chronic cultural dependency. The question may now be asked whether there is a place in our future for indigenous Caribbean political and cultural forms which are appropriate to the needs and sensibilities of our Caribbean people.

My submission is that the case for this lies solidly in the textured history and experience of past and contemporary life and that nothing less than serious study and analysis of that Experience can bring the understanding that we seek. For through such study and analysis of that Experience some important truths will not only unfold, those truths will offer the organic dynamism for action in the service of the change that must come. The release from the dependency complex is therefore *our* challenge and not that of Russia nor the United States — two super-powers which have become the current bogey-men in the vocabulary of both revolutionary and reactionary politics, depending on one's political taste. The alleged imperialist designs on the part of either will succeed only if *we* decide to surrender unconditionally to the geopolitical demands of client-statehood. That we should not, is a cultural imperative which cannot be escaped by those of us who wish not to yield to the standard temptation of searching outside for solutions. The prospects of success are that more agonising if only because the economics of it all are ever so vile.

Yet there are some historical facts surrounding *our* struggles which are worth remembering. Long before many of us heard of Cromwell, Robespierre or Jefferson, of Marx, Lenin or Mao, we in our persons suffered, recognised and consciously resisted the seemingly endless humiliation and indignity rooted in poverty and reinforced by low-class status and ethnic/cultural debasement. What is more, we today have long been attuned to all the strategies of revolt known to our oppressed and deracinated forebears who bequeathed to us a psychic inheritance of great solemnity. That legacy couches not just memories of, but active responsiveness to, such instruments of survival as *armed resistance* utilised throughout slavery and beyond against the monopoly of coercive power by 'the masters', *elusive cunning* employed as moral and tactical defence by the predestined weak against the predestined strong, *religious escapism and opportunism* invoked as appeal to a law beyond the jurisdiction of the 'oppressor', *ethnic self-assertion* and even chauvinism as antidote to the racial conceit of the European overlords, *political nationalism* embraced in the bid for transfer of decision-making power from the metropolitan centre to the colonial periphery and *militant adversary trade unionism* systematically developed as means of survival in an exploitative socio-economic system. None of these devices has been useless, as some among us would have us believe. In fact, in their different combinations they continue still to be indispensable weapons in the defence mechanism of the non-privileged black workingclass poor throughout Plantation America of which Jamaica is a part.

But good as these instruments of survival and growth have been, none has been totally effective in bringing about the sort of liberation dreamed of by so many not only in terms of statutory freedom and constitutional autonomy but also in terms of cultural authenticity and economic control. None of these instruments provided the effective *method* for reaching the New Jerusalem. Accounts of the historical struggle of the Jamaican (and by extension Caribbean) people can indeed point to the persistent inequities and despair among the general mass of the people despite the worthy stated objectives of yesteryear. It makes sense that socialism, with its redemptive ethic (utopian style) and the claim to a *method* (scientific or otherwise) by way of fundamental restructuring of the social and productive relations, should find enthusiastic response from a significant number of people in a society which is still exploitative, racist with respect to its capitulation to Eurocentric indulgences, and paralysed by deepseated dependency. Whether socialism is to be seen as an end in itself or as yet another (and for some the final) strategy in the continuing struggle for a socially just and economically rational existence, is a matter that is likely to be determined by the fact of Jamaican cultural realities rather than by force of Establishment arms. At least, such are the indications of the revolutionary vision of Jamaican democratic socialism which is either denounced as too reformist to be effective or lauded for its inherent humanism and strong moral suasion.[292]

The old liberalism that informed earlier strategies like nationalism and trade union industrial democracy is no longer adequate for progressive programmes of action — not when human rights still come couched in language that would quicker emphasise the individual's right to starve over the society's responsibility to facilitate his freedom from hunger. Worse still, liberalism is seen to have gotten itself inextricably bound to the capitalist market economy. The more sophisticated and conscious among Caribbean progressives would subscribe to the view that liberal democracy is the creation of capitalism. So if tolerance is the essence of liberalism then it tends to lose force in the face of the terrorism of revolutionary impatience and the moral hypocrisy of political opportunism, not to mention the intellectual arrogance evident in

292. Many of the ultra-Leftists associated with the (Jamaican) Peoples National Party would hold the view that socialism prefixed by the word "democratic" and as implemented by the majority Party since 1973 when it was declared is reformist rather than revolutionary. Carl Stone also expressed the view in his article in the Public Affairs column in the *Sunday Gleaner*, Jan. 12, 1975; also article "Our Political Economy" *Daily Gleaner*, Wed., Dec. 28, 1977. The failure of the declaration to put class conflict at the centre of its schema was regarded as one of the signals of its reformist nature. The constant references by the Party leadership to "democracy", "brother's keeper", "care and concern for the poor", and "love" are interpreted as being in the humanist tradition. Theodore Sealy, retired Editor-in-Chief of the influential *Gleaner* newspaper, described the Jamaican Government (1972) as a "humanistic socialist government which was conducting an experiment to see whether it could develop a socialist society without cruelty and repressions" according to a report in the *Daily Gleaner* of December 13, 1977, p. 2.

the self-indulgent journalistic cross-talk which passes off for serious ideological debate in the Jamaican daily press. The hope for the survival of what is good in the old liberalism is seen by others to lie in the active promotion of "people participation" exemplified in certain of our artistic cultural activities but conspicuously absent from many so-called more "important" areas of national life.

Some of the confusion which attends the efforts of those who claim to speak in the name of change in the society results from their ignorance of Caribbean history and in some cases even the lack of a sense of history at all. They often err on the same side as their arch-conservative detractors who would wish the fact of slavery away; and even when they invoke the slave experience (quite reasonably) as an extension of Western Capitalism,[293] they carelessly brush aside the variables of ethnicity, race consciousness, religion and the myriad psycho-cultural legacies which continue to play actively on the real life-experience of the contemporary ills and values of the Caribbean. So while Fidel Castro and the Cubans of revolutionary Cuba are eagerly seeking membership in the Caribbean cultural complex, some of our own progressives like the reactionaries before them and since, are trying to abscond abroad or back into an alien past forged out of the specifics of time, place, psychology and geography of a particular people. We can, for example, think of the Russians who made world history in 1917 by their own efforts or of the English and their Magna Carta.

But it is the *processes* underlying those efforts rather than the product of those efforts which should concern us. And it is the processes of Caribbean existence that will in the end justify the continuing links with the great philosophical and ideological discoveries of the world wherever groups of men and women have fought for freedom and social justice, recognition, status and cultural integrity. The replication of Soviet politburos in Africa

293.   cf. Marx's own description of American colonisation: "The discovery of gold and silver in America, the extirpation, enslavement and entombment in mines of the aboriginal population . . . signalized the rosy dawn of the era of capitalist production . . . Force is the midwife of every old society pregnant with a new one. It is itself an economic power". – *Capital* I, tr. Samuel Moore and Edward Aveling (N.Y. 1967).

and the Caribbean may indeed have no more to recommend it, albeit by our conscious willing choice, than the indiscriminate and, for some of us, imposed replication òf Westminster models in the Commonwealth has been. The question keeps plaguing many who are no less for fundamental change. Can nothing good come out of the Caribbean Experience? Naturally it is we as Caribbean men and women who must supply the answer. As with politics which is concerned with the organisation and mobilisation of power, so with artistic expressions which order and mobilise the complex workings of Man's individual and collective creative imagination. Replication of Bolshoi ballet companies in the Caribbean is no more desired than the promotion of mini-Royal ballet groups proved to be under British colonialism. It is my view that Caribbean dance-art (and there is such a thing) has a responsibility to find its own form and logic both for itself and for the advancement of human artistic experience. On the other hand, the meeting of these distinctly different traditions of dance — these quite different products of a not dissimilar creative process — can set in motion a renewed process of attraction/repulsion, assimilation/rejection, thesis/antithesis into a new synthesis in that endless dialectical process of genesis, growth, maturation, disintegration, regeneration. Such a coming-into-being through cross fertilisation is already the dynamic of Caribbean life and is its greatest cultural asset. Yet, it is always under the threat of being marred by that persistent world-view which postulates that the ingredient from Western Europe is superior to that from anywhere else and particularly from Africa. Have we never wondered among ourselves that it is always we as Caribbean peoples who have had to be sitting the tests and passing the examinations set by Europe?

Granted, the authorities we have been called upon to study have been among the most eminent the Western world has known starting with the King James version of the Bible to secular preachers and thinkers of varying philosophical and ideological hues. But the invigilators have been no less varied and alert in their supervision. We can think of such ones as the British colonial office, and the Christian Church as well as of their able successors, the Eurocentric educators (expatriate and native-born) and the doctrinaire Leftist clerisy who are not only vigilant against cheating but are inclined to dictate to the examinees what actual answers must be written. We now take delight in blaming our Founding Fathers for being Eurocentric Anglophiles who were too eager to convince the British colonial office that they could work a British constitution in Independence.[294] Let us hope that future generations will not have reason to condemn us for doing no less with other outside patrons. The issue in question here is that dependency complex and its likely perpetuation in continuing uneven relationships. The need for intellectual courage suggests itself. In this we are seemingly well exercised by such things as North-South dialogues, and the proposals for a new international economic order — matters on which Jamaica's Prime Minister, Michael Manley, was to become the universally accepted spokesman for the Third World from 1976 on. In addition there are the bold self-assertions of the intrinsic worth of the cultural patrimony of countries all over Africa, Asia, Latin America and the Caribbean. Moreover, the definitive re-introduction into the Caribbean political consciousness of the Marxist perspective[295] is destined to give us a fuller picture of Western civilisation providing, as it were, a welcome antithesis for a prevailing and suffocating capitalist thesis. That the re-interpretation of aspects of our history in Marxist categories must be faced just as the employment of other schemata has been, is part of

---

294.   At the time of writing there was a campaign on in Jamaica to prepare the populace for the rewriting of the Jamaica Independence Constitution (an Order in Council, of the British Government in fact) of 1962. In their zeal some protagonists have been known to discredit the Founding Fathers for their reputed 'neo-colonial' posture said to be evident in the constitutional provisions especially those entrenching the monarchical system, the sanctity of private property and the rigid amendment procedures.

295.   During the thirties in Jamaica a number of Marxists emerged among the Progressive groups calling for the end of the crown colony system. The most famous of them was one H. C. Buchanan. He was mentor to the Marxist wing which developed after 1940 when the People's National Party declared itself a "socialist party." The activists in that wing (the brothers Ken and Frank Hill, Richard Hart and Arthur Henry) were purged in 1952 at the height of Cold War politics. In Guyana the presence of Cheddi Jagan since the early fifties has meant the presence of the Marxist posture in Guyanese politics. Back in Jamaica in 1937/38 there was also connexion (interlocking membership) between the left Book Club and the Writers Circle in the new movement of self-government.

the liberation process of a once hemmed-in society. The idea of an integrated Marxist social science as part of our higher education curricula makes palpable sense therefore. The deepening of insights and widening of vision is the hope of this new awakening. But this depends on the existence of wise, knowledgeable, and academically creative authorities among the teachers and facilitators. Class conflict categories are easy enough to work with: the brilliance of one Karl Marx has already done the original work on this. But to deal with the no less dynamic class/colour correlation as an active, if bothersome, variable in Caribbean development or the psychic and cultural realities of post-colonialism is something that requires intellectual muscle and some real originality. There's the challenge for us! Elsa Goveia's reminder is instructive. "The road to hell is paved with authoritative half-truths," she said. "No one is ever educated or liberated from the past by being taught how easy it is to substitute new shibboleths for old."[296] The impulsive semantic urge simply to call old social categories by new and fashionable borrowings amounts to little more than mechanical labelling. What a contrast to the far more organic manifestations evident in the linguistic defiance by a genuinely Caribbean-rooted protest group like the Rastafarians whose battery of 'I-words' are only a part of their small but pointedly relevant lexicon of normative-descriptive word-symbols. At least they have done more than simply replace the imperial Standard English of Establishment power with French and German derivatives which come from one tradition of nineteenth century European polemical debate. Black Jamaican ghetto-youths object to being referred to as lumpen-proletariat. Not surprisingly our cultural encirclement is once again demonstrated with what is for some a frightening foreboding. Yet the argument that the Rastafarian linguistic technology is far too limited to satisfy the sophisticated and complex conceptual needs of the modernisation and development process of the contemporary Caribbean, is one that cannot be lightly ignored. But what a difference this is to the case of the Tanzanians who can speak of

296. Goveia, Elsa: Review of Eric Williams "British Historians and the West Indies", *Caribbean Quarterly*, Vol. 10, No. 2 (June 1964).

"ujaama" which is said to reflect with cultural accuracy the essence of Nyerere's political experiment much better than the English translation of the Swahili word could.

There will always be room for doubt, then, as to whether an integrated Marxist social science is absolutely superior (for our purposes) to an integrated non-Marxist social science which will have come no less resolutely from Eurocentric traditions. The answer will not be found until the Caribbean seriously looks to itself and courageously continues on that journey to collective self-discovery already charted by a number of our own West Indian historians, social scientists, creative artists, political activists and, indeed, by the common people themselves in their now historic struggles throughout slavery and since. The task is that more difficult since the discovery of the collective self must be achieved in full view of the sometimes blinding influences of other people's experience and with full knowledge of the fact that the process of cross-fertilisation is the inevitable means to cultural advancement and our civilisation's enrichment. The important factor in all this is that our people should be made aware of all the ramifications of this process and not be blockaded from worlds which former conquerors and their aides, the colonialist educators, felt were unpalatable or from those which a new intellectual elite armed with ill-digested Vulgates may now regard as illegitimate for the purposes of the liberation struggle. After all, the logic of independence dictates that we diversify, by our own volition, our sources of knowledge as we are even now doing, as a matter of tactical necessity, our markets and sources for loans and technical assistance.

III

But in diversifying, the full consciousness of the unifying forces of one's own cultural heritage remains crucial to our absorption rate and assimilation capacity with respect to outside forces. One unifying force in the Caribbean heritage is undoubtedly the African Presence. Placing it at the centre of the Caribbean ethos as the mass of our people have long done is not to be mistaken as a perversely chauvinist racist orientation of a contrived integrated

Caribbean civilisation. For this would take us no further away from the racial conceit of Western imperialism which has bequeathed to Western Man a quite indefensible sense of cultural hierarchy whereby things European confidently assume a pre-ordained place at the apex of the pyramid. This is as true of the great philosophical and ideological systems of the Western world (from bourgeois liberalism to Marxism-Leninism) as it is of religion (Christianity), language, literature and artistic manifestations. Imperial *linguae-francae* like English, French, Spanish and Dutch are, after all, the official languages of the creole-speaking Caribbean. One also only has to reflect on the notion of *classical* music, *classical* ballet, Renaissance and Modern Art and *classical* drama (from Euripedes of ancient Greece through the Shakespeare of Elizabethan England to Jean Racine of pre-Revolutionary France). In reality, these are all distillations of specific *European* national cultural experiences though they have been sold to us as the best in *universal* experience. And as seasoned colonials we have been the unquestioning consumers of this received 'universal' culture.

It is against this cultural imperialism and the underlying economic and political domination that Caribbean apostles like Marcus Garvey have rebelled, bequeathing to us a certain tradition of struggle which makes him, significantly, the most popular of our indigenous prophets among the mass of Jamaican people today. It is true that in his rebellion he betrayed admiration for what are the undoubtedly great achievements of Europe and he did not scruple to use the very criteria supportive of the overlords' claim to excellence. But this fact only confirms the dialectical nature of Caribbean existence[297] and the entrapment of Garvey and all who came after in a world where Euro-determinism is total and has somewhat intensified with the growing primacy and impact of Western science and technology. That the access to political

---

297. Derek Walcott expresses this in another way. He says of the patrician writers of the New World — "they know that by openly fighting tradition we perpetuate it, that revolutionary literature is a filial impulse and that maturity is the assimilation of the features of every ancestor" see "The Muse of History — An Essay" in *Is Massa Day Dead? — Black Moods in the Caribbean,* Orde Coombs ed. Doubleday Anchorbooks N.Y. 1974.

power (however limited) is crucial to an initial release from this cocoon Garvey knew too well, as did the Nkrumahs and Nyereres in black Africa and the N. W. Manleys and Eric Williamses in the Commonwealth Caribbean. That economic power is vital as object-ive base for eventual confidence in that cultural authenticity we dream of was well known to early Jamaican Left-wing progressives. Garvey also knew it. He not only proclaimed its necessity, he tried to do something about it though his efforts foundered on obstacles presented by an international economic and political order which concentrated power and influence in the hands of the very over-lords who did not wish to see Africa 'rise up' in the way that Garvey and his followers dreamt it could. This lesson has not been lost on contemporary Caribbean leaders who must find equitable markets for their sugar and bananas, their oil and their bauxite, their cocoa and their coffee so that basic amenities of health, education, housing and jobs can be provided for the millions whose deprivation and powerlessness have led many of them to something worse than violence, *viz* mental paralysis.

When the suffering is compounded by notions of ethno-cultural superiority in favour of those who not only dictate prices on the world's commodity market with no reference to the primary producers but who also remain the prime source of both our polit-ical philosophy and our counter-philosophies, one senses the dire need for us to plumb deeper into the neglected elements of our own experience for appropriate, if not totally new, instruments of development as well as for our own cultural frame of reference. Or must we remain distorted echoes in perpetuity?

That the African Presence in our midst has been one of the most neglected (debased is more to the point) especially in determining our ethos, there can be no doubt. The vast majority of our people can no longer be relegated to being second-class citizens if energies are to be mobilised to building a just and lasting civilisation. The cultural education of our 90-odd percent of Jamaicans of African descent in the appreciation of the real worth of the ancestral inputs of their once forsaken forebears into the making of Caribbean and, by extension, Western society will have to assume top priority in the 'raising of consciousness' among the survivors of the Middle Passage. Revolutionary Cuba's declared entry into the Caribbean not only by geo-political alliance but by the invocation of an 'Afro-Latinity'[298] that is said to be firmly rooted in pre-colonial Iberian-Moorish history, may not be a whim of Fidel Castro's political imagination as some would have it. Rather, it may be the result of an insightful grasp by Cuba's maximum leader of the deeper cultural realities of Caribbean life it terms of the centrality of the African Presence in the cultural calculus. We may as well admit to ourselves the great moral strength that would accrue to Caribbean civilisation were we to eschew once and for all the lingering plantation and colonial assumptions about the natural inferiority of those of its inhabitants who carry the 'stain' of Africa in their blood.

For as long as such assumptions remain a fact of Caribbean existence so long will the submerged ethno-cultural frustrations play their accustomed 'subversive' role in Caribbean social development. Such frustrations are by no means the monopoly of any single racial grouping. For the cultural marginality of the Blacks in relation to the historical/political coloniser-colonised experience is paralleled by the cultural marginality within the society of the latecomers as they relate to the Euro-African creole complex which is still battling for definition and focus. It is interesting to see how the different groups choose to deal with this dilemma. If they are able to shift now from racial considerations to class consciousness, they are no less capable of utilising both categories simultaneously in working out their personal and collective cultural salvation.

So protected by a thick varnish of brash and bravura which serves to conceal a deepset insecurity and a chronic psychological dependency, Caribbean Blacks (i.e. all who willingly admit to the African "stain") will indeed continue in their emotionally wasteful love-hate relationships with the former White 'oppressors.' Caribbean Whites, even in the face of political displacement, are

298. Dr Fidel Castro so declared his identity in a long speech given to a mass rally on October 16, 1977, in Sam Sharpe Square, Montego Bay on his now historic state visit to Jamaica.

likely to receive continuing psychic sustenance for their inherited sense of superiority from the realities of White economic power in the wider world and the persistent dominance of Eurocentric cultural norms within Caribbean society whether these be religion (Christian orthodoxies and their offshoots), political creeds and economic systems (from capitalism/liberalism to socialism/communism), or the fruits of science and technology which are regarded as the special gift of the West to human civilisation. Functional Whites, as new converts, are sometimes far more fanatical than their biological counterparts in their defence of Europe's achievement and the Eurocentric faith.

Blacks will also continue to feel a need to "look down" on the latecomer East Indian and Chinese whose pedigree of indenture may even be made into a liability rather than an asset. Then they will further reserve a visceral envy for and somewhat guarded hostility towards the entrepreneurial Arabs whose rags-to-riches success story, like that of many of our Chinese and East Indian compatriots, becomes ready target for attack in the general condemnation of capitalist exploitation.

Under the circumstances, and if only for self-protection, the newer generations of evolved East Indians, Chinese and Arabs will naturally wish to establish common cause with the symbols and actual holders of economic and cultural power. So, by marrying White and, more importantly, by gaining mastery over the still dominant Eurocentric education (especially in the areas of science and technology), mores and even religion, they are soon numbered among the new Caribbean creoles since they would have met some of the most important criteria traditionally associated with the "making of the West Indian." But as part of their own transculturation they become carriers of vintage plantation prejudices about race, class and colour. Such offspring of latecomers will have unwittingly contributed to the perpetuation of the tradition of African denigration and might even continue to throw up from among their ranks staunch supporters of the view that the native-born and native-bred Euro-African ethos signifies nothing, not having *created* anything.

If Caribbean society is really to enjoy the non-racial

splendour and multi-racial bliss it so frequently boasts about, then logical priority must be given to a final resolution of the inherited conflict between Europe and Africa. The resolution must be in terms that will rid Caribbean society of those imbalances of history which have put people of African ancestry at a clear disadvantage – economically, politically, socially and culturally. The liberation of the entire society from all kinds of racial chauvinism therefore depends, in an elemental sense, on the self-liberation of the 'exiled African.' The operative word is "self-liberation" indicating that the freedom has to be achieved by the efforts of the Blacks them- selves – whether through self-reliance and high productivity, a display of political acumen and the innovative exercise of the intellect, or the vibrant use of the creative imagination for achieve- ment of excellence. Whatever it is, it is going to demand action and concrete results. Otherwise they will still be seen to have created nothing not having achieved their own liberation.

The paradox is that outside assistance which is always forthcoming is also crucial in achieving far-reaching change. French- men have, after all, helped to liberate rebellious American colonists. Englishmen have aided and abetted the demise of a decadent *ancien régime* in the France of the Bourbons. Germans reputedly secured for revolting Russians the authenticity of a leader by facilitating his timely return in the now legendary sealed train. Russia gave succour in more recent times to Castro's cunning Cubans and the Red Chinese to Ho Chi Minh's valiant Vietnamese. Cubans are even now assisting Angolans and the Mozambicans are supporting the guerilla Rhodesians. Our own experience recalls that British liberals encouraged radical and anti-colonial subjects of the Crown, even tutored them, to defy, challenge and subvert the authority of the British Empire and the Crown colony system. Black liberation will indeed continue to need the support of all other racial group- ings within Caribbean society. But lurking behind facades of co-operation and goodwill are suspicions, reservations and even fear for the future which are typical of joint ventures in which there is uncertainty about which partner is likely to be in control.

For despite the evidence of the need of external assist- ance no real struggle for liberation and fundamental change is worth its name unless it is fought and seen to be won by the people for whom the change is intended. The actual liberation cannot be the gift of either a benevolent imperial power in voluntary retreat or a generous senior partner magnanimously refusing to share the spoils. Despite the virtues of internationalism in the wider world, outsiders must be seen to assist, not to take over. As far as Caribbean society itself is concerned, our current cultural fiction of multi-racial harmony will become social fact only when the historic denigration of the African Presence disappears, and disappears as a result of the demonstrated efforts of the Blacks themselves who, after all, are principal "insiders" in this Plantation struggle of the region.

This insider-outsider dichotomy naturally reveals itself in the ethnic/cultural sphere of Caribbean life, especially in the battle to determine the nature of cultural legitimacy within the society. But, more significantly, this has serious implications for that post-colonial dilemma of politics — that is of deciding just where the newly transferred political power will be located and *how* it will be distributed. The region's varying responses to the dilemmas are instructive. In one place, the Blacks (as the first to hold that power since Independence) will probably arrange to prolong their stay in power as "natural heirs" to the British raj by preventing East Indians, who constitute the numerical majority of the population but are culturally marginal, from gaining control of the state apparatus too soon, i.e. before a truly Afro-centred creole ethos is established. This can be done presumably by the employment of electoral devices which are weighted in the Blacks' favour. In another place, the Euro-African creoles may, through fear of an East Indian alternative, decide to retain indefinitely, one of their own as head of government despite the shortcomings of a tired regime deemed to have outstayed its welcome. Still in another place, Caribbean Blacks with an undoubted numerical majority in the population may offer strong resistance to attempts to entrust the leadership of the nation's government to any contender whose forebears are not identified with the struggle of the plantation before Emancipation. The apparent defiance of the reality of numbers in the first two cases cited above and the inherent contradictions bordering on schizophrenia in the third only provide reason for serious study of this Caribbean phenomenon. For it is unrealistic to dismiss the phenomenon as ethnic chauvinism which is alien to the humanist tradition or a will-o-the-wisp illusion that is said to be indulged by those incapable of grasping the scientific laws of economic determinism. To over-emphasize the importance of the race-variable in post-colonial Caribbean politics is to misread, indeed, the total dynamics of our textured existence. But to under-estimate its significance in given circumstances is equally to miss an objective reality of Caribbean existence.

No appeal to such abstractions as pluralism, humanism, nationalism or socialism (democratic or scientific) can be used simply to escape the existence of this reality. They can no doubt be used to temper the viler effects of racism. But what these worthy abstractions must be able to do is to quench the thirst after right-eousness with the hope of recognition and status for the deprived and denigrated multitude, and provide them with the reality of socio-economic betterment and cultural certitude as important pre-requisites for that non-racial ethic which many Caribbean people of all races will see as the cultural counterpart to the economic ideal of a classless society.

If a creed like Marxism is to be a serviceable abstraction in our search for solutions, it were best that we rely less on the literal linguistic symbols which are often inadequate being the *product* of specific times, circumstances and cultural perspectives, and draw more realistically on the *process* so seductively spelt out in the Marxian dialectic which could produce positive results only if applied by resourceful and creative activists and planners who themselves genuinely appreciate the multi-dimensional complexity of our Caribbean existence. In Cuba the anti-racist stance by José Martí, the spiritual father of the Cuban revolution and the assertive mulatto songs of praise by the anti-colonialist Nicolás Guillén are now vindicated in revolutionary legitimation. Though no doubt yet to be fully realised in practice, it is a courageously forward step for a Cuba which not so long ago displayed a vested interest in the deblackening of its ethos. Black people have, therefore, had reason to take the Cuban revolution seriously, at least on this level.

The Jamaica testament to this inevitable fact of Caribbean life had long shown itself in the mettle of our commonfolk, particularly our peasantry, in their language, social institutions and sensibilities. It was Guillén who once wrote:

> "Jamaica says
> she's happy being black
> and Cuba now knows she is mulatta."[299]

He had no doubt heard about Marcus Garvey but he was being over-generous for our society had given Garvey short shrift and pursued its progress in Eurocentric ways with things African progressively tolerated but on terms dictated by the overlord's own standards. Precisely! For even while the revolution of 1938 was ablaze in Jamaican canefields and banana walks, on the urban waterfronts and in the sweat shops, George Campbell, a young and self-aware Jamaian described by the late Norman Manley as "the poet of the revolution" was asking some poignant questions that plagued him out of the Caribbean past. He wailed:

> "Say is my skin beautiful
> Soft as velvet
> As deep as the blackness of a weeping night?
> And my mind?
> Like bright sunlight,
> Wonderful you would be if you were free!
> Say, is my voice beautiful?
> Really beautiful?
> And my strength?
> As fine a music as ever cheered us here,
> Durable as iron
> It's a pity to be with such despair."[300]

Massa day was far from done. Yet all Jamaica was waking up to the fact of what it ought to be because of what it actually was! Edna Manley had herself predicted this in her long acclaimed and now highly symbolic master-work "Negro Aroused" which was carved

---

299. Marquéz, Roberto: *op cit* p. 28.

300. Quoted in *Manley and the New Jamaica* (Rex Nettleford, ed.) Longman 1971, in address "Mission Accomplished" p. 379.

out of mahogany in 1935 in prophetic celebration, as it were, of the soon-to-be-aroused Jamaican collective consciousness against the debilitating ills of a rotting colonial order. For all along it was the people who had had African slave forebears and had suffered the anguish of the early Plantations who were giving the new Caribbean society cultural shape and purpose as they once brought, through their labour, economic significance and prominence to the sugar-producing region. It is obvious that that remarkable Guyanese East Indian leader, Cheddi Jagan, understands this phenomenon if we examine his efforts in the late sixties to identify with the West Indian Black Power movement. His further identification of the *indentured* East Indian labourer with the earlier enslaved African labourer, is clearly one attempt to lay foundations for national unity in his still race-ridden mainland Caribbean territory. But there are problems. For chattel slavery possesses a dimension of suffering qualitatively different to voluntary contract labour in the history of Plantation America. Moreover the time of entry of the East Indians after Caribbean society had consolidated itself in Plantation terms has somewhat robbed the East Indians (as well as other late-comer cultural groups) of full participation in, and substantive claim to, that struggle which is central to the experience of plantation slavery in the Americas. Jagan may have therefore found greater ease or happier ground in a system of political and social thought which lays claim to scientific (sc. non-racist) foundations in the objectification of concrete historical realities into abstractions that can serve the cause of the oppressed anywhere – whether they be forsaken and marginalised Amerindians, ex-slave Africans, indentured East Indians, Chinese 'coolies', exploited urban factory workers, members of the agro-proletariat or whoever may be the economically oppressed of the earth.

Such wholesale commitment to universalism is of major importance to Caribbean development since it introduces new and sharpened tools of analysis and offers yet other directions vital to real solutions. But let me once more make the point: it is a mistake to sacrifice in all this the specificity of racial/cultural concerns which are self-evident in every single territory of the Caribbean. Not only have the vast majority in places like Jamaica been the survivors of an oppressive system, they are still being the survivors of a global conspiracy to keep the Black in his place, whatever his demonstrated potential as a creative resourceful being. The identification by Caribbean leaders with the progressive forces against the apartheid practices of Rhodesia and South Africa is not merely declared in the name of abstract human rights as if to qualify for American aid under President Jimmy Carter.[301] There is a deep emotional self-interest on the part of Caribbean people of African ancestry who no longer wish to tolerate the continuing denigration by the white world of that ancestry.[302]

The assertion, with or without rancour, of faith in the Caribbean's ancestral authenticity becomes then more than an indulgence in personal pleasures of a predominantly selfish kind. Such an assertion becomes integral to the complex process of total liberation from the political, socio-economic and cultural dispossession which is at once the cause, occasion and result of a prolonged dependency. Yet the quest for ancestral certitude cannot be rooted in a narrow cultural nationalism. Rather it has to be informed by wider spheres of experience that revolve around or are in organic relationship with the specificities of Caribbean life and being.

Not least among such specificities is the agony of the struggle in the wider African Diaspora which has nurtured the spirit of oppressed masses of people and the protagonists they threw up in the Garveys, the Booker T. Washingtons, the Fanons, the Césaires, the Malcolm X's and the Martin Luther Kings. It has been

301.   President Jimmy Carter who assumed the Presidency in January 1977 declared that nations receiving aid and friendship from his country, the USA, would be expected to fulfill certain criteria of observance of human rights. It threw American foreign policy immediately into contradictions since each nation's perspective of human rights observance naturally differs one from another depending on the objectives each sets itself for its own development. The debate continues . . . Many countries of the Caribbean give priority to the freedoms from hunger, disease, and ignorance as part of their development thrust.

302.   A Caribbean political leader (Hon. Michael Manley, Prime Minister of Jamaica) was selected to give the keynote address at the conference on Southern Africa held in Maputo, Mozambique on May 17, 1977. The strong anti-apartheid posture taken by the Jamaican Government receives widespread acclamation from the populace which has bred Rastafarians, pan-Africanists, black nationalists and Marcus Garvey.

their deep understanding of the multi-faceted nature of the exiled African's dilemma that enabled those men to chart their own individual courses along universal paths to freedom and dignity for the people in the fight against social and economic injustice and in the quest for a liberating humanism. The African Diaspora continues to be an invaluable source of inspiration for a world-view alternative to the one which would label as inferior all that the victims of the Diaspora have created or achieved. The Rastafarians of Jamaica have attempted such an alternative with not insignificant or unrewarding results for themselves. But the old struggle between Europe and Africa on foreign soil (in Plantation America as well as in Africa itself) continues in ways that force contemporary Caribbean man to identify with the anguish of even the great United States of America which despite its power and military might, is yet to admit of its creolised reality and to liberate itself from its Eurocentric bondage. It is, for example, yet to accept the fact that the only musical vocabulary created by its citizens is the musical vocabulary of jazz, the gift of the Blacks to the continent and the world.[303] However, jazz is yet to earn its classic place of primacy in the musical ethos of Eurocentric America. The European imports still take pride of place at the top of the cultural hierarchy. It is a struggle that is inextricably bound up with Europe's past bid for imperialist domination the world over and with it the proletarianisation of labour by the free-market propensities of profit-hunting members of the expansionist brigades, as well as the superbly orchestrated cultural intimidation of all on the colonial periphery.

The logic and consistency of the phenomenon take us into the context of the coloniser and the colonised, into the world of

---

303. It is a Frenchman, Charles Delaunay, who recently declared the primacy of Jazz music reminding the world that "one can no longer compose or perform today as one did before jazz" in 'Jazz and World Culture' (a Lecture) in *Dialogue* Vol. 10, No. 3, 1977, pp. 77-88. James Baldwin in a review of Stanley Dance's *The World of Earl Hines* is characteristically assertive on the point. "Jazz composers", he says, "were creating American *classical* music. There isn't any other, and the American attempts to deny this have led, among other disasters, to the melancholy rise and fall of the late Elvis Presley, who was so highly paid for having a black sound in a white body." *New York Times Book Review*, October 16, 1977, p. 9.

Prospero and Caliban which the Englishman, William Shakespeare, explored in his play *The Tempest*, with full knowledge of Elizabethan expansionist zeal that flourished in his day. This play has, of course, been made immortal for some of us through the device of the set-book in the old Cambridge University School Certificate English Literature examinations. It has understandably been used by scholars and students of imperialism as point of departure for psychological analyses of the political and cultural domination in the modern world.[304] For the civilising mission of Prospero was simultaneously a controlling device to keep the alleged beneficiaries of such an adventure in cultural subjugation. "Colonialism [after all] demands that the native wilfully repudiate himself and acknowledge European spiritual and political order."[305] In so far as the native (black, white, yellow or brown) is still forced by institutions, mechanisms, processes or psychological pressures to repudiate himself in the service of values and norms of an outside power and culture, to that extent he continues to be colonised. This is therefore bound to be something of more than hypothetical interest to the Caribbean citizen whether he be East

304. Hegel's *Phenomenology of the Mind* (see argument on Master and Slave) Chap. 4, Jean-Paul Sartre's *Being and Nothingness* (Tr. Hazel E. Barnes) N.Y. 1953, Chap. 3, and Frantz Fanon's *Black Skin, White Masks* (Tr. Charles L. Markmann, N.Y. 1967) esp. Chaps. 1, 4 & 7, all offer excellent insights into the psychology of dependency. Fanon's work cited here gives an excellent gloss on *The Tempest*. Aimé Césaire adapted the play in his *Une Tempete* (Paris, 1969) and O. Manoni's classic "Prospero and Caliban: The Psychology of Colonization" (N.Y. 1956) on the Malagasy rebellion all use Shakespeare's play as a point of departure. Bruce Erlich discusses Shakespeare's "colonial metaphor on the social function of theatre" as part of a symposium on a Marxist Understanding of Shakespeare. And Roberto Retamar of Cuba offered a piece "Caliban" in the special issue of *The Massachusetts Review* Winter-Spring 1974, pp. 7-72 in which he reviews much of the literature on the Prospero-Caliban theme reminding us of the Barbadian novelist, George Lamming's own contribution in his *The Pleasures of Exile* (London 1960). The debate as to the psychology of Caliban as the colonised prototype will no doubt continue. The Journal *Caliban* addresses itself to new world writing and has as its editor, Roberto Marquéz with advisers of the pedigree of Guillén, René Depestre, Retamar, Sylvia Wynter and Edward Brathwaite. It is published in the U.S.A.

305. Erlich, Bruce: "Shakespeare's Colonial Metaphor: On the Social Function of Theatre in *The Tempest*" *Science and Society*, Spring 1977, Vol. XLI, No. 1, pp. 43-65.

Indian, Chinese, Arab, White, Brown, Black or Amerindian. Who wants to be the continuing echo of what occurs elsewhere?[306]

But since Caribbean cultural and political realities suggest a continuing colonisation of our people, the conscious repudiation of the colonial dictate that we repudiate ourselves provides a central dynamic in the struggle for liberation, especially now that we do have a modicum of formal political power to take decisions in our interest. I do not expect a government of any independent Anglophone Caribbean state, for example, to indulge the whims of the old colonial power by thoughtlessly upholding irrelevant and impractical Anglo-Saxon norms over well tried and serviceable creolised Caribbean forms in the areas of artistic manifestation, religious expression, family patterns, or language use. This is not in defence of throwing babies out with the bathwater; rather it is to advocate recognition of the fact that the baby has an existence separate from the bathwater. The repeal in 1976[307] by the Government of Jamaica of a long-standing and reprehensible English-derived law depriving children born out of wedlock of certain rights in the society is the sort of action I expect of an independent society in repudiation of the colonising ('civilising') cultural norms of the external (European) power. The legalisation by Guyana of obeah, an African-derived religious practice, was a similar effort.

But even if governments fail to recognise their duty in such particulars we now know enough about colonialism and the psychology of domination to be encouraged in the view that while a colonial power can control (civilise) the colonised in all that calls for external compliance, the colonised can never be totally controlled in his perception of his own subjectivity or in all the wilful thoughts and acts that are experienced in the inner landscape of his individual, colonised person. It is this ultimate area of seeming inviolability, however limited, that has provided Caribbean slaves, colonials, labourers, lumpen proletarians and sufferers alike with the stamina to withstand the worst consequences of oppression

306. Retamar, Roberto: *op cit* p. 7.

307. Status of Children Act, 1976, legitimising *inter alia* some 70 percent of Jamaica's population.

and to repudiate through strategems and strategies of myriad kinds the 'oppressor's' demand for self-repudiation among the oppressed.

Foremost among the strategies has been the fullest possible exploration of that process which draws on the individual and collective creative imagination. And whether for escape, protest, or confrontation, the exercise of that creative imagination has remained a major instrument of liberation in the Caribbean cultural and political experience. Small wonder, then, that the Caribbean creative artist has been in the vanguard of a genuine cultural revolution throwing up creative acts of genuine achievement that have in turn informed, inspired, and must continue to interact with, other aspects of a genuine movement for deep-rooted change in our Caribbean.

There is, however, a paradox in all this which needs to be articulated. Whatever may be the outcome of that deep-rooted change, it will not itself be free from the severest tests of the 'colonial' relationship. In other words if the new masters choose to become Prosperos, they will discover that they too will soon have their Calibans and Ariels who will be no less eager to become free of a debilitating dependency. Oppressive military juntas or corrupt and cynical elected representatives get their just rewards in due course. An elitist intellectual vanguard will also discover Ariels and Calibans a-plenty among the proletariat in whose name they purport to speak, just as the Mother Country found rebellious souls among her deceptively docile Caribbean, African and Asian wards. Here the analogy ends.

For many of us that Shakespearean colonial metaphor has long given place to social reality in Caribbean life and experience. The specific experience has taught universal lessons. For out of that reality have long come rebel spirits that have yearned to be free not as Ariels or Calibans but as flesh-and-blood guerillas, mock minstrels (like Fools in universal classic drama), preachers, scholars, political activists and creative artists — universal beings all, who are to be found wherever there is a fight for freedom and human dignity and against imperialist cultural penetration.

Nowhere is that spirit of freedom, and the full play of the creative impulse, more needed than in the field of science and technology seen as a dominant force in the development process in the Third World of which Jamaica and the Caribbean are a conscious, active, part. It is through that creative 'genius' residing in the collective consciousness and a will to innovative action that policy-determiners and decision-takers in the public domain will achieve the fruits of development after which the Caribbean and the rest of the Third World hanker so badly. The signs of 'progress' are perceived by many Caribbean planners in terms of fairly rapid technological and economic modernisation on the one hand and, on the other, the rationalisation of the bureaucratic apparatus of the nation-state into an effective and efficient instrument of policy-implementation. It is a fact that such goals are sometimes preceived with equal passion by advocates of both the liberal-nationalist and the Marxist-socialist models of development. And it is a further fact that these development goals are inspired by the demonstration effect evident in the record of achievement in the metropolitan centres located anywhere between San Francisco and Moscow. Yet it is the cultural hegemony of these very metropolitan centres that we reject. Here is the unending paradox: we hanker after the fruits of metropolitan technology and economic prowess while we reject metropolitan cultural dominance by asserting a collective identity rooted in our own historical heritage. Such a heightened contradiction is commonplace but it nonetheless requires from our collective consciousness a sensibility that will guarantee a mature resolution of the conflict in the neo-colonial situation. Otherwise we are likely to stand condemned as 'jokers' before a world that may one day have cause to take us seriously.

But how do we in the meantime get that world to understand that the "universal" goods of scientific and technological development must be made to work within the framework of political and cultural experience specific to this or that people? For what happens to a society which may not be in a position to "develop" in the sense we all now understand the term "development"? What for example, if our natural resources are insignificant in supply, or if our energy-base is inadequate, or if our soil for agriculture is poor and our arable land insufficient, or that climatic conditions are unfavourable? Such realities of Caribbean life summon up creative effort by those who plan for the better future. No less is demanded if some resources do exist but are subject to the hegemony of transnationals and other exploitative entrepreneurial mechanisms in the developed world. The indigenisation of scientific research and the building up of institutional networks to serve as infrastructure for development programmes within the region do require intellectual daring from the inquirers and creative thought and action among the politicians and technocrats. Such, indeed, are the imperatives of change in the groping Third World and these imperatives have a way of transcending ideological boundaries though to many progressives the "socialist solution" offered by the experience of Moscow, Peking and Havana means specifically the hope of rapid technological-economic advance in the interest of the majority while Western bourgeois-liberalism means traditional and slow economic growth and structural dependency.

But Caribbean leaders need a "third eye" in all this. I mean, by this, no more than an insightful grasp of the meaning and portent that inhere in such events as the threat of worldwide famine, the energy crisis and population pressure, all of which have shaken man's faith somewhat in the erstwhile hallowed myth of an inevitable linear progress. There are, after all, limits to economic growth and the proffered benefits of material progress. The fact is being discovered significantly, at a time when the Third World are just becoming free to address with passionate self-interest, their own growth potential.

But, with this we must live and at least take the initiative in finding alternatives to those development theories which have tied Caribbean planners to the view that industrialisation has a logical and temporal priority in the entire scheme of things. For it is to be seriously contemplated whether the options open to the Caribbean are as many and accessible as developmentalists of differing — and opposing — ideological persuasions like to claim. Moreover, should we not now disenthral ourselves, eschew the platitudes of the the political-cultural cant borrowed from the developed world and, while not attempting to re-invent the wheel, test the established inventions of the science and technology revolution against the objective realities of our situation. We need, moreover, to engage in the sort of fundamental research that will lead us to the "knowwhy" as well as the "knowhow" of man's existence and his relation to the physical environment he inhabits.[308]

It is that knowledge of our capacity to create, to be conscious that we have a collective consciousness, to be able to take off our spectacles and inspect them, – in short our capacity to innovate, reflect and evaluate – that will enable us to utilise rationally the offerings of science and technology which remain one of Western man's best gifts to his modern self and one of the finest manifestations of human creativity.

All our people – and especially the disadvantaged mass – can be said to have been involved in the creative process, in the sense of helping to forge a new order and perspective out of the raw stuff of Experience. The collective, ancestral, anonymous Caribbean wellspring dismissed by some as folk art, romanticised and mimicked by others as folklore, remain the strongest, surest source and expression of the Caribbean artistic cultural process. We must, however, also look closely at the Caribbean creative artist who has been most *consciously* at the centre of that process, articulating it, giving it focussed directions in varied artistic expressions and evaluating its consequences. The creative artist understands as part of his stock in trade the dialectical process expressed in the struggle between the forces of colonialism and liberation, between domination and the spirit of self-determination. Whether he be reggae artist or calypsonian, choreographer, playwright, poet, novelist, painter or sculptor, the Caribbean creative artist has confronted the contradictions of Caribbean life (class and colour conflict included) through the repudiation of the narrow cultural indulgences of a dominant superordinate class and by way of affirmation of the rich cultural products that have come out of the experience of the disadvantaged and deprived classes. Such classes have themselves thrown up creative artists a-plenty in any case. Such artists have most of them known nothing but struggle and so

308. See *White Paper on National Institute of Higher Education* (Research Science and Technology) Republic of Trinidad and Tobago, 1977, pp. 3-7).

they have had to deal with the dynamics of change designed to take our society away from the exploitation of man by man to the celebration of each human being's creative talent regardless of race, colour or social origin. The performing arts, the world of music, and all the varied creative acts that call for collective action have traditionally been among the most effective means of promoting equality, a sense of self-worth, and even economic justice among different groups of Caribbean peoples drawn from a wide cross-section of the society. We should want more of this not less. No *major* creative artist has up to now joined the fugitive middleclasses in the latter's escape from the threat to their privileges, which is how these fugitives have viewed the new thrust for real change in Jamaica from the mid-seventies.[309] For the Caribbean creative artist has long addressed himself to the negation of that negation-of-self which he knows is the essence of colonial domination. If he is pro-Caribbean or dares to recognise and assert that he in fact exists and is therefore on the side of his own liberation, he has to be anti-imperialist — a phrase he might not even utter since he has other and rather positive ways of expressing the thought. One has therefore got to look at the artist's *action* (his work) and less to his rhetoric for testament of his place and purpose. And even when he does speak about his work, the vernacular he employs naturally carries the stamp of his endeavours own inner consistency, logic and methods just as the disciplines of politics and economics purport to do for their practitioners. This should not detract how-ever, from the force and impact of the creative artist's role and place in Caribbean or any society's devleopment. Nor should that posture of contempt which is reputedly taken up against Caribbean creative efforts by certain Caribbean creative artists who either are

---

309. The country's most internationally acclaimed reggae artist did leave the country to live in the Bahamas but only after there was a threat on his life which reputedly forced him to reside in the nearby Caribbean island from which he tours. Two accomplished but by no means major artists have also left (for Miami) where they find a ready market for their compositions among the self-exiled Jamaican community. Their presence there may be explained in terms of good business prospects. Commercial artists of their standing could presumably find foreign currency stringencies in Jamaica hard to bear. Such major reggae artists as Toots Hibbert and Jimmy Cliff continue to make Jamaica their place of residence.

in self-exile in the metropoles or are living in agony as resident strangers in their own homelands.[310] The creative artist understands very well the phenomenon of perpetual crisis, this being a normal condition of his occupation. But the really good and effective creative artist also has a deep understanding of the regulative principles that underlie all change and the crisis which change inevitably brings. His work is nothing more than the product of the simple genius of coping with the dialectical tension of such an existence. In short the creative artist's achievement and potential for action in the Caribbean is something that political decision-takers in pursuit of that kingdom of necessity would be imprudent to ignore. And long after the mere politicians are forgotten, the Guilléns, the Louise Bennetts, the Edna Manleys, the Derek Walcotts, the René Depestres, Aimé Césaires and such others will be remembered along with the ancestral mass of ordinary Antillean souls who gave to our individual artists their sense of purpose. The great innovative nation-builders who will have led, directed and articulated the political/cultural struggle will naturally live. For they, too, will have created![311]

But the Caribbean creative artist, like his counterpart anywhere, deeply understands the dictum that universal paths are made by specific journeys. José Luis Mendez is therefore right: the best way for the creative artist to make his contribution to the

310. One such West Indian is credited with the *obiter dicta* that having created nothing (the Caribbean) has achieved nothing. This is not the view of all artists in self-exile, many of whom like Andrew Salkey, George Lamming, Samuel Selvon of the immediate post-war generation of West Indian writers operating out of London where the publishing technology was located, still write with the soul of the Antilles and have kept in touch with the source of their literary energy. Wilson Harris who went later is himself no advocate of the notion of Caribbean "cultural inauthenticity."

311. The list of such innovative Caribbean nation-builders is already long. Names like Toussaint L'Ouverture and Henri Christophe (Haiti), N. W. Manley and Alexander Bustamante (Jamaica), Eric Williams (Trinidad & Tobago), Grantley Adams (Barbados) all come to mind. Michael Manley of Jamaica already displays innovative capacities and Forbes Burnham's Cooperative Republic experiment in Guyana is undoubtedly significant. Fidel Castro of Cuba will most certainly command many pages in Caribbean and world history in the future, as will the great Caribbean thinkers such as Marcus Garvey and Frantz Fanon.

revolution is for him to regard his particular field of endeavour seriously as art — be it music, dance, literature, painting or sculpture.[312] For it is through the practice of his art (a form of action) that his commitment and contribution will attain direction and purpose. There are two inescapable tests that must be passed by the creative artist — a knowledge of his subject and excellence in the performance of the art. Otherwise life and the revolution are impoverished.

So to declare the validity of Caribbean Theatre or Caribbean Literature without addressing oneself to the constant practice and development of the craft that underlies such an expression is to end up with banalities or worse, with manifestos that should more appropriately come from the politician who is in any case better suited to such a task. There can be no substitute for the long arduous application of intellectual and physical energy to the forging of vocabularies of artistic expression that are true to the life challenges of Caribbean society. Among those challenges is the question whether art is a mirror of reality, or whether it is, as one Marxist critic aptly puts it, "a relationship between [creative artist] and audience conversing about reality, mediated by social struggle and by the artistic-intellectual languages of comprehension available to [both artist and audience]."[313] The dynamics of such a relationship is certainly what has moved much of what are today regarded as *Caribbean* art-expressions. And the openness of Caribbean society, in terms of our diverse cultural influences provides both audience and creator with a richness and variety of "artistic-intellectual languages of comprehension" that have to be taken into account and assessed, utilised, ignored or discarded. This is why the cavalier dabbling by well-meaning but often quite misguided visionaries of 'cultural progress' who are themselves unable to submit to the demands of study and analysis of cultural action will always end up with the facile clichés of a self-indulgent mysticism

312.   Mendez, José Luis: "Problems in the Creation of Caribbean Culture" *Caribbean Quarterly*, Vol. 21, Nos. 1 & 2, pp. 7-8, see footnote 142 above.

313.   Erlich, Bruce: *op cit* p. 64.

or the vulgar pursuit of an empty social realism. Professional critics, whose aesthetic sensibilities are out of tune with the times and realities of a post-colonial and more culturally self-aware Caribbean will themselves be equally perverse. One can still find in Jamaica such persons armed with a white-settler mentality. They make the common mistake of assuming that the promotion of things Jamaican is Black chauvinism[314] − forgetting, conveniently, the racial conceit which has accompanied the enslavement and colonisation of people like ourselves and which has served to downgrade what our own people have created. The generations since 1938 have happily been questioning all this and Eurocentric compatriots, like some of their resident expatriate cohorts, abhor the 'insolence' of such self-assertion. They would rather have us parade as second-rate Picassos and Stravinskys rather than be our original selves. How similar is this attitude to the one taken by others of us who would equally wish to be imitation Maos and imitation Lenins just as we have been imitation Platos and imitation Aristotles! Some of us continue to depend too much on the manipulation of foreign symbols and too little on the mobilisation of our own internal creative energies!

The articulation of a Caribbean aesthetic is indeed part of that struggle for cultural identity. But there are awkward problems other than those earlier mentioned. In poor societies like our own, some of the viler consequences of an inherited socio-economic system that sanctifies venality, are already evident among our artists and cultural agents. For artistic expressions become part of the syndrome of private ownership to be bought and sold and traded for profit to the highest bidder. The release of artistic activity from the realm of work-*only*-for-commercial-profit can indeed be justified on the grounds that it is a necessary *social activity* (as education and public libraries have come to be accepted) and therefore qualifies for adequate expenditure from the public purse. Complementary to this is the rendering of services by creative

---

314. A good example of this is the article "Fruits not only Roots" written by Harry Milner, in the *Sunday Gleaner* of July 17, 1977, in response to the television version of Alex Haley's American bestseller *Roots.*

talents, who can afford it, with no expectation of remuneration but who function with a spirit of public service as do the internationally acclaimed National Dance Theatre Company of Jamaica, the Jamaican Folk Singers and the Little Theatre Movement. This is a major consideration in poor developing countries like ours where scarce money resources often provide ready excuse for national neglect of artistic efforts and cultural development programmes. The case of Jamaica may be regarded as an exception to this well applied rule. But Jamaica has not escaped other well-known indulgences such as that which views creative artistic activity as some exclusive private domain to celebrate a self-imposed solitude. I share the view that artistic activity becomes little more than a self-indulgent affair when it merely affords an affluent few a "kind of privileged despair." There is the need, then, to educate our young and the public at large in the belief that art is a social activity which "speaks to the whole society, explaining to us why we are alive and how we are responsible one to another for our joint interdependent survival."[315]

That both Christian and socialist sensibilities are supportive of such a view is bound to be good news for the complex Caribbean soul who is marinated in religious orthodoxies but is nevertheless desirous of fundamental social change and with it the equitable redistribution of power and profits. I believe that the intense moral suasion that is implied in the notion of art as a social activity is not alien to the Caribbean psychic inheritance. Despite the strong and sturdy individualism of the people, a great many of our artistic manifestations that are of value did after all emerge out of *collective acts* which facilitated self-reinforcement, regeneration and survival among the forebears of the majority of the region's inhabitants. Such artistic manifestations as do find refuge in rhetorical gestures of despair or in frivolous commodity art designed to serve a cynical and prematurely decadent clientele, are not likely to produce the cultural confidence which is the society's objective. Nor will a blind obedience to solitary egos purporting to be in exclusive grasp of some divine gift of grace provide the answer.

---

315. Tynan, Kenneth: *op cit.*

Indeed, those "personal artists" who ostentatiously declare that they care little whether their poetry or their novels are read, whether their dances are taken notice of or their music heard, whether their plays are attended or their paintings and sculpture seen are merely indulging rhetoric for effect. For, save in rare eccentric reclusive cases, such 'self-sufficient' artists do in fact depend heavily on an "audience" for moral sustenance if not for bread.

The reason for such a position is sometimes given as a genuine fear of the corrupting influence that certain kinds of audience have on the cultural process and the creative arts, especially when they come clothed in the politician's garb. But this is to fail to appreciate the fact that political action and cultural action are different aspects of the same process of growth — both concerned with people being at the centre of the cosmos. A twentieth century European theatre authority avers that "all drama is ... a political event [since] it either re-asserts or undermines the code of conduct of a given society."[316] 'National theatres' are indeed ritual affirmations of nationhood and what convenient and effective means they are for keeping the works of certain creative artists alive — whether it be Shakespeare, Molière and Racine, Goethe or the Abbey Theatre playwrights! They are all national monuments in their respective polities. In any case if one is consciously involved in helping to build a nation and shaping a society, as Caribbean politicians undoubtedly are, one is automatically in the creative process, not unlike the very process that engages the artist forging form out of substance.

I would indeed contend that the only politician who can expect to be taken seriously in a society like ours is the one who not only displays demagogic prowess and skill in electoral combat but also possesses the sort of artistic and cultural sensibilities that will enable him or her to grasp the deeper issues of our society and

316. Esslin, Martin: *An Anatomy of Drama,* Hill and Wang, N.Y. 1977, p. 29. Cp. Fidel Castro's view that "Our standards [in evaluating cultural and artistic creations] are political. There cannot be aesthetic value without human content or [if it is] in opposition to man, justice, welfare, liberation, and the happiness of man." (Quoted by Michael Myerson, *op cit* — see footnote 125 above).

face them squarely even at the risk of losing power at the polls. Such a politician must be prepared to believe in the educability, if not the perfectibility, of the human being and in man's capacity to create. Such a politician must be prepared to go beyond his outward loyalty to partisan faction and seek after the inner substance of the fundamental issues of what is a complex, dynamic and changing society. If he is unable to do this he has no right attempting to lead any nation in the region at this time. As for culture and the national interest there is point, indeed, to a reputedly Russian advice which goes: "It is not the Ministry of Culture that one worries about: it is the culture of the Minister."[317]

This is not to say that the politician must usurp the function of the artist *per se,* no more than he can that of the priest, whatever may have been his electoral pledge to deliver the people out of bondage and give them the key to the gate of some new Kingdom.

Rather, the artistic input into cultural development and social change may best be realised through restoring the creative arts to their primary function – that of recreating for every individual the "fullness of all that he is not, the fullness of humanity at large" and giving him power, purpose and faith to assume "any form and [to] lead a thousand lives without being crushed by the multiplicity of his experience."[318]   The texture of our Jamaican and Caribbean life is the result of such multiplicity of experience. Our continuing survival is proof positive of our capacity to cope, powerless perhaps but purposeful and amply endowed with the gift of faith. Protest, criticism and revolt are all a necessary and inescapable part of the collective strategies of a harassed people anywhere. But so is the celebration of life and of the very miracle of survival. So, too, is the celebration of the demonstrated resourcefulness of villages and ghettos and of the regenerative sources of ancestral

317. Attributed to Isaac Stern, the violinist who told it at a ceremony in tribute to Livingstone L. Biddle Jr., recently appointed Chairman of the US National Endowment for the Arts. See *Newsweek,* Dec., 12, 1977, p. 93.

318. Fisher, Ernest: *The Necessity of Art* (1963) quoted by K. Tynan *(op cit)* Fisher, who is a Marxist, is an Austrian critic.

energy. And so are the exultation of the invincibility of the human spirit and the acknowledgement of the sheer intelligence of our forebears who have left us such treasured legacies as hope and courage. It is in the celebration of all such things that lies the irony of contradictions which in turn challenges us to sanity and a determination of the will — these indispensable weapons in the struggle for total liberation.

Such a liberation constitutes the fact of power for *all* the people — finally decolonised and released from the psychological paralysis of dependency.[319] It also constitutes, through the opportunity and will to work, the means to food, shelter and clothing for the deprived multitude as well as freedom from fear, hunger, disease and ignorance which are the declared objectives of a programmatic progress to real political and economic democracy. But such a liberation constitutes, no less, the gift of self-confidence, the fullest awareness of the creative impulse and the power of its varied expressions in the identity of self and the building of a civilisation. Above all, total liberation is nothing if it does not constitute, in addition, the gift of faith in and respect for the validity of our own Experience to the point where that Experience no longer stands indicted in our own eyes for being innocent of theory and empty of Explanation. Despite the clinging colonial biases and the constant quest outside ourselves for the promise of liberation, increasing numbers of us are discovering some challenging truths about ourselves through cumulative study, unique insights, and the hard fact of existence. Many of us have discovered that there is no basis in fact for this relegation of ourselves to being a mere footnote to Europe's history and experience, nor for the charge frequently levelled against us that we are the irredeemable victims

---

319. The late Harold Simmonds, St. Lucian folklorist and artist said the following in a BBC Broadcast — "Little Galleries" back in 1948: "What is certain is that if a strong Art is to flourish in the West Indies, it must not be rooted in European Art, nor blossom in forms that bloomed and served its purpose fifty years ago or more . . ." Quoted by Pat Charles in her paper "The Arts in a Small Society" (mimeographed). Ten years earlier Norman Manley had said "We can take everything that English education has to offer us, but ultimately we must reject the domination of her influence, because we are not English and nor should we ever want to be." (See *Manley and the New Jamaica* ed. Rex Nettleford, Longman 1971, p. 109).

of primitive innocence and intellectual poverty. None of these myths of Caribbean existence have successfully withstood the test of close and serious examination of our historical experience. For in this Experience are to be found a richness of texture, a dialectical complexity and a creative dynamic in the resolution of conflict and the forging of definitive forms — all of which are seen by many as the greatest authenticated source of energy summoning us who live in the Caribbean to a determination of the will and a creative urge in continuing what is aptly called "the struggle." For as long as our people have cause to harbour a feeling of having been wronged and deprived, and to be without a sense of place or purpose, so long will that battle be waged for cultural integrity and identity no less than for social justice and economic freedom.

There is, then, a grave responsibility on our part to create a society and bequeath a civilisation in which future generations of Caribbean men and women will enjoy cultural confidence as a matter of course and have their creative potential actualized in the crafting of cultural products of excellence that will in turn enrich, elucidate and celebrate life. We will then be released from the scourge of a demeaning dependency, the clumsiness of self-indulgent revolt, and the debilitating self-destructiveness of hate and revenge. That will be the day when our lingering sense of shame will dissolve in the unequivocal acceptance of self as it emerges from a history that is replete no less with ennobling acts of invention and triumphs than it is with degradation and defeats. That will be the day when our people will no longer feel uneasy for being indebted to Europe, Africa or wherever may contribute to our nurturing. For the gift of influences will be like fertilisers to the soil, with our capacity for free choice and our own experience — hopes, fears and aspirations — as the soil. That will be the day when self-contempt will vanish in the face of a growing self-confidence and when pride that is puffed up will be so replaced by a self-assured humility that no one will find it tactically necessary to "accuse great art of feudalism and excuse poor art as suffering."[320] That will be the day when

320. Walcott, Derek: "The Muse of History — an Essay" in *Is Massa Day Dead? — Black Moods in the Caribbean*, Orde Coombs, ed. Doubleday, Anchorbooks N.Y. 1974, p. 4.

the essential unity of man will triumph over the cleavages of race, class and cultural capacities. That will be the day . . .

Yet we need in all honesty to remind ourselves that "revolutionary culture produces enthusiasm and because such enthusiasm relates to spasms of power and is subject to disenchantment, it is shortlived and antagonistic to discipline."[321] Indeed, the old cultural values which once divorced the creative imagination from the realities of practical experience can no longer serve the Caribbean. By the same token, human progress is nothing if it promotes material welfare without providing for the enrichment of the human spirit. The quest, then, demands sustained energy, rigorous effort and discipline – without the terror of coercion, the heartlessness of bureaucratic cynicism, or the totalitarian monopoly of organisation. Not that we can expect to have crops "without plowing the ground" or "rain without thunder and lightning" or "the ocean without the awful roar of its waters,"[322] as an American slave forebear so insightfully described the agony of choice that inheres in all process of growth, change and development. "It's a hard road to travel and a mighty long way to go" is the opening line from a popular hymn frequently sung in the revivalist rituals practised by the mass of the Jamaican people. That journey, long begun by those who went before, is for *us* and no one else now to continue. As the poet, Dennis Scott, once declared:

> "It is time to plant
> feet in our earth. The heart's metronome
> insists on this arc of islands
> as home."[323]

321. Walcott, Derek: Article on the Jamaican Dance Company, *op cit.*

322. Attributed to Frederick Douglass, the celebrated American slave-born freedom-fighter by Basil Wilson in his reference to the clear uneasiness evident among some leading Jamaican newspaper columnists concerning the state of affairs in a changing Jamaica. See "Jamaica's Leading Columnists," *Sunday Gleaner,* Dec. 25, 1977, p. 9. The article was first published in the *Amsterdam News* of New York.

323. Excerpt from poem "Homecoming" by Dennis Scott, Jamaican poet-playwright and former dancer with the Jamaican NDTC. He directs the teaching programme of the Jamaica National School of Drama.

Indeed, this arc of islands *is* home. To the vast majority of Caribbean souls there will be none other. And for many among that significant minority who will have departed from or abandoned the arc, life back in the region will always summon a return to a homecoming as has been the case with so many an *émigré,* be he artisan or artist. The return can never be a turning-back for there is no turning back. The Caribbean experience is, instead, a pursuit of life complete with the contradictions of the bitter with the sweet, great hope and much travail. It should not then be made the cause for flight despite the push of Third World dross or the pull of metropolitan lustre. Life in the Caribbean is, at this stage of the region's development, a particular and special form of action which, like a great work of art, must respond with imagination and daring to the most challenging historical tensions we can never escape. No less a response is demanded of us all, by the creative tensions of our post-colonial Caribbean now in the final quarter of a century that has not only mothered our discontent and fed our turbulence but has also nurtured our aspirations and promised redemption.

Index

Abrahams, Carl 38
Africa/Africans 2, 3, 4, 6, 7, 10,
11, 13, 18, 23, 25, 26, 28, 30, 39,
42, 47, 51, 52, 60, 63, 67, 68, 69,
72, 84, 167, 185, 190, 202, 206,
207, 208, 210, 211, 215
   Afro-Latinity 205
   Euro-African 208
   solidarity with 212
African Diaspora 212, 213
African Festival of the Arts 175
African Presence 204, 205, 208, 211
Alonso, Alicia 28, 65
America 26, 27, 67
   Latin 149-185
   North 11, 12, 16, 28, 31, 32,
   52, 77, 79, 150-151, 153, 161,
   185, 195
Amerindian 2, 39, 60, 185, 211,
215
Angolans 207
Antigua 158
apartheid 212
Ariel 216
artistic and creative
   consciousness 224
artists 154, 184, 188, 220
Association of Caribbean
   Universities and Research
   Institutes (UNICA) 162-163
Augier, Roy 160

Babylon 11
Barn Theatre 103
Barnett, Sheila 99
Baugh, Cecil 40, 96
Baxter, Ivy 27, 100
Belize Festival of Arts 158
Bell, Wendell 92
Benjamin, Walter 60
Bennett, Louise 15, 32, 34, 113,
221
Bennett, Wycliffe 31, 32

Bertram, Arnold 70
Bolivarian Society 125
Boxer, David 39
Braithwaite, Lloyd 160
Brathwaite, Edward Kamau 15, 16,
17, 59
Brazil 28, 153
Britain, United Kingdom 12, 27,
28, 31, 32, 67
British Council 33
   Empire 207, 208
   Museum 39
Brown, Aggrey 133, 134
Bruckin party 37
Burke, Edmund 7
Burnham, Forbes 152, 153

Caliban 214, 216
Calypso 22
Cambridge University School
   Certificate Examinations 214
Campbell, George 210
Canada 153
capitalism 197, 198, 200, 206, 223
Caribbean Artists Movement
   (CAM) 159
Caribbean Common Market,
   Caribbean Community
   (CARICOM) 174, 175
CARICOM Seventh Heads of
   Government Conference 175
Caribbean cultural separateness
   150, 160, 168, 171
Caribbean Experience 189-193,
   195-199, 219-227
Caribbean Festival of Arts
   (CARIFESTA) 152-154, 175
Caribbean News Agency
   (CANA) 135
Caribbean Quarterly 158
Caribbean Union of Teachers 176
Carib-Indians 2
Carnival 154

Carpentier, Alejo 14
Carter, President Jimmy 212
Castro, Fidel 9, 65, 198, 205, 207
Ceramics 40, 96
Césaire, Aimé 14, 153, 212, 221
change in society 193-199, 216-221
Chinese 6, 12, 32, 42, 51, 52, 69,
185, 193, 195, 206, 211, 215
  Red- 207
Christian, Christianity 18-21, 133, 187,
203, 206, 224
cinema, film 35
class 11, 20, 204, 206
Cliff, Jimmy 23, 53, 56
Collings, Dr Dorothy 138
colonial, colonisation, decolonisation,
  post-colonial, anti-colonial 67, 68,
  70, 77, 91, 94, 111, 137, 149, 161,
  172, 176, 181, 193, 200, 205, 207,
  209, 211, 213, 214, 215
Columbus, Christopher 60
commodity prices 204
Commonwealth Caribbean 11, 14, 17,
83, 127, 151, 156, 158, 159, 160,
171, 174
communications media 126-140, 176,
194
communication support development 127
Community Cultural Centres 114
Conjuntos Folkloricos 28
Copyright Law 74
Costa Rica 12
Craft Development Agency 94
craft work 40, 41
  development 85, 105, 143
creative arts 21-43
creative imagination 216, 221-223
creative process 219-222
creolisation 2, 10, 181-185, 191, 208
Crown Colony System 207
Cuba, Cubans 6, 9, 12, 28, 30, 149,
150, 153, 154, 171, 190, 198, 205,
209, 218

Modern Dance Company 28
National Ballet of 28
cultural dependency 192, 195,
197, 200, 205, 216
  deprivation 204, 212
  development 83-105, 124-126,
  145, 155-157, 161, 165, 167,
  169, 174, 175, 176, 188, 193,
  199, 201, 205, 215, 217, 218-229
  domination 48, 52, 68, 71, 126,
  149, 171, 172, 173, 176, 181,
  191, 199, 200, 201, 202, 203,
  206, 213, 214, 215, 216, 217,
  223
  dynamics 181, 219-230
  financing 140-146, 166, 174,
  177, 223-224
  identity 187, 202, 205, 211, 223
  indices 13, 165, 169-170, 174,
  186
  integration 151-180
  pluralism 1-43, 47, 48, 50, 171,
  173, 189, 199, 202, 209
  policy 87-91, 126-140, 153,
  155-157, 159, 165, 167-169,
  170-173, 175, 176-178, 182,
  188, 193, 195, 217-229
  preservation 11-118,
  137-140, 144, 153, 155, 166,
  169
  superiority 204, 206
Cultural Training Centre 95, 98,
105-109
  cost of 96, 110
Cumfeh 18
Cundall, Frank 111, 118
Cuthbert, Marlene 134

dance, dance art, dance theatre
27-31, 107, 199, 221,
daCosta, Yvonne 100
Dawes, Carroll 102, 103
Dawes, Neville ix, 4, 111

Depestres, René 221
Destine, Jean Leon 28
development 218
drama 31-37
Drummond, Don 23
Dunham, Katherine 28
Dunkley, John 38

East Indians 4, 6, 25, 32, 51, 69,
185, 206, 208, 211, 215
economic power 204
Eddy Thomas Dance Workshop 100
education and training in arts and
    culture 94, 173-175
education/educators 201
    European education 199, 206
electronic media 128-130
Emancipation 3, 8, 18, 51, 62
emigrants 12, 13
Engels 8
Epilogue 181
Eurocentric, Eurocentrism 8, 10, 17,
21, 26, 29, 31, 52, 66-68, 70, 84, 85,
89, 112, 133, 137, 167, 172, 173,
176, 193, 197, 199, 200, 202, 203,
206, 210, 213, 223
Europe, Europeans 2-6, 7, 9, 14, 17,
26, 32, 40, 41, 42, 47, 48, 51, 52, 53,
57, 59, 60, 63, 66, 67, 71, 203, 207,
215
Exploratory Committee on Arts and
    Culture, 1972 42, 87-91, 92, 95,
    137

Fanon, Frantz 64, 65, 192, 193, 212
Federal Theatre Company 33
Figueroa, John 161
Five Year Plan 84, 85, 95
folk music 23
Folk Music Officer 24
Folk Music Research Unit 23, 24,
41, 97, 109, 113

Fowler, Greta 34
Fowler, Henry 31, 34
Franklin Town Centre 115
Fraser, Dorothy 100
French aid to American rebels 207

ganja (marihuana) 20
Garvey, Marcus Mosiah 32, 37, 40,
42, 43, 71, 192, 203, 210
Germans 207
ghettos 11, 23, 27, 48, 53, 89
Gleaner, Daily 134, 135, 136
Gordon, Shirley 161
Goveia, Elsa 58, 60, 160, 192, 201
Graham, Martha 101
Guillén, Nicolás 9, 15, 126, 209,
210, 221
Guyana 6, 18, 20, 69, 151, 152,
172, 190
    National Council of History and
    Culture 155
    University of 163

Haiti 28, 152, 153
Hall, Douglas 160
Harder They Come, The 35
Harris, Wilson 14
Hearne, John 14, 66, 67
Henzell, Perry 35
Hibbert, Toots 23
Hill, Errol 33
Hill, Frank 112
Hillary, Sam 33, 103
historiography 60
history 198
    the study of 58, 59, 60, 61, 189
Historical Gallery 115
historical sites 116
Ho Chi Minh 195, 207
Holder, Boscoe & Geoffrey 27
Hosein, Everold 130, 131
Huie, Albert 38, 96

ideology 204, 206, 208
immigrant 12
imperialism 208, 213
    educational 214
indentured labourers 6, 211
Independence, self-government 192,
    200
indigenisation 3
individualism 105, 127, 188, 224
industrialisation 216-219
information 126-146
Institute of Jamaica 62, 71, 96,
110-122, 125, 139, 140, 141, 142
    African Caribbean Institute of
    Jamaica 112-113, 117, 141
    African Museum 115
    Chairman of 159
    Count Ossie Rastafarian Centre 125
    Cultural Heritage Series 117
    Historical Gallery 115
    Jamaica Journal 31, 94, 114, 116
    Jamaicans of Distinction Series 117
    Junior Centres 114, 141
    Natural History Division 120, 141
    Publications Division 116, 141
Institute of Social and Economic
    Research 160
Integration and Cooperation with
    Latin America 149-178
Inter-American Council for Education
    Science and Culture (CIECC) 93
    (CIDEC) 166
Inter-American Foundation 144
Inter-Governmental Committee on
    Caribbean University Education 159
international funding 143-145, 163,
168, 169

Jagan, Cheddi 211
Jamaica Agency for Public
    Information (API) 137
Jamaica Artists and Craftsmen Guild
125

Jamaica Broadcasting Corporation
93, 129, 140
Jamaica Daily News 134
Jamaica Federation of Musicians
125
Jamaica Festival Commission 24,
41, 63, 94, 110, 122, 124, 125,
140, 142
Jamaica Journal 31, 94, 114, 116
Jamaica Labour Party, 49, 86
Jamaica Library Service 93, 119,
139
Jamaica Philharmonic Orchestra 25
Jamaica School of Art 38, 40, 96,
97, 105, 106, 107, 108, 109, 141,
157
Jamaica School of Dance 29, 96,
99, 101, 107, 108, 109, 125, 141,
144
Jamaica School of Drama 36, 96,
102, 107, 108, 109, 141
Jamaica School of Music 23, 24,
26, 96, 97, 98, 99, 107, 108, 109,
125, 140, 141
Jamaica Social Welfare Commission
93
Jamaica Welfare Limited 41, 124
Jamaican Folk Singers 24, 72, 97,
125, 143, 153, 224
Jamaican Georgian Society 125
Jamaican Government 56, 83, 89,
91, 99, 103, 110, 113, 128, 134,
136-140, 158, 176
Jamaican Movement for the
    Advancement of Literacy
    (JAMAL) 55, 139, 140, 142
Jamaican theatre 31
Jamaican Tourist Board
    (Domestic Marketing Board) 116
James, C. L. R. 58, 60, 192
jazz 213
Jews 9, 42
Johnston, Hazel 28

Kapo 39, 40
King, Martin Luther 212
Kitchener, Lord 23
Kumina 18, 37

Lamming, George 14
language 13-18, 191, 201, 203
Lannaman, Gloria 129
Lebanese 4, 12, 42, 185, 206, 215
Leeward Islands Arts Festival 158
Lenin, Leninism 7, 9, 77, 195
Lewin, Olive 23, 113
Lewis, C. Bernard 114, 120
Lewis, Ed Bim & Clover 35, 36
Lewis, Rupert 43
lexicography 16, 201
liberalism 197
libraries 137-141
literature 222
Little Theatre Movement 34, 35, 36, 95, 96, 102, 125, 142, 224
Locke, John 7
Lomax, Alan 113

Machel, Samora 72
Mais, Roger 64
Manley, Edna 39, 40, 84, 96, 210, 221
Manley, Michael 42, 79, 85, 86, 91, 200, 204
Manley, Norman Washington 40, 41, 42, 49, 64, 67, 83, 84, 124
Mansilla, H. C. F. 171
Mao Tse-tung 195
Marcuse, Herbert 7
marginality 12, 205, 208
Marley, Bob 23, 26, 52, 53
Marquéz, Roberto 186
Marriot, Alvin 40
Martí, José 9, 126, 150, 195, 209
Martinique 28, 153
Marx, Marxism, Marxist, neo-Marxist 7, 8, 9, 57, 58, 64, 77, 78, 79, 171, 172, 193, 195, 200, 201, 202, 203, 209, 217

mass media 11, 73, 126-140, 194, 198
Matthews, Basil 17
McBurnie, Beryl 27
media policy 129-131, 136-137
Mendez, José Luis 75, 221
mento 48
Mexico 153
Military Museum 115
Mill, J. S. 7
minstrelsy syndrome 186, 187
Minister of State for Culture (and Information) 42
Ministry of Education 93, 95
misreporting and misrepresentation 127
Montserrat 158
Moncrieffe, Barry 100
Moodie, Vera 96
Morant Bay Rebellion 62
Mozambicans 207
multi-racialism 4, 9, 207, 208, 211
Museums and Archaeology 114, 115, 125, 141
Museum of Folk Art and Technology 115
music 22-27, 97, 213, 222
education in 98
Mystic Revelation of Rastafari 37

Naipaul, V. S. 14
nationalism 209
National Council on Libraries Archives and Documentation Services 138, 140
National Dance Theatre Company 29, 72, 94, 95, 96, 99-101, 125, 142, 143, 224
National Deposit Library 138
National Gallery of Art 113, 117, 140, 141, 142
National Institute of Craft 143
National Library 114, 118-119, 138

national motto 5
National Pantomime 34, 35, 72
National Trust Commission 41, 62, 94,
115, 122, 140
National unity 1-43
nationalism 4-6
Natural History 114
Negro Aroused 210
Netherlands Antilles 153
new international economic order
200
newspapers 134, 135, 136, 198
Nkrumah, Kwame 204
Nyerere, Julius 7, 72, 190, 202, 204

Obeah 18, 20
Office of the Prime Minister 140
O'Gorman, Pamela 98
Organisation of American States (OAS)
93, 144, 151, 165, 167, 168, 170, 173,
174, 177
Olympia International Art Centre 125
Order of National Heroes 62
"Out of Many, One People" 5

painting 37-40, 106
Panama, Panama Canal 12, 172
Pan-American Development Fund 168
Papiamento 14, 17
Parboosingh, Karl 37
Parry, John 160
Pasuko, Berto 27
Peking 218
People's National Party 49
People's Theatre 34
planters, plantations, plantation
system 3, 12, 30, 42, 69, 70,
149, 187, 190, 196, 206, 208,
211, 213
political power 208
political system 194
politicians 225
Port Royal 115

Portrait Gallery 115
poverty 53, 54, 181, 196, 212
press freedom 127-129
Proctor, George 120
Production Plan, 1977 143
proletariat 6
Prologue xv
Prospero 214, 216
Puerto Ricans 152
Pukkumina (Pocomania) 18, 37

race 4-8, 193, 204, 205, 206, 207,
208, 223
racism 8, 9, 10, 32, 51, 52, 69,
196, 202, 203, 209, 215
in politics 208
Radio Jamaica and Rediffusion
(RJR) 34
Ras Jose 37
Rastafarians, Rastafarianism 16,
20, 37, 48, 49, 71, 86, 113,
187-188, 201, 213
rebellion against Euro-determinism
203, 216
Reggae 48
regional universities 162-163, 173,
177
Reid, Vic 15
relationship between artist and
audience 222, 225
religion 18-21, 133, 187, 190, 196,
203
Repole, Dahlia 121
Requa, Barbara 99
Retamar, Roberto Fernandez 179
Revels in Jamaica 31
revolution, revolutionary 9, 47, 65,
75, 181, 193, 195, 205, 211, 216
Reynolds, Mallica (see Kapo)
Rhodesia, Rhodesians 212, 207
Rhone, Trevor 35
Ricketts, Patsy 100
Rock Steady 22

Rodney Affair 49
Rodney, George 38
Rodney, Walter 60
Rose, Bert 99
Russian, Russians 29, 195, 198, 207, 217, 218
Ryman, Cheryl 100

Savacou 159
science & technology 76, 205, 206, 216-217, 218
Scientific Research Council 120
Scott, A. D. 125
Scott, Dennis 35, 103
sculpture 211
Seaga, Edward 23, 41, 84, 113, 145
Selassie, Haile 72, 187
self-liberation 207
Selvon, Samuel 15
Shakespeare, William 31, 214
Shango 18
Shearer, Hugh 72
Sherlock, Sir Philip 42, 111, 114, 161, 162
Ska 22
slaves, slavery 1, 4, 211
   character of 186
Smith, M. G. 1-2, 5, 21, 160, 192
Social Development Commission 140, 143
social sciences 162, 165, 202
socialism 78, 150-151, 171, 190, 192-195, 196, 197, 206, 209
socialist 9, 190, 218, 224
   transformation 192-197
South Africa 212
Sparrow, Mighty 23, 26, 52, 126
sports 186
Star, The 136
Status of Children Act, 1976 215
Stone, Carl 54
Surinam 153
Swahili 202

Tanzanians 201
Tempest, The 214, 216
Ti Jean 34
television 128-130
theatre 31-37, 102-115, 222
Things Jamaican Limited 143
Third World 217, 218
Tito, Marshall 195
Tivoli Gardens Centre 114, 125
Todd, Edwin and Maribel 40
trade unionism 196
Trinidad 6, 18, 22, 27, 69, 72, 74, 129, 151, 152, 154, 172, 176,

ujaama 7, 190, 202
unemployment 53, 105
UNESCO 93, 138, 144, 153, 168, 170, 171, 172, 173, 177

Vaz, Noel 34
Venezuela 153
Verity, Robert & Carmen 114
Vietnamese 207
voluntary cultural contribution 124, 188

Walcott, Derek 14, 33, 34, 36, 37, 103, 154, 184, 221
Warner-Lewis, Maureen 67
Watson, Osmond 38
Washington, Booker T. 212
West India Reference Library (WIRL) 62, 93, 114, 117-120, 138, 141, 142
West Indian Federation 152, 160
West Indies, University of the 16, 33, 62, 93, 112, 113, 119, 121, 153, 155-156, 163
   Creative Arts Centre 50, 142, 144, 159
      occupation of 50
   Engineering Department 158

Extra Mural Studies 33, 100, 152,
157, 158, 159
Faculty of Natural Science 120
Institute of Mass Communication 130
Library School 138
Libraries of the 139
White, Dorcas 127
whites, functional whites 101, 206
Williams, Eric 58, 60, 126, 192, 204
Williams Lavinia 28
Williams, Ranny 34
woodcarving 39
working class 6
Wright, Richardson 31
Wynter, Sylvia 66, 67

Yard Theatre 37
Yugoslavia 195